Dictionary of Personal Development

Paul Tosey PhD

and

Josie Gregory PhD

Human Potential Research Group
School of Educational Studies
University of Surrey

WHURR PUBLISHERS
LONDON AND PHILADELPHIA

First published 2002 by
Whurr Publishers Ltd
19b Compton Terrace, London N1 2UN, England
325 Chestnut Street, Philadelphia PA19106, USA

British Library Cataloguing in Publication Data
A catalogue record for this book is available from the
British Library.

ISBN 1 86156 281 0

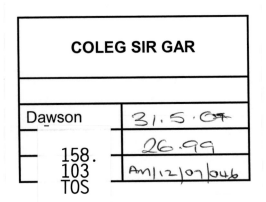

COLEG SIR GAR	
Dawson	31.5.07
158. 103 TOS	26.99
	AM/12/07/046

Printed and bound in the UK by Athenaeum Press Limited,
Gateshead, Tyne & Wear.

Contents

Preface

Why a dictionary of personal development?

Personal development, with its modern roots in the growth movement of the 1960s, may be experiencing a renaissance. Businesses are realizing more and more that soft skills are key to performance, are clamouring for their staff to develop 'emotional intelligence', and are beginning to embrace the idea that spirituality and the workplace might be related. Formal education based substantially on experiential learning and attending to emotional development is still at the leading edge, certainly in higher education. The UK government is actively promoting 'lifelong learning', emphasizing both emotional and spiritual dimensions of healthy citizenship.

At the University of Surrey, we work with facilitators of human development and change. Their roles embrace organizational consultancy and management training, group leadership, education, community development, counselling and therapy. This dictionary arose from a wish to create a guide to terms commonly found in these diverse but overlapping contexts of personal development work. There appears to be much cross-pollination of vocabulary, and our students often comment on the wide range of jargon they encounter. So this is quite deliberately not a discipline-based or profession-based approach. People who facilitate personal development, and those who seek development for themselves, encounter a language that is mixed and diverse, a multi-cultural cookbook of human potential.

We have aimed to give a reliable guide to the origins, meanings and usage of terms commonly found in personal development. We view the book less as a convergence on definitive meanings than as a gateway, a reference guide that is also a point of departure to myriad fields and topics concerned with human experience and development.

Selection

Our aim has been to select around 500 of the most prominent terms, concentrating in the main on the following fields:

Adult and Experiential Learning; BodyMind Development; Counselling; Gestalt Therapy; Groupwork; Humanistic Psychology; Jungian Psychology;

Interpersonal Skills Training; Management Development; 'New Age'; Neuro-Linguistic Programming; Psychology; Psychosynthesis; Spirituality; Systems Thinking; Transactional Analysis; and Transpersonal Psychology.

We did not attempt to include healing or alternative medicine within our scope.

We also bring some biases to our selection. First, we emphasize the 'inner' dimension of personal development and take a holistic view of the person – mind, body, emotion and spirit. There are intrapersonal, interpersonal, social, organizational, cultural and transpersonal dimensions to personal development, though here we address mainly the intrapersonal, interpersonal and transpersonal.

Second, we have emphasized 'development' as connoting learning, growth and realization of potential, rather than as remedial or corrective. This is not a clinical dictionary, although many terms in common usage have technical or clinical origins. In such cases we have aimed to acknowledge those origins so that professional as well as more vernacular meanings are indicated.

Third, we have reflected a range of concepts and practices that we use in the Change Agent Skills and Strategies MSc course at Surrey. Among other things this programme espouses humanistic values and emphasizes research as a mode of personal development.

Format and conventions used

Cross-references are in SMALL CAPITALS, sometimes to a variant on the actual entry (e.g. PROJECTED referring to an entry titled **projection**).

We have referred to internet-based resources as well as other literature, but ensured that the book stands on its own, especially for those readers who may not have internet access. We have concentrated on websites that seem well maintained, authoritative, and (so far as we can tell) likely to remain accessible.

We mentioned above that we see this book as a gateway. An unexpected joy of compiling the dictionary has been the opportunity to discover a wealth of reference sources available on the internet. In addition to listing sources referred to in the text (cross-referenced as RESOURCES), we have included a selection of helpful and relevant websites. These include contact details for professional associations, growth and development centres, and so on.

A full list of bibliographical references is also included at the back of the book.

Disclaimer

Inclusion of terms referring to practices or bodies should not be taken as approval or recommendation of those practices or bodies. The authors do not accept responsibility for, and do not endorse the content of, any service or website listed here.

About the authors

Paul Tosey, BSc, MSc, PhD, FRSA, is a senior lecturer in the School of Educational Studies, University of Surrey. He was founding Director of the MSc in Change Agent Skills and Strategies, and is current peer Director of the Human Potential Research Group. He is a Master Practitioner of NLP.

Josie Gregory, BA(Hons), PhD, CTA (C) (UKCP), PGCEA, Dipl Hum Psychol (IDHP), RGN, is a lecturer in the School of Educational Studies, University of Surrey. Former peer Director of the Human Potential Research Group, she is current Director of Studies for the MSc in Change Agent Skills and Strategies. She also runs a small psychotherapy, organizational consultancy and clinical supervision practice using a variety of humanistic models.

Acknowledgements

We wish to thank the many colleagues and associates who have contributed terms or material to the dictionary:

Jocelyn Barker; Christine Bell; Kate Brightwell; Nick Duffell; Dorothy Hewerdine; Diana Howlett; David Jaques; Carol Laughlin; Duncan Lockett; Nic Marks; Jane Mathison; Jan Mulreany; Emilie Myers; John Nugent; John Pearson; Hilary Pinder; Martin Pollecof; Sheila Ritz; Graham Robinson; Wendy Rose; Sue Saxby-Smith; Peter A.C. Smith; Julie Soskin; Mal Tanner; Geoff Thompson; Peter Woods.

In addition we wish to thank Denis Postle for his invaluable feedback and advice; and many other colleagues, friends and family for their help, support and patience.

Dedication

This book is dedicated to our teachers in personal development.

Some are recognizable teachers, such as John Heron, John Mulligan and Meg Bond, who, with others, organized and facilitated the IDHP 2-year postgraduate Diploma in Humanistic Psychology and Facilitator Training. Sadly this is no longer running at Surrey, but it has left its hallmark on the hearts and minds of many who attended the course. Other teachers are less obvious, but equally important. These are my peers on all the personal development courses I have attended and my students on the MSc in Change Agent Skills and Strategies who through their feedback and challenges continue to facilitate my personal development.

A very special mention to my former therapist Sue Fish who, even through her final months on this earth, gives out love and wisdom.

Josie Gregory

Many people helped introduce me to personal development, particularly staff and peers at the University of Bath in the early 1980s. They include Judi Marshall, Adrian McLean, Peter Reason, Reg Hamilton, Peter Hawkins and Judy Ryde. I have gained invaluable learning from my various therapists and counsellors over time. At Surrey, John Mulligan was the peer Director of the HPRG when I joined in 1991, and was the instigator of the MSc Change Agent Skills and Strategies. This has proved an endless source of personal development, and has brought me into contact with scores more teachers, the programme participants. My thanks to all these people.

Paul Tosey

abreaction the clinical term for CATHARSIS. Considered to be an instinctive and unconscious emotional release, in response to a RE-STIMULATION of previous emotional TRAUMA.

accelerated learning refers to a variety of methods that claimed to engage faster or more efficient learning. An example source in this genre is Meier (2000).

These methods often use the 'whole brain' (see LEFT-BRAIN/RIGHT-BRAIN) or the 'BODYMIND', and/or counter various assumptions and practices of traditional, formal education. For example, they may use Howard Gardner's theory of multiple INTELLIGENCES rather than traditional IQ.

Examples of forms of accelerated learning include speed reading, BRAIN GYM and SUGGESTOPEDIA.

acceptance Maslow comments on self-acceptance as a characteristic of psychological HEALTH as follows: '. . . healthy individuals find it possible to accept themselves and their own nature without chagrin or complaint or, for that matter, even without thinking about the matter very much . . . One does not complain about water because it is wet, or about rocks because they are hard, or about trees because they are green' (Maslow 1970: 155–56).

Dryden (1998) is a useful recent source on self-acceptance that uses a RATIONAL-EMOTIVE approach. Acceptance can also refer to acceptance of one's circumstances or fate.

acting into when a person is emotionally distressed, but appears to be repressing the emotion through body armour (see CHARACTER ARMOUR) or social conditioning, a co-counsellor or therapist can encourage the person to intentionally act into the feeling to create a muscular pathway for its release. This 'acting into' can be shaking and trembling if fearful, sobbing if grieving and shouting and pounding if angry. The very act of working into the feeling often produces real and profound CATHARSIS.

acting out an unaware spilling out of distress into areas of life not intended to be influenced by the distress.

As in physics, all energy is utilized whether in its true form or as displaced or transmuted. All emotions – anxiety, anger and grief – need to be, and will be, expressed in the person's physical and/psychic system. The same applies to positive emotions; acting out, however, is a distress-driven behaviour.

The difference between acting out and ACTING INTO is that acting out is neither spontaneous nor intentional. The behaviour can be described as COMPULSIVE.

Within TRANSACTIONAL ANALYSIS theory, 'acting out' is similar to Fanita English's (1971) concept of RACKET feelings, when authentic feelings are covered up by more permissible feelings with a culture or family. If a family tolerates expressions of sadness but not anger, then the person could develop a sadness racket, with anger being repressed. Such sadness will not be authentic and eventually will result in psychological stress. As a development of rackets, all forms of psychological GAMES (within TA) are a form of acting out.

action inquiry a particular mode of ACTION RESEARCH developed principally by American educator Bill Torbert (see Torbert 1991; Fisher, Rooke and Torbert 2001): 'By *action inquiry* we mean a kind of behaviour that is simultaneously inquiring and productive. It is behaviour that simultaneously learns about the developing situation, accomplishes whatever task appears to have priority, and invites a redefining of the task if necessary' (Fisher and Torbert 1995: 13).

The key word here is 'simultaneously'. Torbert advocates action inquiry as a form of research-in-the-moment, a mindfulness of behaviour, emotion, thought and intuition. As a management practice, Torbert claims that the action inquiry enables personal and organizational transformation. It is controversial as a mode of research – see, for example, Donald Schön's foreword to Torbert's *Power of Balance* (1991).

action learning a form of learning through experience, action learning was originated by Reg Revans (1983) in the 1940s as a means to improve UK coal production. It appears in numerous variants, but typically is based on the following tenets:

- Participants tackle real problems (no 'right' answer) in real time
- Participants meet in small stable learning groups ('Sets')
- Each Set holds intermittent meetings over a fixed program cycle
- Problems are relevant to a participant's own workplace realities
- A supportive collaborative learning process is followed in a Set
- Process is based on reflection, questioning, conjecture and refutation
- Participants take action between Set meetings to resolve their problem.

Action learning encourages REFLECTION and promotes insightful inquiry with perceptive partners in situations where solutions are not always obvious. It leaves responsibility for implementation of the solution in the participant's hands. The individual makes sense of an experience by conceptualizing it and generalizing the replicable points, and plans future actions based on the learning gathered. In this way the action learning Set provides a 'safe practice field' where the participants' mental models and future actions are shaped and reshaped.

Mike Pedler (1997) provides a useful overview of action learning.

action profiling a profiling method based on choreographer Rudolf Laban's model of human movement (see Ramsden 1992). Action profiling itself was developed by Warren Lamb, a management consultant, who applied these principles to work settings. Based on observation of natural movement, action profiling relates the range and variety of a person's physical movement to psychological preferences in decision-making, using three dimensions of *attention*, *intention* and *commitment*.

action research intervention in a real-life situation, rather than detached or reflective study, is the essence of action research. As a form of personal and professional development, action research involves testing or extending practice and monitoring the effects.

The origins of action research lie in Kurt Lewin's work on changing attitudes in the 1940s (Lewin 1947). He used Action Research to investigate social practices like factory production, social policy issues and group decision making and leadership. His cyclical 'plan, act, review' model resembles Kolb's EXPERIENTIAL LEARNING CYCLE.

Action research became a recognized form of academic and practical research, particularly in the field of organizational behaviour – in this respect it differs from the more exclusively pragmatic concerns of ACTION LEARNING.

A recent variant developed in the education sector emphasizes the personal and professional development of the individual practitioner, through action (McNiff et al. 1996). This differs from the emphasis of 'classic' action research on social change through the study of human systems in action, and/or problem solving by participants rather than outside experts.

adult see EGO STATE.

affect, education of the this form of education (also called emotional education) developed as a pivotal change strategy within the HUMAN POTENTIAL movement in the 1960s. Heron (1982), among others, identified the need for emotional education to counteract the prevailing dogma of centuries during which the intellect was viewed as the prime attribute distinguishing man from animals. Such dogma supported the education of the intellect and the suppression of innate (animal) emotions. In established education the development of cognitive and behavioural skills was emphasized far more than subjective experience, particularly emotional experience. This is considered oppressive and alienating, limiting the psychological and spiritual growth of the person, and contrary to the HOLISTIC philosophy of humanistic education.

Affective education addresses EMOTIONAL COMPETENCE, such as the capacity to manage and express effectively frustration, grief, joy and excitement, and familiarity with CATHARSIS. It can take many forms, such as PSYCHODRAMA, ROLE-PLAY, peer counselling (see CO-COUNSELLING), OUTWARD BOUND courses, music, song and dance, physical activities and animated interpersonal dialogue.

The place of affective education is made explicit in Heron's model of MANIFOLD LEARNING, and continues to be promoted by the Society for Effective Affective Learning (see Resources).

affection a feeling of liking, loving, or empathy for another person. 'The affect' refers to the emotional dimension of experience.

The role of affection in human relationships is the subject of Bowlby's ATTACHMENT theory, a psychoanalytic approach. Bowlby says: 'the core of what I term an "affectional bond" is the attraction that one *individual* has for another *individual*' (1979: 67).

affirmation affirmation provides impetus to move towards a chosen outcome or away from an unwanted current situation. Affirmation is common in NEW AGE sources but is a long-established practice. 'There are many practical applications of the principle that what we affirm and program into the unconscious belief system, we tend in subtle ways to bring about . . . The basic principle has long been a core idea in the esoteric inner-core understandings of the world's spiritual traditions' (Harman 1988: 77).

Assagioli (1992) positions affirmation as the step that follows a decision to change but before the act of planning what will be undertaken. The process of affirming an image makes it stronger and more effective by activating the creative energies needed to achieve the outcome. Harrison (1995: 145) underlines the requirement to be determinedly honest about all aspects of the current reality.

Affirmation can be both an INTRAPERSONAL and INTERPERSONAL process. Intrapersonal affirmation enhances a personal conviction that a change will be accomplished. Interpersonal affirmation supports the intrapersonal process by, for example, clarifying the image, or endorsing the individual's process. A facilitator may support the person's process of commitment to an outcome rather than influence the outcome itself.

aggression literally the ability to step out or towards. It is a common misconception to believe that aggression is necessarily negative (its contemporary usage in language suggests as much). In personal development, sufficient aggression in the sense of being able to assert oneself, and take action to meet one's needs, is considered important for healthy functioning. For example, 'Perls conceptualized aggression in terms of its original root of "to reach out", and wished to re-establish its true biological function (which is not senseless discharge) but rather application of one's will to bring about relevant change in one's environment' (Clarkson 1989: 10).

alchemy historically, alchemy was the precursor of modern chemistry. It sought to understand the nature of matter and transformation; the goal of alchemy was to perfect everything in its own nature. Jung (1968d) became interested in it after a lengthy study of Gnosticism, and reading Richard Wilhelm's *The Secret of the Golden Flower*, a translation of a Chinese manual of spiritual alchemy (Wilhelm and Jung 1992).

Jung approached alchemical texts as though solving the riddle of an unknown language. He believed the Alchemists' quest was essentially symbolic, expressed through often abstruse and archetypal motifs. Just as the Alchemists were seeking the 'unknown substance', so people were driven to assimilate into their lives that which was mysterious and paradoxical.

Jung identified with the Alchemists' quest and viewed them as projecting their inner processes of INDIVIDUATION on to the material they were investigating. He extended the analogy to analysts, who sought to mediate between the contents of unconscious forces and the conscious self in the process of individuation. Alchemy was for Jung what sexuality was for Freud; an ultimate explanatory principle for the mysteries of the unconscious.

Alexander technique invented and developed by F. Matthias Alexander (1869–1955), the Alexander technique is a process through which the physical body is aligned (e.g. MacDonald and MacDonald 1998). The principle is that alignment not only promotes healthy physical functioning, but also contributes to psychological and emotional well-being. John Dewey took lessons with Alexander over a 35-year period, and they both believed strongly in the importance of the BODYMIND principle.

Alexander was born in Tasmania, and was pursuing a career in drama when he experienced great strain in using his voice. Although nothing medically wrong could be found, he became unable to speak effectively in public. In attempting to correct this he spent many hours observing himself speaking, in a mirror. He noticed subtle differences in the alignment of his head and neck when his voice felt free, and realized that this was not a problem of voice per se, nor even of the alignment of his head; his vocal performance was affected by his entire body posture.

From this developed what became known as 'the Alexander technique', and 'the principle that each of us functions as a whole and, first, to effect change that leads to improvement, one must learn to consciously prevent unwanted, unnecessary and harmful habits (such as undue muscular tension and effort). Because these habits occur repeatedly through our everyday life and hence become unconscious, part of the process of learning and applying the Alexander Technique is to become aware of what it is that we are actually doing' (The Society of Alexander Teachers UK website – see Resources).

The technique typically involves gentle realignment of posture by, or guided by, a trained practitioner. Exercise might involve maintaining this alignment when, for example, getting into and out of a car. There is an emphasis on interfering with unhelpful habits, which the technique calls 'inhibition'.

alienation a state of feeling distanced, isolated or estranged from society, or work, or oneself.

There are differences of meaning in various fields of usage. In sociology, writers such as Marcuse and Fromm use the Marxist idea of alienation of workers from the means of production in industrial society – the worker as a commodity or 'human resource', rather than as a human being who could find fulfilment through work.

In personal development, alienation is most likely to denote a sense of estrangement from self, of lack of meaning or of being disconnected from our inner nature or purpose.

John Rowan (1998: 184, for example) has argued that many forms of research are unnecessarily alienating, especially that they are inappropriate and potentially invalid as ways of understanding human experience. He has advocated more HUMANISTIC, collaborative forms of inquiry that have been developed in practice by, for example, Peter Reason (1994).

altered state an altered state of consciousness (ASC) is a qualitative change in attention, awareness, and consciousness, sometimes measured by changes in brain-wave patterns.

Experiential inquiry into radically altered states was at its zenith in the 1960s and 1970s. This included, but was not confined to, experimentation with 'mind-altering drugs' such as LSD (see Rowan 1993: 42 on Stanislav Grof). Contemporary strands of interest are represented, for example, by John Heron's (1987) explorations of other realms of consciousness.

However, many altered states are 'normal'. As Charles Tart (author of the classic *States of Consciousness*) says: 'Dreams could be called a rather "ordinary" altered state of consciousness, experienced to various degrees by most people. Then there are the extraordinary ASCs, induced sometimes by meditation, sometimes by psychedelic agents, sometimes by extreme stress, etc., altered states which are much more difficult to talk about . . . But in terms of the question of "Who am I?" the spectrum of altered states is a dramatic reminder that we may be much more, much different than just our ordinary state, our ordinary self' (Tart 1997: 192–93). Modalities such as NLP also take the view that everyday consciousness consists of varying STATES, and that it may be misleading to mark these out as extraordinary through the label 'altered'.

anal stage the second stage of human PSYCHOSEXUAL DEVELOPMENT within the Freudian (psychoanalytic) school. The anal stage occurs between the ages of 18 months and three years and is characterized by an investment of LIBIDO (sexual energy) in the anus with the child's attention on the function of defecation and bowel control. There are two main functions, holding back and giving up. Should the child get very anxious either through physical illness or psychological stress, the potential response is to FIXATE or freeze their development at this stage manifesting a personality trait of either anal-retentiveness (withholding) or with an anal-expulsive character (messy, dirty, wasteful and extravagant).

In common usage, the descriptor 'anal' usually refers to anal-retentive behaviour or characteristics.

anchor in NLP, anchor denotes any stimulus or representation that becomes connected to or associated with an internal response (including emotional states). Once established, the anchor can be 'fired' intentionally to trigger the response in question. The metaphor of the anchor denotes the way in which a ship's anchor ties the ship to a stable point of reference. NLP has many techniques for utilizing anchors (e.g. see O'Connor and Seymour 1993).

An anchor is a type of association and usually occurs naturally. Some people, for example, associate spiders with fear or panic. The sound of a particular person's voice may be associated with pleasurable times we have spent with them. Hearing their voice triggers our feelings of pleasure. Anchors can also be a product of conditioning. For example, red becomes associated with danger and hence triggers caution.

Anchoring derived from MODELLING the work of Milton Erickson, the American hypnotherapist. Bandler and Grinder's use of anchoring is described in *Frogs Into Princes* (1979). Robert Dilts distinguishes NLP's concept of anchors from straightforward behavioural CONDITIONING. He says: 'In the behaviorist's stimulus-response conditioning formula, however, the stimulus is always an environmental cue and the response is always a specific behavioral action. The association is considered reflexive and not a matter of choice . . . Rather than being a mindless knee-jerk reflex, an anchor becomes a tool for self-empowerment. Anchoring can be a very useful tool for helping to establish and reactivate the mental processes associated with creativity, learning, concentration and other important resources' (Dilts 1999).

andragogy the teaching (and learning) of adults, as opposed to pedagogy, which refers to the teaching and learning of children. Malcolm Knowles (1980) is credited with being the principal writer on the notion of andragogy. This reflects a concern, emergent in the 1970s, that a classroom-style, teacher-led approach, as used in school education, was not suitable for adults.

Andragogy is associated with principles of SELF-DIRECTED LEARNING and a negotiated approach to education through the use of LEARNING CONTRACTS. The notion of andragogy has been re-evaluated, not so much because it is mistaken about the learning needs of adults but because the suitability of 'pedagogy' for children is questioned.

anger anger is one of the most difficult emotions for many people. At root it is a healthy response to threat, associated with the 'fight–flight' response (Goleman 1996: 59–65).

In families, work organizations and communities people often tread a tightrope between expressing and suppressing their anger. Not only do social structures often give people cause to feel threat, becoming therefore a source of anger, but they also have norms that lead to expressions of anger being frowned upon. If a person vents their anger they risk being penalized. If they suppress it, they may either turn it inwards or risk a destructive eruption when the pressure can no longer be contained.

Personal development has emphasized the need for many people in Western society simply to get in touch with and become more familiar with anger. The less able we are to express anger, the greater the chance that it will spill out or become represented in rigidities in the physical body. In CO-COUNSELLING, for example, there are techniques for expressing anger in a safe environment. Being able to express anger towards another person cleanly, dealing with whatever issue is at hand without escalating into a personal attack and creating lasting resentment, is an aspect of EMOTIONAL COMPETENCE. Recent years have seen 'anger management' courses become popular, particularly because many celebrities have been participants.

To achieve an authentic and socially acceptable expression of anger is very challenging. Many theorists and practitioners (such as Wilhelm Reich) might argue that social strictures and norms need to change, rather than the burden being on the person to regulate their energies and emotions too carefully. But some disciplines (e.g. BUDDHISM) see anger as an undesirable emotion that should be calmed and TRANSMUTED into a more positive state, rather than expressed through CATHARSIS.

anima a term used in Jungian psychology, *anima* comes from the Latin for air, breath, life, soul; in other words, the animating principle in a living being. The modern psychological sense was given by Jung in *Psychological Types* (Jung 1971; see also Hillman 1985).

The anima represents the feminine principle in the male. It is the ARCHETYPE of the eternal feminine with both creative and destructive aspects. Men carry this archetype with them just as women carry the masculine principle of the ANIMUS, as an unconscious inner image of woman and the feminine.

These unconscious inner images are fantasy figures, represented on the collective level by gods and goddesses, film stars, celebrities, rock stars, and contrasexual icons of any kind. In relationships with the opposite sex, people project facets of their unconscious contrasexual images on to the partner, seeing them not as they are but according to this model in their psyches, endowing them with highly exaggerated characteristics, both positive and negative. The anima is the unknown woman inside the man which he has had to disown in order to be a man; in order to become a whole being he needs to discover this contrasexual side and integrate it into his conscious personality.

The concepts of animus and anima have been extensively criticized by post-Jungians and others as too polarized, belonging to an essentially masculine and patriarchal culture which stereotyped and over-romanticized women (Claremont de Castilleja 1973). It is now thought more useful to think of animus and anima as archetypal principles in both men and women.

animus the masculine principle in Jungian psychology. Jung wrote more about the ANIMA than the animus. He proposed that the animus represented the masculine principle. This was responsible for the ability to rationalize, and representative of spirit and religious or philosophical ideas. It was also considered to embody the creative principle (see, for example, McNeely 1991).

The concept of animus has come in for considerable criticism. Jung held that the animus in women was responsible for 'an inexhaustible supply of illogical arguments and false explanation', because it could be expressed through being quarrelsome and opinionated. He disapproved of the tendency for women to enter masculine professions. These notions are indicative that Jung held women to be of less worth, implying that they did not possess their own abilities to think and reflect. Their role was essentially to be the *femmes inspiratrices* for the more active males of the species. Contemporary Jungians, however, tend towards the notion that both animus and anima are active principles in the psyches of both the sexes.

anthroposophy anthroposophy is a movement derived from theosophy (the title combines the prefix *anthropo-*, referring to human beings, with the latter portion of theosophy). It was founded by Rudolf Steiner, an Austrian thinker known for his interests in consciousness and spirituality (see, for example, Steiner 1993; Gulbenkian 2000; a useful internet source is the Rudolf Steiner archive – see Resources).

Steiner advocated the need for a deeper understanding of the world and human history through knowledge of the inner and spirit worlds, and believed that a human capacity for direct apprehension of the spiritual could be reawakened.

Anthroposophy is applied through Steiner or Waldorf schools, which provide a form of alternative education. There is debate about the extent to which the curriculum and philosophy of these schools is based on Steiner's esoteric philosophy; however, many welcome the emphasis on developing the imagination, and on nature, ritual and mythology.

anxiety a heightened emotional subjective state characterized by trepidation about events, either internal (within the person) or external (within social, political and environmental relationships). Overstimulation of the autonomic nervous system, which is involuntary, results in heart palpitations, sweating and HYPERVENTILATION with agitated thinking and sometimes agitated behaviour.

There are differences in the way anxiety is treated in different therapies. For example, Freud and his followers were concerned mainly with dysfunctional aspects of (neurotic) anxiety. Fritz Perls saw 'excitation' as more positive, a creative tension, but one that could turn into anxiety if not expressed or acted upon (Clarkson 1989: 10). Rollo May (1996, originally 1950) challenged the notion that health means living without anxiety and argued that anxiety is an essential part of the (contemporary) human condition. Anxiety or angst is a fundamental of EXISTENTIALISM (where angst means to want something one fears and is central to the conception of original sin). May attributes to Thomas Wolfe, the novelist, the observation that anxiety hinges on the ability to accept psychological autonomy.

Anxiety can range from mild excitation to a feeling of dread with no obvious justification. It can be free-flowing when there is no particular focus, or phobic when linked habitually to one event or object. Anxiety can manifest with the phenomenological experience of ALIENATION; of loneliness, feelings of not being valued and the experience of not being loved. External causes of anxiety can be social or cultural alienation or over-adaptation to others, financial instability, and rapid changes in family roles and values, particularly if experiences are perceived as imposed and when CHANGE is happening on too many fronts at the same time.

APEL the Accreditation of Prior Experiential Learning.

'APEL is the accreditation of prior experiential learning, that is, the award of credit for learning based on prior experience – from work, community or volunteer experience – which has not previously been assessed and/or awarded credit. By converting informal learning into certificated learning, APEL provides cost-effective routes to qualifications. It has potential significance for people who, through life and work experience, have learned knowledge, skills and analytical abilities that are comparable to those in a higher education award' (Learning from Experience Trust 2000).

APEL has developed in adult education (see Evans 1992) as a means of recognizing, and often of giving formal credit for, prior practical learning from experience (APL, the Accreditation of Prior Learning, usually refers to credit that can be transferred from previous formal study). APEL is significant in relation to widening access to further and higher education.

archetypal psychology the term 'Archetypal Psychology' was first used by James Hillman in the 1970s (see Hillman 1983). Its historical origins lie in the Eranos Conferences, begun in 1933 at Ascona in Switzerland, which aimed to explore the connections between Oriental spirituality and Western psychology.

Central to this approach is the notion that imagination (see IMAGINAL) is the main vehicle through which the human PSYCHE expresses itself, spiritually, psychologically and bodily. It is concerned with fantasy, imagination and MYTHS for its material. It claims not to be logical in the Western sense, and to concern itself with body, SOUL and SPIRIT as a unity, rather than the Cartesian dualism and platonic idealism of the Jungian tradition.

Archetypal Psychology differs from (Jung's) analytical psychology in that it deliberately affiliated itself with the arts, culture and the history of ideas, rather than medicine and psychiatry. It set out to de-PATHOLOGIZE psychology, and to view any human experience as a rich source of archetypal information. The therapeutic approach is to use the clients' imagination to understand the underlying archetypal patterns in their lives. Feelings are viewed as part of the imagery, rather than factors to be addressed on their own. See also ARCHETYPE.

archetype an unconscious psychic matrix which moulds an individual's experiences. Jung's specific psychological use of the term dates from 1919 (Jung 1969: para. 270; see also Rowan 1993: Von Franz 1997).

Both Jung and Freud believed that the PSYCHE patterns our experiences according to innate models, the psychic equivalent of the instincts (Jung 1968b). In Jung's conception, each archetype of the COLLECTIVE UNCONSCIOUS sums up the entire biological experience of a particular type of relationship or experience. In situations that resonate, via emotional attunement, with similar situations from mankind's past, the relevant archetype determines the structure and parameters of experience. So every newborn human being projects onto the woman nurturing it the archetype of the mother and acts out the archetype of the child. The woman does not, however, behave only as a type: she is an individual person with individual characteristics that make her relationship with this particular baby unique.

In this way a COMPLEX develops – personal experiences that colour and customize the individual's mother complex accrete around the generic mother archetype. Our personalities consist of the totality of these complexes; according to Jungian psychology, our psychological task is to integrate them into our conscious awareness.

At all levels, both individually and collectively (i.e. as a whole nation or culture), the archetypes set patterns which determine the kinds of experience we can have and the ways we can perceive and relate to the world. These patterns are known only through their partial manifestations in people's behaviours, being particularly observable in connection with the PRIMAL experiences of life (birth, sex, marriage, parenthood, death). They can also be seen in certain images from dreams, fantasies, fairy tales, legends, myths, and religions. Images and motifs from all of these frequently show remarkable and otherwise inexplicable similarities.

Among the most important of the inner personalities that appear to us in our dreams and fantasies are the mother, the SHADOW, the ANIMA or ANIMUS, and the wise old man or woman. The shadow, anima/animus, and SELF are particularly significant and have been called the archetypes of development, for they represent the major stages of psychological progress. Not all archetypes, however, are aspects of the merely human: some, such as river, ocean, and mountain, reflect aspects of the natural world. The archetypal is collective, suprahuman, and overpowering for individual human beings. Precisely because of this it can enchant us with a fascinating numinosity – whether in the heightened life of a film or in a sexual infatuation – and overcome our reason and our will with irresistible emotional power.

A modern application in personal and organizational development is the work of Carol Pearson (1991). Here, archetypes are used as a powerful tool for engaging people at a deep level of awareness, exploring and valuing the 'shadow' self (both personal and organizational), and recognizing mismatches and conflicts and their impact.

arousal stimulation into a state of wakefulness. 'The level of arousal of your body – how activated or relaxed it is – affects your mind at all levels. Fluctuating arousal is a normal part of life but sometimes you may fail to notice that it is running very high or very low so that you are either agitated or sluggish. For this reason it is useful to be able to raise or lower your level of arousal at will' (Postle 1988: 194).

arts therapies the arts therapies are modes of therapy that use art forms as ways of working. The principle is that the arts help particularly to engage the non-cognitive and non-verbal dimensions of being, and encourage an HOLISTIC approach.

The major forms of arts therapy are Art Therapy; Dance Movement Therapy; Dramatherapy; and Music Therapy. Art media (drawing and painting, sculpting, movement, music, drama, play, creative writing and storytelling) are frequently used more informally within experiential workshops and training courses.

Assagioli's Egg Roberto Assagioli's famous Egg Diagram (e.g. Assagioli 1975b: 17) is a map of human consciousness according to his principles of PSYCHOSYNTHESIS.

The Egg is an attempt to offer a more complete model of the human conscious than that of Freud or Jung. Assagioli had no quarrel with either but he took the map a stage further. To the idea of the subconscious, which he called the Lower Unconscious, he added a further dimension – the Higher Unconscious, or Superconscious. This consisted of elements which were not repressed but which were as yet undeveloped, or not yet identified. Amongst these he included values, meaning, purpose, qualities, and aspects of the spiritual life. Awareness and IDENTIFICATION could expand or contract into all these realms, mediated by the personal self or 'I', which was in turn a reflection of the HIGHER SELF.

This inclusion radically altered the context of psychology from a need and drive based battleground to one where humans were striving to integrate both what their conscious identities had previously omitted and that which was yet unrevealed to them. In this way Assagioli made sense of his own spiritual background and paved the ground for the HUMANISTIC and TRANSPERSONAL psychologies that followed.

assertiveness a person's ability to act in his or her best interests, understanding what he or she needs and wants, and appropriately seeking the necessary gratification without undue ANXIETY (see Hare 1996; Back and Back 1999).

Verbal assertive behaviour is the ability to express oneself honestly and to exercise our rights while being mindful of others' needs and wants and taking them into account. Assertiveness is related to SELF-ESTEEM, for example, through accepting our rights as appropriate, feeling GROUNDED and willing to engage in relationships. Assertive behaviour is a characteristic that is both person and situation specific.

The following examples are taken from Huss (1990).

To act in one's own best interests: refers to the capacity to make life decisions (career, relationship, life style, time activities), to take initiative (start conversations, organize activities), to trust one's own judgement, to set goals and work to achieve them, to ask for help from others, to comfortably participate socially.

To stand up for oneself: includes such behaviours as saying 'No', setting limits on one's time and energy, responding to criticism, or putdowns or ANGER, expressing or supporting or defending one's opinions.

To express honest feelings comfortably: means the ability to disagree, show anger, to show affection or friendship, to admit fear or anxiety, to express agreement, or support, to be spontaneous, all without painful anxiety.

To exercise personal rights: relates to one's competency (as a citizen, or consumer, as a member of an organization or school or work group, as a participant in public events) to express opinions, to work for change, to respond to violation of one's own rights, or those of others.

To not deny the rights of others: is to accomplish the above personal expressions, without unfair criticism of others, without hurtful behaviour towards others, without name-calling, without intimidation, without manipulation, without controlling others.

Thus, assertive behaviour is a positive self-AFFIRMATION, which also values the other persons in one's life.

assessment centre an assessment centre is an organizational event with programmed activities for the purpose of appraising, or assessing the COMPETENCE or suitability of, existing or prospective employees. The experience is usually intended to be developmental for the person undergoing assessment. Assessment centres typically use, for example, PSYCHOMETRIC tests, group exercises, ROLE PLAYS and developmental interviews to give FEEDBACK.

associated in NLP, this refers to experiencing the world directly, with sensory awareness (i.e. through our own eyes, and with feelings and body sensations). This is contrasted with 'disassociated'. In a disassociated state, a person experiences the world as if detached from their own body – unaware of, or detached from the sensations arising from, feelings, and observing oneself rather than experiencing from 'inside'.

Both associated and disassociated states have their uses. A person cannot feel 'fully alive' unless they are associated. Also past events can be re-experienced more vividly (literally) if one can recall them as if *in* the experience again now. It can be appropriate to be disassociated in order to detach (at least temporarily) from traumatic or otherwise unpleasant feelings. For example, disassociation is used intentionally within the NLP 'phobia cure'. What is not thought to be helpful is a chronic disassociated state (i.e. being 'cut off from feelings'). In NLP terms, a person is better off when they can choose when to be associated or disassociated.

astrology a branch of knowledge concerning correlations between configurations of celestial bodies (especially sun, moon and planets) and life on earth (e.g. Harvey and Harvey 1999).

Though its antecedents go back several millennia, modern astrology started to take shape in the Near East after 600 BC. Originally the words *astrologia* and *astronomia* were interchangeable: both meant study of the heavens, be it for pure scientific knowledge or for the purpose of divination. However, by the seventeenth century astronomy was used for the former and astrology for the latter.

There are as many branches of astrology as aspects of life, but most astrology is concerned with (1) delineating character (e.g. by using sun-signs); (2) predicting events and experiences for individuals, companies, nations, or any other kind of entity; or (3) determining the best time to do something. Generally, it will involve drawing up a diagram showing the positions of the celestial bodies for a significant moment in the matter under consideration (e.g. for character delineation, the individual's birth).

Much astrological literature needs to be approached cautiously. Nevertheless, the validity of astrological correlations is increasingly accepted in scientific circles. Causal mechanisms have been suggested but it seems most likely that astrology is an expression of acausal SYNCHRONICITY.

Recently several new schools of Psychological Astrology have developed. Liz Greene (e.g. 1990) is well known for her thorough, Jungian-influenced approach to astrology in relation to personal development. Another, called the Huber School (Huber 1991), has reinterpreted traditional astrological symbolism in the light of Esoteric Astrology (Bailey 1970) and PSYCHOSYNTHESIS. This claims to give access to individual potential, environmental conditioning and learning from previous lives.

attachment a concept popularized in the 1950s and 1960s with Bowlby's Attachment Theory (1969). This theory elucidates the importance of emotional bonding between the infant (age 0 to 12 months) and their primary caregiver. This is considered a 'healthy symbiosis' in most schools of psychology.

Attachment theory developed out of research conducted to understand the origin, function and development of the child's early socio-emotional relations. Attachment or bonding is a behavioural process with FEEDBACK mechanisms allowing the infant to correct behaviour if there appears to be a discrepancy with what is necessary to attain the desired goal. This behaviour is not instinctual, and has a degree of INTENTIONALITY (i.e. to increase the proximity of the caregiver). Affectional bonds are formed as a result of interaction with the attached figure. Emotional life is seen as dependent on the formation, maintenance, disruption or renewal of attachment relationships.

attention a state of alert awareness to internal and external environmental stimuli. Psychologically, attention means the selective retention of reflective experience. To attend to an event may entail unconsciously applying a hierarchy of criteria through which we decide what is, and what is not, significant in our experience (Spinelli 1989: 24).

It is impossible to attend to all available stimuli in the environment, so we focus on what we choose, or believe is significant, so excluding other stimuli from the focus of our attention. Attention is therefore selective.

In the SELF-HELP technique of CO-COUNSELLING, attention means deep listening to the cues and insinuations of what another is saying and doing. It may involve all the five senses, kinaesthetic, auditory, visual, tactile, and olfactory. Giving full (free) attention to the other person is the first of the three helping CONTRACTS and many would say the most important. In co-counselling, giving full attention means that the counsellor listens attentively without interrupting and without non-verbal interference apart from a steady gaze. It implies that the counsellor 'brackets', or sets aside, their own interpretations, concentrates on the client's story and their needs, and lets go of any need to take action.

attitude originally, to 'have an attitude' meant to hold a certain physical posture (e.g. 'a threatening attitude'). As the discipline of psychology developed, the question of why the person might adopt such a physical stance moved to making inferences about the mental state of the individual. Thereafter, attitudes referred to the psychological perspective a person applied to people and situations.

As a psychological construct, attitude means to have a predisposition to identify, in a discriminatory fashion, objects and events and to react to them in a personal, evaluative way. Attitude development is in effect a process of classification – for example, of types of people according to class, race, jobs, belief systems and so on, or about the physical world, art or history – to which evaluations become attached.

Attitudes may be either positive or negative depending on the judgements and responses of the individual. Attitude researchers rely on persons' own accounts of their predispositions or on inferences made through observation. Attitude questionnaires are the most common form of social surveys used within social and political sciences.

Many researchers and authors assert that there is a hierarchy of how people categorize and evaluate themselves, others and events. Beliefs and opinions are more specific members of the hierarchy, attitudes being slightly broader, and sentiment and 'interests' more basic, with VALUES being broad tendencies towards a person, object or event. Attitudes are seen as underlying predispositions with expressed opinion their overt manifestation.

attunement felt resonance with the worldview of another being or object; being fully aware of the sensing, thinking, feeling entity, communicating that back to the person or thing attuned with while still recognizing one's separate identity.

Heron (1992) speaks of attunement in the same breath as indwelling, resonance, participating in and harmonizing with the cosmic world and all the material and non-material aspects of it. Attunement resembles emotional EMPATHY and in this sense is encouraged by psychotherapists (Erskine 1993) as a means of understanding the client and a form of intersubjective communication.

In REIKI, attunement refers to the process through which a person becomes able to channel universal healing energy. More generally, attunement refers loosely to the notion that a person is or can become 'tuned' to the universe, nature, divinity, and so on. It is also a core concept in some modes of healing.

aura a field of subtle energy that surrounds the body. There are said to be various layers, linked to the CHAKRAS, and corresponding to colours and aspects of the psyche (as suggested, for example, by the American psychic Edgar Cayce). Those who claim to see auras may attempt to assess health or psychological dispositions from the depth and quality of the aura's colour (e.g. Brennan 1988).

authenticity authenticity refers to being true to oneself. In HUMANISTIC PSYCHOLOGY, authenticity is seen as a desirable goal because it relates to emotional awareness, freedom from social repression of thoughts and feelings, and direct, honest communication. Rowan (1993: 46) cites Maslow's notion of being 'authenticated' in relation to being 'fully human' and self-actualizing, and notes that Ken Wilber associates the issue of authenticity with the CENTAUR stage of development (1993: 121). The question of what constitutes authentic existence has been considered by philosophers such as Camus, Sartre and Kierkegaard.

The quest for authenticity is prominent in GESTALT. Clarkson and Mackewn (1993: 9) note that authenticity is an EXISTENTIAL principle and means 'choosing to live with integrity, to face, without self-deception or game-playing, the fact that we are free and responsible and yet at the same time condemned to die'.

But authenticity is far from a straightforward concept. It may be appropriate, for example, to ask 'authentic in relation to what or whom?', rather than to treat authenticity as an unquestioned ideal. In the humanistic tradition and in personal development more widely, it is usually thought desirable for the practitioner to be authentic in the sense of owning up to their vulnerabilities, and saying what they really mean. Authenticity to one's own feelings is likely to be helpful for those who previously have been inauthentic in this respect, but this is still a particular form of authenticity. The principle of being true to one's feelings can be in conflict with social and ethical considerations. A person might treat other people's needs and feelings as impediments to their own authenticity, and dismiss others' responses to his or her behaviour as either their own problem or their PRO-JECTION. Similarly objectionable would be the practitioner who cites their own authenticity as a mark of superiority over others. COMPULSIVE authenticity is likely to be the mirror opposite of compulsive social repression.

authority the legitimate power or capacity to direct; or the quality associated with someone who is considered to hold such power ('She has an air of authority'). The tendency to obey authority was illustrated frighteningly by the experiments of Stanley Milgram (e.g. Buchanan and Huczynski 1997: 258).

The notion of authority has several aspects. In organizations and societies, authority can be bestowed to those in particular ROLES. Usually, the higher the status of these roles the greater is the authority. Thus managers typically have a degree of legitimate authority to take decisions and give instructions of various kinds. Using this power in a dictatorial manner is what is meant by 'authoritarian'.

Weber (for example, Buchanan and Huczynski 1997: 365) identified three types of authority: traditional (e.g. the 'divine right' of kings), legal-rational (based on rules, as with roles in work organizations), and CHARISMATIC (derived from special qualities the person themselves is perceived to possess).

Those in positions of authority then may become identified with this power and be known as 'authorities' or 'authority figures'. Here, the concept of TRANSFERENCE becomes important. People learn about authority from their first experiences of authority figures, their parents (and often authority is associated more with fathers, nurturing parenting with mothers). As we grow up we meet more authority figures – teachers, bosses and so on – onto whom we may transfer the feelings and dynamics we experienced and learnt from parents (Freud associated authority figures with the SUPEREGO). Thus someone who reports that they have difficulty with authority figures may well have unresolved issues left from their relationship with their parents. In practice, the quality of relationships with authority figures is also influenced by the degree to which we subordinate ourselves, or consent to the exercise of authority.

Personal development is also concerned with the authority we give to ourselves – our capacity to be the author of our own experience and choices.

autogenics autogenic means 'self-generating'. Autogenics is essentially a method of relaxation based on self-hypnosis. Using simple mental exercises, it links mind and body to achieve states of deep relaxation. According to the British Autogenic Society website (see Resources), the person attains a 'passive concentration', a state of 'alert but detached awareness'. 'Autogenic Therapy' was developed by Dr. Johannes Schultz (1884–1970), a psychiatrist and neurologist who was influenced and supported by Freud, drawing on research which noted that simple verbal exercises to induce hypnosis led to a state of well-being. Schultz helped patients achieve a similar state by attending to sensations of heaviness and warmth in the limbs. This state is considered helpful for stress management and many stress-related conditions. It is claimed to be simpler and more generally acceptable (at least to the conservatively-minded) than hypnosis, YOGA, TRANSCENDENTAL MEDITATION, and the like. There is no link to any religion or particular philosophy.

autonomy autonomy has many definitions, from fields such as philosophy, developmental psychology, education and psychotherapy. Philosophically, autonomy means self-rule and is the right of the self-conscious adult with long-term aims (Raphael 1994: 133). Heron (1999: 335) defines autonomy as 'a state of being in which each person can in liberty determine and fulfil their own true needs and interests'. May (1996) believes that for a human to be autonomous he or she must also have developed a sense of responsibility to him- or herself and to others. Learner autonomy is an educational concept related to SELF-DIRECTED LEARNING.

The main therapeutic intention in TRANSACTIONAL ANALYSIS, for example, is to help the client to achieve autonomy, through SELF-AWARENESS, creativity and INTIMACY. Here, autonomy means to respond to personal and social reality in appropriate ways from the adult EGO STATE, rather than act out of, for example, distressed child SCRIPTS.

autonomy lab 'Autonomy Lab' is the name given by Roger Harrison in the 1970s (e.g. see Harrison 1995) to an educational format that he developed in response to misgivings about T-GROUPS, and observations about differences between American and European experiences of T-groups.

Harrison describes his aim as to 'produce the creative tension of the T-group lab without using groups'. He experienced T-groups as a practitioner, and also conducted research into participants' experience of them. He challenges the notion held by T-group trainers that 'equated openness with competence'.

Instead, Harrison suggests a negative correlation between a person's emotional expressiveness and their rating (by other group members) as constructive and helpful: '. . . group members saw emotional expressiveness and willingness to confront as aggressive and unconstructive, even after (or perhaps *especially* after) they had been through a T-group in which such expressiveness was promoted and valued' (Harrison 1995: 37).

A feature of the Autonomy Lab is that 'people choose their own activities, pace, timing, and partners. They come and go as they please, and so each chooses the level of stress and confrontation at which he or she wants to operate' (Harrison 1995: 65). A related method is Harrison Owen's OPEN SPACE TECHNOLOGY (1995). In both these formats, the key issue for effectiveness is of how people respond to the relative lack of boundaries. See also Heron (1999: 276).

avoidance an attempt to escape a potentially embarrassing or anxiety-laden topic, object, or encounter. For example, a group might begin to talk endlessly about a relatively unimportant topic. This could be an avoidance of the task in hand, or of an uncomfortable decision that must be made.

Avoidance of conflict is very common. Avoidance is not necessarily deliberate or conscious. ATTENTION is selective and partial so in a sense we must always be avoiding – in GESTALT terms, it is impossible to make all awareness figural at once (Clarkson 1989: 102).

awareness a state of being aware. GESTALT in particular emphasizes the value of present-time, sensory awareness. This encourages a focus on what we sense and feel HERE AND NOW. In Gestalt it is suggested that people spend much of their existence thinking about the past or the future. Personal development will often lead to enhanced sensory awareness and emotional sensitivity.

The idea that 'mindfulness' in everyday awareness can transform our experience is a frequent theme. For example, John Rowan (1998: 161 et seq.) advocates the development of a particular form of awareness or consciousness, less focused or concentrated than usual, and a whole-body rather than intellectual awareness. He likens this to Freud's 'free-floating attention' and calls it 'listening with the fourth ear'. In NLP a related distinction is made between a defocused, expanded peripheral vision and foveal (focused) vision.

A classic book of awareness exercises is Stevens (1971). See also SELF-AWARENESS.

baggage baggage refers to problems, attitudes, hang-ups, grievances and the like that a person carries with them. The implication is that such baggage is unnecessary and weighs us down; also that it is unhelpful to transport it into new situations. People are, however, generally quite possessive about their baggage and reluctant to be parted from it.

behaviour modification behaviour modification, sometimes known as behaviour therapy, is a systematic approach to changing behaviour through the application of the principles of conditioning (Sarafino 1996; see also BEHAVIOURISM). In a nutshell this seeks to reinforce desired behaviour and to suppress undesired behaviour.

Behaviour modification is a standard approach in clinical settings for a variety of behaviour patterns. Behaviour modification is also common in child development and school education.

Common techniques of behaviour modification are aversion therapy (associating current behaviour with an unpleasant stimulus); systematic desensitization (reducing the intensity of response to a stimulus) and biofeedback (enabling better self-regulation of a physiological response to a stimulus).

The same principles are applied commonly in organizations, for example, to produce employee CONFORMITY to desired organizational norms and targets. Methods in organizations typically involve systems of reward and sanction (Buchanan and Huczynski 1997: 103). In such settings the label 'behaviour modification' is less likely to be used or made explicit.

Behaviourism Behaviourism is that school of psychology which seeks to explain behaviour in terms of observable responses to environmental stimuli, and without attempting to understand mental processing or subjective experience.

Behaviourism was introduced in 1913 by J.B. Watson who was influenced by the conditioned-response experiments of Pavlov. Pavlov's investigation of the conditioned reflex had shown that dogs could be conditioned to salivate not just at the sight of food, but also at the sound of a bell that preceded food. This is 'classical' conditioning.

B.F. Skinner (see Skinner 1971; Wright 1987), the major modern proponent of Behaviourism, concerned himself exclusively with the relationship of observable responses to stimuli and reward. He considered that our behaviour is moulded by the consequences generated by our past behaviour. Consequently, what we have already learned to do we can change by learning new patterns of behaviour.

Skinner developed the idea of shaping. By controlling the rewards and punishments given in response to behaviours, we can influence and shape behaviour. This is the principle of BEHAVIOUR MODIFICATION as a change technique.

HUMANISTIC criticisms of behaviourist approaches attack their reductionist view of the person (e.g. Rowan 1998: 10–14), although they acknowledge that behavioural methods can be effective in some circumstances.

being can refer to 'human being'; being as 'existence'; and also to a state of 'being' in contrast to 'doing'.

According to Teilhard de Chardin (1959), 'being' means to place one's ATTENTION on the work of reflecting deeply on spiritual and emotional essence, nature, and so on. Erich Fromm (1978) contrasted 'having' and 'being'. Rowan (1998: 104) cites an extract from Rollo May's work that illustrates the primal, existential experience of being.

HUMANISTIC psychologists explore what Maslow (see Maslow 1968) called SELF-ACTUALIZATION. Maslow contrasted 'being values' (B-values), being-cognition, and being-love, with 'deficiency values' (D-values). 'Being' has a transcendent and mystical quality that is associated with PEAK EXPERIENCES.

In personal development work, intentional reflective practice is advocated to increase self-knowledge and knowledge of our relationship with others and with nature. Balancing attention between actively being-in-the-world, and reflecting on being, is highly valued.

beliefs beliefs are very generalized concepts that influence how people think and act. They are wide ranging explanatory principles that may be held by individuals or groups. They act as conceptual filters through which individuals' experiences are perceived, coded and made meaningful. Usually people select information that supports or strengthens their beliefs.

Shared beliefs produce social cohesion. They cover a variety of experiences, such as the meaning of life and death, suffering, right and wrong, the construction of an individual's identity, tasks in life, relationships, roles and other life experiences. Beliefs appear to be intrinsic to human life. They often create expectations about how things 'should' be. Many beliefs operate unconsciously, and are influenced by language. It is now increasingly surmised that a person's beliefs can influence such factors as health, recovery from illness and the ability to tolerate crises.

Beliefs may be limiting or generative. Therapy (e.g. RATIONAL-EMOTIVE BEHAVIOUR THERAPY) often addresses limiting beliefs and results in their modification so that individuals acquire a new outlook on themselves and their lives.

Different theories and models of personal development define and approach beliefs in varying ways. NLP, for example, has developed techniques and processes for working with beliefs, which are understood to encompass a range of attitudes, beliefs, values and assumptions (e.g. Dilts 1991). In Dilts' model of NEUROLOGICAL LEVELS, 'belief' is a level higher than 'capability', implying that change at the level of beliefs will have an effect on a wide range of capabilities.

'big chicken' in personal development groups, participants typically bring personal issues to work on. A subtle form of competitiveness can be conducted through the (subjectively perceived) importance of the issues presented, to the extent that participants feel they can only raise an issue if it is very substantial – i.e. a 'big chicken', enough for everyone to feed on. If unchecked, this can create a heavy group energy, with a tacit norm that only weighty and serious matters are legitimate.

Bioenergetics Bioenergetics (also referred to as Bioenergetic Analysis, or bioenergetic psychotherapy) is a BODY-MIND psychotherapy developed by Alexander Lowen (e.g. Lowen 1976). Lowen trained with Wilhelm Reich, and subsequently founded the Institute for Bioenergetic Analysis in 1956.

According to Lowen and Lowen (1977): 'Bioenergetics is a way of understanding personality in terms of the body and its energetic processes. These processes, namely, the production of energy through respiration and metabolism and the discharge of energy in movement, are the basic functions of life.'

Bioenergetics assumes that mind and body reflect each other, such that, for example, childhood traumas are 'stored' physically, and manifested through structure, movement and/or breathing patterns. Psychological DEFENCES are represented in the body, and they affect emotional well-being by decreasing a person's ENERGY level.

Bioenergetic therapy attends to muscle patterns, posture, breathing, movement, and emotional expression. Sometimes using specific exercises to release tensions, it works towards increasing a person's capacity for spontaneous and creative self-expression.

biography biography is a method of personal development that places developmental issues in the context of the person's whole life and circumstances, thus taking into account their PERSONAL HISTORY.

Hunt and Sampson (1998) explore (auto)biography as a therapeutic tool, particularly its influence on the self and personal development, drawing on theory and practice from psychoanalysis, the philosophy of language, literary and social theory.

Autobiographical writing is used as a personal, and management or leadership, development tool by American educator Bill Torbert (Torbert and Fisher 1992).

BioSpiritual focusing a practice for accessing spirit-based body wisdom, which is claimed to represent a pastoral and theoretical shift away from dualism between body and soul in Western spirituality.

In the early 1970s, Peter Campbell and Edwin McMahon (Campbell and McMahon 1985; McMahon 1993), psychologists of religion and Jesuit priests, began exploring the link between FOCUSING and SPIRITUALITY. Their particular interest was in what distinguished healthy spirituality from addictive or abusive religious practices. They discovered a bridge through the body into the experience of spirit or bodily-felt meaning, which they concluded came as a spontaneous gift or surprise. They posited that a necessary precondition for this is what they termed Caring Feeling Presence. This internal experience has similarities with Carl Rogers' (1961) UNCONDITIONAL POSITIVE REGARD, and is the principal feature that distinguishes BioSpiritual Focusing from Gendlin's Focusing.

body language a general term for that part of NON-VERBAL COMMUNICATION which is conveyed through body posture, gesture, movement (including breathing patterns) and facial expression (e.g. Pease 1997).

In modes of development such as NLP, body language is treated as a highly significant channel of communication. Body language can be used intentionally, for example, to develop RAPPORT.

Some sources seem unduly concerned with using body language to tell whether a person is lying; or keen to identify universal meanings for body language. However, while there are clear cultural patterns (e.g. the 'Gallic shrug') it is generally considered safer not to jump to conclusions about the intended meaning of an individual's body language.

bodymind 'bodymind' refers to the principle that human beings are whole systems, mind plus body, and especially that we can best understand health and development through this perspective. It is a label used in many fields, including healing and alternative therapy.

Thinkers such as John Dewey have advocated the idea of bodymind unity. This is opposed to the dualistic principle embedded in much scientific and medical thinking in the West, which treats the mind and body as essentially separate. In this view, apart from occasional PSYCHOSOMATIC (literally mind-body) symptoms, a person's thoughts and emotions are seen as having peripheral significance for their health.

Many methods of personal development explicitly utilize the bodymind principle, though in varying fashions. These include ALEXANDER TECHNIQUE, BIOENERGETICS, BRAIN GYM, FOCUSING, KINESIOLOGY, NLP and SUGGESTOPEDIA.

bodywork refers to a very wide range of therapies (e.g. BIOENERGETICS; Gerda Boysen's biodynamic massage), modes of development (e.g. MASSAGE) and techniques that work primarily or directly with the body. Wilhelm Reich (see e.g. Boadella 1991) is a key figure whose work has influenced many of these approaches.

The body is always relevant, and usually important, in HUMANISTIC approaches to personal development, which generally embrace the BODYMIND principle. This quite deliberately runs counter to the cognitive, intellectual emphasis of mainstream education, and social embarrassment about the human body. Bodywork can be direct and powerful precisely because it bypasses the rational mind and the potential distractions of a 'talking' therapy.

Rowan (1996) provides a useful introduction to bodywork in humanistic psychology.

boundary a term with similar meaning but varying usage in a number of personal development theories. A boundary generally is the border or perimeter of a psychological entity or field of awareness. Examples are the notion of ego boundary, and group boundary. A boundary does not exist in its own right. To cross a border or boundary means to declare an intention, a wish to recognize and to engage with the object or person on the other side. This intention may not be conscious.

GESTALT uses the term 'contact boundary' to denote the place of a person's encounter with others and the outer world. It is concerned with the quality of contact a person is able to create. The concept of boundary disturbance is also important (see GESTALT CYCLE). 'Boundary management' is a core concept of the Tavistock approach to understanding social systems (see Resources).

In the personality theory of TRANSACTIONAL ANALYSIS, 'ego boundaries' refer to the self-contained energy within each EGO STATE. In the healthy personality, ego boundaries act as containment of energies. Berne stated: 'ego boundaries appear to function like complex membranes of highly selective permeability. Inappropriate permeability of the boundaries between the Adult and the Child ego states may give rise to any of a special group of symptoms called 'boundary lesions' (Berne 1961: 63).

The notion of professional boundaries refers to practitioners working within a context of philosophical, ethical and practical standards. This is a controversial topic (see G.O.R.I.L.L.A. website in Resources).

brain gym a systematized form of Educational KINESIOLOGY developed by Paul Dennison, an American educational therapist, initially in order to help people with learning difficulties, but available generally to enhance learning, creativity and enjoyment.

As with kinesiology, the emphasis in Brain Gym is on the relationship between body movement and brain functioning. There are connections with the LEFT-BRAIN/RIGHT-BRAIN principle. Bodily coordination and integration are significant not only physically but also mentally, and Brain Gym uses movement to enhance neural pathways. For example, the 'cross crawl' is a movement based on a baby's crawling, which is believed to develop connections between the two hemispheres of the brain.

According to the Educational Kinesiology Foundation in the USA (*see* Resources), 'The Brain Gym movements integrate the brain . . . allowing information to flow easily from the senses into memory and then out again as new learning.'

brainstorming a creative problem-solving process whereby a person or group generates ideas without censoring or evaluating them (see Buzan 2000), akin therefore to FREE ASSOCIATION. The principle is that by 'turning off' the judging, censoring part of the mind (which many associate with the LEFT BRAIN) people can freely produce creative, nonsensical ideas which they might otherwise dismiss as irrelevant or stupid. Often these provide useful connections or new ways of perceiving a problem. A brainstorming session may last a set length of time (e.g. 10 minutes), or until the flow of ideas has dried up. Participants then move on to exploring and evaluating the brainstormed ideas.

breathing the quality and rhythm of breathing is significant in many BODY-MIND modes of personal and transpersonal development. Breathing is a PRIMAL experience – we literally depend on it for life. Also, as John Rowan notes (1993: 192), breathing works on physical, emotional, intellectual and spiritual levels.

There are many varieties of breathing in personal development. Ancient modes of development such as YOGA, for example, have sophisticated and complex understandings of the importance of the breath. Breathing also has a significant role in MEDITATION, REGRESSION, REBIRTHING; and VOICE WORK. A popular contemporary source on breathing is Hendricks (1995).

brief therapy brief therapy is a methodology for enabling clients to solve problems rapidly and effectively. It developed mainly from the therapeutic work of Milton Erickson (see Zeig and Munion 1999) and the cybernetics of Gregory Bateson, and is now practised widely. Its approach is essentially constructivist, in that it believes in giving higher priority to people's views of their problems than to the presenting contingencies. It is practised with individuals and families (see de Shazer 1988; Zeig and Gilligan 1990).

Brief Therapy originated in the USA. Among its main developers were the Mental Research Institute in Palo Alto (Watzlawick et al. 1974). It distinguishes itself from other therapies by claiming not to be dependent on elaborate theories about the human psyche, but rather to treat each individual's construction of their world as unique to them. It believes that the therapist's main task is to 'map' clients' constructs, then reconstruct the problem so that a solution is possible that matches clients' abilities. It abjures interpretation and PATHOLOGIZING. It is decisively goal-oriented, so that initial sessions are spent finding appropriate, achievable, well formed goals, and identifying evidence by which clients can know when these have been achieved. The therapy takes as long as the client needs to achieve the goal.

The therapist's approach is direct and interventive. It usually involves setting clients tasks to be completed before the next session. Sometimes these may intentionally be PARADOXICAL INJUNCTIONS or DOUBLE BINDS. Some traditions of brief therapy use teams of therapists to debate clients' problems in their presence, thus clients gain other perspectives and become involved in finding resolutions. Sometimes hypnosis is used.

Brief therapy has been criticized for not exploring underlying causes of problems, and being too mechanical.

However, there are many conditions for which it seems to work well.

Buddhism an Eastern philosophy and religion that has become very popular in the West. Buddha means 'one who is awake'. The Buddhist notion of non-attachment refers to perception that is unattached to any particular goal, theory or values (Harman 1988: 70). Buddhism sees suffering as the result of such attachment.

Buddhism probably originated in India, and spread to China and Japan. Zen is a Japanese form of Buddhism that became popular in the West as a result of books such as Herrigel's *Zen in the Art of Archery* (1972), and then Robert Pirsig's *Zen and the Art of Motorcycle Maintenance* (1974). The goal of Zen Buddhism is to develop an enlightened, tranquil mind.

Tibetan Buddhism is another strand that grew from Indian Buddhism. Tibetan Buddhism is very TRANSPERSONAL in nature; perhaps the best-known written work is the Tibetan Book of the Dead (H.H. The Dalai Lama 1998).

John Heron has critiqued Ken Wilber's work for what he (Heron) perceives to be the Buddhist perspective in Wilber's writings on transpersonal psychology, particularly the fundamental idea that this world and the self are illusory. Also Buddhism has no theory of, for example, repression of emotion, which some see as a limitation on its value in personal development.

buzz group a small group convened in the middle of a workshop or lecture. The purpose can be, for example, to discuss and respond to workshop or lecture content. This creates a change of attention and format; the 'buzz' comes from the sound of several groups in discussion.

career development career development and professional development of various kinds can support and enhance personal development. They can, however, provide a quite watered-down form of personal development, perhaps limited to INTERPERSONAL SKILLS and omitting to touch the 'inner' dimension that may be more difficult to address in professional or work settings.

catharsis the release, discharge or expulsive expression of emotions. In most forms of personal development work, catharsis is encouraged as a means of releasing blocked energy, often emotional energy, through crying, expressing grief through sobbing, or expressing ANGER through loud sounds and storming movements.

Most therapies agree about the benefits of spontaneous expression of feeling through behaviour and encourage catharsis to achieve this end. CO-COUNSELLING places particular emphasis on catharsis. There are different views in FOCUSING (where premature discharge may interrupt the emergence of the relevant symbol) and NLP, where cathartic release of distress is more a by-product than a means to insight.

In PSYCHOSYNTHESIS and other TRANSPERSONAL work catharsis is regarded as a 'process of becoming pure'. Heron (1992: 65) suggests that techniques such as catharsis are essential for spiritual development, because of the need for self-creation through undoing the 'negative psychological effects of the wounding and splitting of the infant psyche'.

celebration in CO-COUNSELLING, celebration of ourselves and our strengths and qualities is encouraged as a counter to social norms of self-effacement and putting ourselves down. Many people have been brought up to believe that appreciating ourselves and our achievements is self-aggrandizing and boastful. Celebration is an act of AFFIRMATION and self-EMPOWERMENT.

centaur the centaur stage of development in Ken Wilber's writing (Rowan 1993: 121) is the beginning of TRANSPERSONAL development. Wilber says: '. . . because consciousness is no longer identified with any of these (lower) elements to the exclusion of any others, all of them can be integrated: the body, the PERSONA, the SHADOW, the EGO – all can be brought into a higher-order integration . . . This integrated SELF wherein mind and body are harmoniously one, we call the "centaur". The centaur: the great mythological being with animal body and human mind existing in a perfect state of at-one-ment' (Wilber 1980: 45).

Wilber's model of levels of CONSCIOUSNESS (see Rowan 1993: 102) is a detailed synthesis of many traditions. Its three broad, principal stages are the pre-personal; the personal; and the transpersonal.

centred generally refers to being physically and mentally balanced. For example, in Taoist practice, centring refers to adopting an aligned posture combined with a calm mental state. Left and right sides of the body are in balance, with the centre of gravity at the point known in TAI CHI as the *tan tien*, located approximately two inches below the navel. The mind is quiet, alert but relaxed, and focused on the present.

chakras *chakra* is Sanskrit for 'wheel'. The chakra system is an approach to understanding people – and humanity more broadly – as flows of energies. In its simplest and typical form, there are seven main wheel-like centres located in the body, from the root chakra at the base of the spine to the crown chakra at the top of the head. These consist of three lower centres linking with the physical, emotional and lower mental; the fourth or middle centre is the heart that is the bridge between spirit and matter; and the three higher centres are connected to creative communication, visionary intuition and divine connection (see, for example, Ozaniec 1990).

The system has existed in various forms, probably for millennia. It comes principally from Hindu tradition, and is an integral part of that philosophy and spiritual discipline, but chakras or their equivalent appear in many other cultures including China, and the West. These have points in common, but also differ in many details.

The chakras are variously associated with colours, sounds and more. Each chakra has psychological and spiritual significance too, being associated with different qualities or dimensions of experience and consciousness. The root or base chakra, the *muladhara*, is associated with KUNDALINI energy, which traditional yogic techniques attempt to release.

Chakras are referred to in many sources on health (Brennan 1988), personal development (Judith 1996), and organizational change (Tosey 1999). Caroline Myss emphasizes the developmental aspect: 'The chakra system is an archetypal depiction of individual maturation through seven distinct stages . . . we ascend toward the Divine by gradually mastering the seductive pull of the physical world. At each stage we gain a more refined understanding of personal and spiritual power, since each chakra represents a spiritual life-lesson or challenge common to all human beings' (1997: 68).

change change is an almost ubiquitous concept, and a theme of interest that traces back to Herodotus's observation that 'all is flux'. It is elusive to define. Whilst in common-sense terms everyone may know what they mean by change, it needs careful handling in whichever field it appears.

How we think about change is significant. Typically, 'change' is intended to indicate some identifiable difference in quality or state. But usually this means contrasting 'change' with 'stability'. Some would argue that stability, or at least the notion that stability is the norm, is an illusion. COMPLEXITY THEORY, for example, sees what we perceive as stability to be a temporary order or pattern within a constant flux. Another useful perspective is provided by Watzlawick et al.'s (1974) idea of FIRST AND SECOND ORDER CHANGE.

In terms of personal experience, there are several models of change based on the notion of TRANSITION. These emphasize that external changes, or changes in circumstance (e.g. moving house, redundancy, organizational restructuring, and so on) typically involve loss and a process of emotional adjustment.

Change has been a leitmotiv of recent decades, especially in the world of business. It seems to have become a truism that our lives are characterized by change; that change is increasingly more rapid (a notion popularized by Alvin Toffler in the 1970s); and that change is threatening. But the validity of such claims merits scrutiny.

The effectiveness of practitioners in the personal development field seems predicated on their ability to produce or facilitate change. In this sense change implies improvement, progress or success. Much research in the fields of counselling and psychotherapy is concerned with testing efficacy, treating these human modalities through a medical frame of reference. The validity of this is open to debate. A consequence is that we might need to be cautious about claims, if practitioners have a vested interest in demonstrating that change has occurred.

change agent a person who has a role, legitimized by an organization or community, to facilitate change in that setting.

The label 'change agent' became popular in the late 1980s and early 1990s, along with the substantial attention given to change management. It can encompass many types of role, both internal and external to the membership of that setting, such as consultant, manager, trainer, developer, FACILITATOR and so on.

The Surrey Masters degree in Change Agent Skills and Strategies has a more particular emphasis on change agency in human systems, whether INTRAPERSONAL, INTERPERSONAL, group, inter-group, organizational or inter-organizational, through a facilitative, educational and generally CLIENT-CENTRED approach. We emphasize the need for the change agent to have experienced their own change before facilitating change for others.

channeling the PSYCHIC process by which an individual receives communication from another state, dimension or higher level of CONSCIOUSNESS in order to receive inspiration, teaching and advanced SELF-AWARENESS (see, for exam-

ple, Hastings 1991; Harman 1988: 73).

Although channeling is mostly practised by psychics and mediums it can occur spontaneously through inspirational writing, music and art, where a presence outside or beyond the individual appears to be part of the creative process.

chanting the practice of using voice and the resonance of the body for MEDITATION, achievement of an ALTERED STATE, or generally to enhance well-being. Chanting is used in many traditions (e.g. forms of BUDDHISM) as a spiritual and/or community practice (see, for example, Rowan 1993: 193). In meditation, a person might chant a mantra (literally 'instrument of thought' in Sanskrit), a word or phrase traditionally given by a guru. Chanting in pregnancy and childbirth is now being advocated by Frederick LeBoyer (*see* the 'Global Ideas Bank' in Resources). Chanting and related techniques are often incorporated into VOICE workshops.

character armour Wilhelm Reich (and followers, see, for example, BIOENERGETICS) believed that psychological and emotional trauma is stored in the body (see Reich 1972). Over time these can become chronic rigidities or tensions of the musculature and posture.

Reich referred to these as 'character armour', in the sense that they form a container for deeply-held distress and a barrier against sensory experience, spontaneity and the expression of emotion.

Rycroft (1971) underlines Freud's influence on Reich's work and notes that character is a development of Freud's notion of a DEFENCE. According to Rycroft, Reich maintained that character 'was the essential defence in all cases and that civilized Western man was imprisoned in a character-armour, which prevented him, in general, from expressing his spontaneous feelings of love and hatred, and in particular from experiencing orgasm' (Rycroft 1971: 29).

This view was criticized by Fritz Perls (see GESTALT) who felt it important to own the repressive intent of the armour as part of the self, rather than to alienate it from the self.

charismatic leadership charisma means personal power, from the Latin meaning 'a favour specially vouchsafed by God; a grace, a talent' (Heron 1999: 215).

Charismatic AUTHORITY is one of three forms of authority identified by Weber. Whereas Weber's use of the term denotes the source of the authority, charismatic leadership refers to influencing others through a felt sense of personal power, PRESENCE, style and manner of being. Charismatic presence is expressive, that is, full of self-confidence and high SELF-ESTEEM.

Charismatic leadership is not intrinsically benevolent. While it may enable others through its self-empowering way of being and behaving, it may also be manifest as an autocratic and controlling power.

check-in a period of time at the beginning of a group session for participants to arrive and prepare for the group's task. Typically, a check-in is a space for participants to 'park' issues that are on their minds; to declare what is 'on top' for them (i.e. uppermost in their awareness); or to share news. A practice used by John Southgate is for people to talk in pairs or threes about 'traumas, trivia and joys' before the group session itself begins. This enables participants' energy to focus on the HERE AND NOW.

Usually, participants choose whether to speak or not. A common recommendation is that contributions are received in silence (with non-verbal acknowledgement) so that the check-in is a process of arrival and not a social chat. However, check-in may be a fertile source of content for the session, especially if the group's purpose is to study its own process and dynamics.

It is also common to have a 'check-out' at the end of the session. This functions as a closing and offers participants the chance to leave behind whatever they do not wish to take, psychically speaking, into the outside world.

child all personality models offer theories on child development – Freud's psychoanalysis, Bandura's Social Learning Theory (i.e. childhood vicarious learning), Piaget's cognitive developmental stages, and Kohlberg's MORAL DEVELOPMENT, to name but a few. A model of child spiritual development can be found in Ken Wilber's work (Wilber 2000b).

Aspects of the child as a dimension of personality include the compulsive or traumatic child (Heron 1992), the free child, or INNER CHILD, and the facets of the Child EGO STATE in TRANSACTIONAL ANALYSIS.

circle dance circle dance is a form of community dancing that has a unique place in the personal and professional education environment. Based on traditional forms of central and eastern European folk dance, the overt aim is to give people in groups a sense of pleasure and purpose in 'moving together', reflecting solidarity in their community. Originally the traditional dances marked agricultural seasons such as the onset of winter, stages in someone's life (weddings, etc.) and events in communal life, e.g. release from OPPRESSION.

Circle dance was originally developed as Sacred Dance (Heligtanz) by Bernhard Wosien, a German ballet teacher, following his observation of the ritual nature of Balkan dances, and was brought by him to the Findhorn Foundation in 1978. Its flow into the USA is marked generally by its link with NEW AGE philosophies, for which it has been criticized there. Circle dance in the UK is now established as a thriving and networking community, with over 250 groups nationally.

The dances can represent and manifest stages, seasons and events of an individual or a group's 'inner life'. Teams can debrief dancing together as models of how they operate at work – are they all, for example, 'dancing to the same tune'? The metaphor of 'being in step with each other' is also powerful. Handholds are indicative of a community's strength, such as the Turkish 'pert' in which people are linked very closely together like a solid wall that no outsider can penetrate.

Reflection is used by established circle dance groups as well as in personal development contexts, team building and community building (see, for example, Jackson 1999; Marshall and Reason 1997).

client a person who receives services. The client is the person to whom, or for whom, the personal development practitioner delivers their service.

The term 'client' is usually preferred to the more clinical 'patient' in personal development work. This underlines the principle that the client is not ill (see PATHOLOGIZING), and often that the practitioner is not providing treatment or cure but is facilitating the client's ability to be self-directed. See also CLIENT-CENTRED.

In some contexts, especially in organizational CONSULTING, it can be hard to identify who the client is – or, there is a need to work with various different types of client (see Cockman et al. 1998). Thus the participant on the training course is one type of client; the manager of the department in which the benefits of the training are expected to be realized is another; and the senior manager authorizing the budget expenditure is yet another.

Issues of power in client relationships have been highlighted by Jeffrey Masson (1992), among others, in the field of psychotherapy.

client-centred the principle that the professional helper attends principally to, and is guided by, the client's needs. This is differentiated from an expert stance, where the helper is more likely to prescribe solutions for the client (as in a traditional General Practitioner–patient relationship).

The notion of client-centredness has its source in humanistic therapist and educator Carl Roger's emphasis on being PERSON-CENTRED and non-directive (Rogers 1951, 1961). Rogers emphasized UNCONDITIONAL POSITIVE REGARD, an atmosphere of respect and acceptance through which the client can, to a great extent, find their own way through their problems. The intention of the approach is therefore to promote client self-directedness and to avoid creating DEPENDENCE on the practitioner. This has been extended to consulting (Cockman et al. 1998), where the principle is that the client is often the best person to generate the solution to their problem, as well as to other helping relationships.

Among the issues with a client-centred approach (see, for example, Masson 1992) is the extent to which the helper's expertise, directing and prescription are covert rather than absent (see POWER). Thus a helper or facilitator who claims to be non-directive and client-centred may be unaware of, or in denial about, the ways in which their behaviour is directive and expert-led, and may hide their lack of experience and competence in a client-centred approach.

coaching a notion imported from sport to business and other organizational settings. Coaching is usually, and primarily, a process in which a facilitator – often an external trainer or consultant – assists a manager to perform better (see Whitmore 1996). Coaching will often concentrate on skills and behaviour, for example, through REHEARSAL, but also involving reflective, verbal sessions. A variant is the type of coaching influenced by Timothy Gallwey's INNER GAME approach.

In practice, coaching and MENTORING may be very similar. Both refer to a helping relationship, usually one-to-one, that is seen as acceptable for managerial staff – because connotations of counselling or psychotherapy are avoided – within a business context. There is debate in the field currently about definitions of mentoring and coaching; and this impinges too on workplace COUNSELLING.

co-counselling a form of client-directed, peer COUNSELLING. Through mutually assisted SELF-HELP, individuals draw on the same principles as, and seek to gain the outcomes of, personal growth and transformation offered in professional counselling and psychotherapy.

Co-counselling is derived from Re-evaluation co-counselling (called Re-evaluation Counselling Communities in the USA). The founder, Harvey Jackins (Jackins 1970), created the method and techniques in the 1950s as a result of helping another man work through emotional distress which seemed to free the man to resolve his own problems. Jackins observed the natural healing power of CATHARSIS which seemed to un-block the person from rigid patterns of thinking and behaving to a more constructive re-evaluation of his life and the motivation to change his way of living without the need for qualified and expensive professional helpers (counsellors and psychiatrists).

For various philosophical and ideological reasons Re-evaluation Counselling did not expand in Europe to the same scale as the USA. The European co-counselling community wanted to create more autonomous cells within an international co-operative framework; hence Co-counselling International was founded in the UK (Heron 1974b; see Resources).

The purpose of co-counselling is to provide peer facilitation (working through an appropriate CONTRACT) to express and release DISTRESS, which is impeding the person's growth. Co-counselling theory asserts that traumatic experiences from the time we are born lodge in the psyche causing unaware, compulsive, maladaptive and rigid behaviour patterns, and that this distress needs to be expressed and released if the person is to develop (Heron 1998a). Once the distress is released the person is encouraged to gain insights about the distressed patterns of behaviour and, through their own efforts and natural healing ability, find solutions to ongoing problems. In this sense, co-counselling is client-directed as well as client-centred.

Co-counselling involves an initial 40-hour training in which participants learn to take both client and helper roles, and practise simple but powerful techniques for working with their problems. Reciprocity is an essential requirement of co-counselling in that each person takes equal time in the different roles of the helping process. It usually involves a two-hour session. Participants typically then join a co-counselling community, or network, and continue to co-counsel with other trained peers.

co-dependence co-dependence (sometimes codependence, or codependency) is a term with varying usage. Some have portrayed codependency as a catch-all, addictive disease of Western society. In this sense codependency refers to a lack of trust or confidence in oneself, a dependency on external factors for everyday living, and perhaps a tendency towards self-destructive behaviour.

Co-dependence is also used increasingly to refer to relationships in which one person effectively colludes to enable a dependent to avoid the reality of an addiction (e.g. drug or drink problem). See also TWELFTH-STEP PROGRAMME.

Literally, co-dependence indicates a form of symbiosis (life together, or a mutually beneficial partnership) in which partners are in complementary RELATIONSHIP. In a couple, one partner might be recognized as being overtly dependent on the other and perceived as the 'weaker' partner; for example, where one is sick and is nursed by the other. But the apparently stronger partner can also have a need to be in this type of role, which they cannot perform without the other. This partner is therefore co-dependent, in the sense of being dependent on having a dependent. See also DEPENDENCE and COUNTER-DEPENDENCE.

co-facilitation co-facilitation occurs when a group educational experience is directed and managed by two people. Given the type and demands of experiential work in medium to large groups, co-facilitation is a popular practice. With two experienced group facilitators, issues of boundary keeping, holding legitimate AUTHORITY cooperatively within the facilitation contract and managing emotional and unconscious group processes can all be addressed more effectively. Two facilitators allow for a more even distribution of the PROJECTIONS and TRANSFERENCE that inevitably occur in experiential groups.

Co-facilitators often carry the YIN AND YANG, the masculine and feminine energies of the group, and will sometimes also re-stimulate family dynamics of two parents with participants as siblings. In distressed or uncreative groups (Randall and Southgate 1980) the co-facilitators will at times mirror 'good parent' and 'bad parent' transference.

An advantage of co-facilitation is as a professional development strategy, perhaps using SELF AND PEER ASSESSMENT of facilitator practice. It is also very useful as a training model with a senior facilitator working with an apprentice facilitator. See, for example, Knight and Scott (1998).

collective unconscious Jung's concept of the instinctual, innate part of an individual's UNCONSCIOUS, common to the entire society or even species.

Jung's theory (see Jung 1968b) originated in his observations of PSYCHIC phenomena which appeared to be both non-personal and universal. The further down we dig, the more we meet material that is incommensurate with a Freudian personal unconscious based on personal relationships. We meet dreams and fantasies which are of great emotional power yet exhibit myths and motifs that are not part of the individual's past experience and, moreover, are extremely widespread. These primordial images are what Jung later called ARCHETYPES.

The experiences that have fed into the collective unconscious are those of our entire species and even its biological antecedents (an idea which finds recent support in the theory of morphic resonance – see Sheldrake 1988). Each of us contains within us physical and neurological structures we have inherited from our evolutionary past (Sagan 1977): the neural chassis, which controls autonomous body functions, we have inherited from fish; the reptile brain that we still possess (the r-complex) cold-bloodedly controls our territorial instincts and aggression; the limbic system – the mammalian brain – gives us emotions and empathic relationships, and consequently the possibility of interpersonal connectedness and social units; and the neocortex, or primate brain, governs higher brain functioning which requires a greater level of consciousness – reasoning, deliberation, linguistic skills, vision and complex perceptual tasks requiring a greater sensitivity to external stimuli.

Jung's view of the collective unconscious is that it appears able to act in a realm outside of time and space. Contact with this limitless reservoir of human experience and supra-human potentialities can, however, be perilous. The numinosity and overwhelming emotionality associated with collective contents can result, for the individual, in delusions, inflation, and megalomania, and, for society, in mass psychoses (disturbed, delusional mental states). If, on the other hand, its contents are handled well, then conscious integration of what it has to offer can lead to beneficial personal growth.

communication refers to many different processes and phenomena relating to the exchange of information and meaning between people (e.g. Hartley 1999). The particular view one takes of communication will depend on the perspective chosen. Dozens of fields of study and activity exist, all with varied approaches.

The sphere of personal development is concerned with communication in the following respects, for example:

- the achievement of clear, or non-distorted, communication between people (such as developing the capacity of two persons in conflict to listen to, and hear, the intent and concerns of the other)
- the field of NON-VERBAL COMMUNICATION
- the capacity of an individual for self-expression (whether in verbal or non-verbal media)
- interpersonal skills of communication (e.g. LISTENING; presentation; ASSERTIVENESS).

A cybernetic or SYSTEMIC view of communication challenges the very common linear (transmitter–receiver) view that communication reaches across a gap between one being to another. The work of Bateson (1973) and others argues that communication needs to be thought of as a relational circuit in which FEEDBACK is necessarily, and significantly, present.

In both personal development and organizational change, clients often state that the problems are primarily to do with communication. Communication is pervasive in human interaction so this is invariably true in some respect; but it is often a PRESENTING PROBLEM.

community building Community Building is M. Scott Peck's method of group facilitation and development. The purpose of Community Building is to create community, based on principles of tolerance and love, at local, national and international levels. Its ultimate purpose is to transform society and take the first steps to world peace.

Community Building was founded by Scott Peck, a practising psychiatrist, in 1984. Initially it was called the Foundation for Community Encouragement as an antidote to what Scott Peck termed the 'fallacy of rugged individualism' that he perceived created much mental stress and ill-health in America.

His work is based on personal experience and practice, as well as Wilfred Bion's theory of 'Basic Assumptions', and other principles of GROUP DYNAMICS. However, Scott Peck clearly differentiates the attainment of 'community' from the Tavistock (see Resources) notion of 'working group', which he says, 'suggests efficiency and effectiveness, but does not imply the love and commitment, the sacrifice, and the transcendence to build community' (Scott Peck 1990: 108). According to Scott Peck, groups that attempt to form themselves into community routinely go through certain stages, usually in the following order: pseudocommunity, chaos, emptiness, community.

Scott Peck's model is seen by some authors (e.g. Senge et al. 1994; Weisbord 1987) as applicable to organizational change interventions.

compassion an undefended response of LOVE, expressed through service, to another who is suffering. It may also be an expression of love and acceptance of oneself.

It is held in both Eastern and Western religious traditions very similarly. Rinpoche (1992) describes it within Tibetan Buddhism as arising from an awareness that one is the same as another, that it is an expression of unconditional love, that 'it is not true compassion unless it is active, and blesses and heals all those involved'.

Vardey (1995: 91), in writing of Mother Teresa's way, describes how 'love is expressed first in being with before doing to someone', and also that without love, action is social work, not compassion.

Compassion also has real results. Suffering can be relieved, but it can also be changed. Heron (1981: 30) writes of how CATHARSIS and TRANSMUTATION are 'two ways in which an un-seen reality moves in the resolution of human suffering'. This view is strongly represented in the traditions described above, and can also be found in the symbols of passion and rebirth at Easter.

competence competence as a quality refers to the ability to perform effectively. A competence is a capacity to apply skill, knowledge and attitude in order to create effective performance (in the USA, the term 'competency' is more widely used).

The notion of competence entails a performative view of KNOWLEDGE. Cognitive or conceptual knowledge is usually needed to underpin a competence, but is not a competence itself.

A competence-based approach to development may attempt to break performance down into tangible, measurable competencies. This has the intention, and to some extent the advantage, of making it easier to learn and assess skills. However, the approach can become reductionist and driven by a desire to measure, thus reducing complex human capacities to whatever can be codified and assuming that the sum of these parts is equivalent to the whole.

In education, competencies are associated with the trend towards defining learning outcomes (what learners will be able to do as a result of their study). In business, competencies may be used as a basis for identifying training needs, job design, performance management, succession planning, career development and recruitment.

complex a term introduced by Carl Jung that refers to a set or aggregation of (usually) unconscious ideas that result in habitual emotional dispositions, patterns of behaviour and thought. It is usually used in clinical contexts but sometimes in wider usage. For example, an 'inferiority complex' refers to a feeling or attitude of inadequacy and low SELF-ESTEEM, for which the person may habitually try to compensate.

The classic 'Oedipus complex' was named by Sigmund Freud. It refers to the myth of Oedipus, who unwittingly killed his father then married his mother. Freud considered this to be a phase of child development, characterized by sexual attraction towards the opposite-sex parent and hostility towards the same-sex parent.

complexity theory complexity, and notions of complex adaptive systems, are not yet (to our knowledge) applied directly to personal development. However this is an influential set of emergent ideas that is informing understanding of organizations and social systems, and processes such as leadership (see, for example, Phillips and Shaw 1998). It offers an alternative perspective on the relationship between individuals and their organizational and community settings.

'Complexity refers to the condition of the universe which is integrated and yet too rich and varied for us to understand in simple common mechanistic or linear ways. We can understand many parts of the universe in these ways but the larger and more intricately related phenomena can only be understood by principles and patterns – not in detail. Complexity deals with the nature of emergence, innovation, learning and adaptation' (Santa Fé Group 1996, cited in Battram 1998: v).

compulsive compulsive behaviour is a compelling, non-reflective response to events. The intrapsychic component is a degree of stress or irritability that needs to be repressed or managed by

31

controlling emotional distress and fear of rejection. Interpersonally, while mostly unconsciously driven, the compulsive person experiences a distressed, overwhelming urge to re-enact a situation, or endeavour to take control of a situation through psychologically defensive manoeuvres.

In TRANSACTIONAL ANALYSIS, compulsive behaviour can be thought of as operating from a 'Be Perfect' and a 'Please Others' DRIVER, being indecisive and tending to procrastinate. More seriously the person may have difficulty with intimate relationships as she or he tends towards expressing emotions of anger, frustration and irritability rather than love and spontaneity. The person may have workaholic tendencies with a great eye for detail and will put work before friends and social activities.

Heron (1992: 53) gives a graphic definition of the compulsive person as 'the wounded psyche [that] has defensive splits and repression', the result of either foetal stress or birth trauma or childhood trauma or a combination of all these. Whereas for Heron not all the trauma is intentional, the major cause is 'treacherous handling from parents and other adults' (1992: 55), resulting in the psychic splitting off of emotions, intellectualization as a defensive strategy and an absolute fear of getting things wrong, hence becoming rule-bound as another defensive strategy.

A compulsive intervention is one type of DEGENERATE facilitation. This comes from the facilitator projecting his or her own needs for help onto the other (participant/student/client) and then inappropriately RESCUING the other.

conditioning see BEHAVIOURISM.

confidentiality confidentiality is often an implicit contract in both work relationships and personal development work. The need for confidentiality is usually linked with the need to build and maintain trust. However, it is often made explicit and in many cases forms part of the ethical code of practice in helping relationships.

conflict conflict can be intrapersonal (for example, between SUB-PERSONALITIES) or interpersonal. Many people find interpersonal conflict extremely difficult to handle, to the extent that they avoid it where possible. Others seem to take a perverse pleasure in agitating and stirring up conflict. Thus to be comfortable with conflict seems relatively rare.

Theoretical perspectives on conflict also vary. For example, some theories of organizational behaviour assume that conflict is dysfunctional, and therefore is negative and needs to be minimized. Other (e.g. radical) theories see conflict as inevitable and not only irresolvable but also a creative tension with potential to enable movement and change (e.g. Buchanan and Huczynski 1997: 633 ff). The point here is that it may be important not to treat conflict as necessarily an interpersonal issue, even if it manifests as a dispute between individuals (see, for example, PSYCHOLOGISM).

A prominent reason for calling on a FACILITATOR – in families, groups, organizations, communities, and so on – is to resolve conflict. Conflict resolution methods include negotiation, mediation, and arbitration. See also Postle (1988: 94, 186).

confluence a confluence of rivers is where two currents or streams become one. In GESTALT therapy, confluence is the merging of, for example, two people's perceptions or views such that they can no longer be told apart.

Confluence is one type of BOUNDARY disturbance to the GESTALT CYCLE (e.g. Clarkson 1989: 55) and refers here to an inability to differentiate self from the environment. This may be manifested, for example, as a marked difficulty with endings and separation. A confluent parent may treat a child as an extension of themselves, and expect the child to have similar thoughts, feelings, needs and ambitions.

conformity much personal development work is geared towards increasing personal choice. In many ways people are subject to pressures to conform – in the family, in school, and in society at large – to prevailing norms and other people's EXPECTATIONS (see, for example, SHOULDS). These pressures were illustrated graphically by the experiments of Asch (Buchanan and Huczynski 1997: 252), in which individuals' judgements were swayed by the prospect of being out of step with the group majority.

The 1960s in particular is seen as a decade of social REBELLION in which the authority of such norms was questioned, and in which the GROWTH MOVEMENT flourished. This trend was symbolized in popular culture, by, for example, pop groups such as the Beatles and the Rolling Stones; and in literature by books such as Joseph Heller's *Catch 22*. Many people experienced this as a permission to explore their IDENTITY and to question their ROLES in society.

congruence congruence refers to consistency between thoughts, feelings and behaviour (including non-verbal behaviour). It is emphasized in Carl Roger's PERSON-CENTRED approach to counselling and education.

According to Grinder and Bandler, the founders of NLP: 'The term *congruency* is used to describe a situation in which the person communicating has aligned all of his output channels so that each of them is representing, carrying or conveying the same or a compatible message. When all of a person's output channels (body posture and movements, voice tonality and tempo, words) are representing the same or compatible messages, the person is said to be congruent. Other people's experience of a congruent human being is usually described in terms of that person having personal presence, knowing what he is talking about, being charismatic, dynamic and a host of other superlatives . . . The term *incongruent*, then, applies to a situation in which the person communicating is presenting a set of messages carried by his output channels which do not match, are not compatible – this person is said to be incongruent. Other people's experience of an incongruent person is confusion, saying that he doesn't know what he really wants, is inconsistent, untrustworthy and indecisive' (Grinder and Bandler 1976: 45–46).

However, congruence does not necessarily entail honesty, sincerity or AUTHENTICITY. Confidence tricksters are successful precisely because of their ability to communicate congruently.

conscious as a noun (the conscious), the domain of awareness that typically is contrasted with the UNCONSCIOUS ('subconscious' usually refers to whatever is unconscious, or out of awareness, but can be brought into the conscious domain). Also, as an adjective, 'conscious' refers to the state of being awake, and aware of oneself and outer sensory reality. A conscious act is one intentionally carried out.

There are many maps of the territory of the conscious and unconscious mind (see Rowan 1993). Freud's model of consciousness considered three areas. The subconscious consisted of repressed or split-off elements in conflict with the conscious, and a more fluid intermediate area called the preconscious – the realm of DREAMS and slips of the tongue – where elements were awaiting conscious attention.

Jung added to this personal map an area he called the COLLECTIVE UNCONSCIOUS, which consisted of universal, cultural, or archetypal elements, which humans had in common, and by which individuals were influenced. Assagioli added to Freud and Jung's work with a further dimension, the Higher Unconscious, or Superconscious (see ASSAGIOLI'S EGG).

Gregory Bateson (1973) used the phrase 'conscious purpose' to refer to human action intended to engineer nature, but which lacked understanding of the whole system and its ecology.

consciousness the phenomenon of awareness of existence, identity, and experience. This is taken by many to be a defining characteristic of the human condition; but the understanding of the nature of consciousness is an enduring philosophical as well as psychological puzzle.

Not surprisingly there is little agreement about the nature of consciousness, although many see it as the basis of all existence, not just a human awareness of an outer reality. Various metaphysical positions are summarized by Willis Harman (1988: 25–39; see also the Institute of Noetic Sciences in Resources).

Consciousness is a state of wakefulness, often contrasted with ALTERED STATES. Thus consciousness refers to AWARENESS, or to being (fully) conscious. In this sense it is linked to notions of PRESENCE and ATTENTION.

The refinement of consciousness is seen as a developmental goal in some traditions. For example, Ken Wilber refers to the attainment of 'higher' forms of consciousness and the notion of 'awakening' (Wilber 1980). He comments (Wilber 1996b) as follows: 'And when we pause from all this research, and put theory temporarily to rest, and when we relax into the primordial ground of our own intrinsic awareness, what will we find therein? When the joy of the robin sings on a clear morning dawn, where is our consciousness then? When the sunlight beams from the glory of a snow-capped mountain, where is consciousness then? In the place that time forgot, in this eternal moment without date or duration, in the secret cave of the heart where time touches eternity and space cries out for infinity, when the raindrop pulses on the temple roof, and announces the beauty of the divine with every single beat, when the moonlight reflects in a simple dewdrop to remind us who and what we are, and when in the entire universe there is nothing but the sound of a lonely waterfall somewhere in the mists, gently calling your name – where is consciousness then?'

consciousness-raising consciousness-raising groups became popular in the 1960s. Their purposes were partly political and partly personal and developmental. They tended to focus on forms of OPPRESSION, particularly through race and GENDER, and to liberate participants from dominant social practices and forms of thought that they might have INTROJECTED. The notion seems to come from the Marxian idea of 'false consciousness', which suggests that people can develop beliefs, attitudes and behaviours that are at odds with their origins and best interests – for example, a woman espousing or enacting sexist attitudes that others would see as contributing to that person's continued oppression. See also CRITICAL REFLECTION.

A different usage has a more spiritual spin, with the aim of personal development more than political action. Here, the 'raising' is to do with achieving a 'higher' or more refined level of CONSCIOUSNESS.

consulting consulting can refer to many varieties of professional activity. There is no clear definition or agreed practice.

As a trade or profession, (management or organizational) consultancy (Kubr 1996) may be thought of as an independent advisory service contracted to organizations to provide technical knowledge and skills in the analysis and solution of problems. Consultants may even help, when requested, in the implementation of these solutions (see, for example, Maister 2000). An internal consultant is a person who is formally an employee of the client organization for whom they provide consultancy. An external consultant is independent, often a person working freelance.

The term 'consultancy' still covers a vast range of approaches and disciplines, however. Consultants may be offering expertise in business strategy, accountancy, engineering, marketing, public relations and more (including, as the cynical joke goes, the ability to charge you for borrowing your own watch to tell you the time – see Block 1981: 1). The most relevant to personal development is the typically human focus of the ORGANIZATION DEVELOPMENT consultant.

Regarding consulting as a process or activity, Peter Block says: 'You are consulting any time you are trying to change or improve a situation but have no direct control over the implementation' (Block 1981: v). Consulting in this sense is a skilled process that many people, and not just designated consultants, may use within their professional role. See also CLIENT-CENTRED.

contact contact is a core concept of GESTALT (Clarkson and Mackewn 1993: 55) and a stage in the GESTALT CYCLE (for example, Clarkson 1989: 33). Contact refers to full, present-time, sensory awareness of self and other, or self and external world. The principle is that a healthy personal BOUNDARY enables good contact. Too rigid a boundary, or too inward a focus, keeps attention and energy away from the world. Too fluid and permeable a boundary, or poor awareness, makes for insubstantial and vague contact. Gestalt acknowledges that each person will experience a rhythm of contact and withdrawal, sometimes referred to as contact styles. A good account is that by Parlett and Hemming (1996).

contract in any personal development work there is a contract, whether explicit or implicit, between the practitioner and the client. This might typically cover, for example, the agreed purpose of the work; the mode of working; the responsibilities of the parties; and the fee and duration. A contract might also make reference to the practitioner's professional code of conduct or ETHICS.

In most modes of personal development, clear contracting is considered good practice. Management CONSULTING emphasizes the significance of contracting for all the subsequent work. In many therapies the practitioner is required to inform the client about relevant details and gain the client's consent before starting.

In experiential groups and training courses the contract may be less formal, but is still important. Often it takes the form of negotiated GROUND RULES. Where a contract is left unstated or implicit the potential for misunderstanding, or for disempowerment of the client, is greater.

In CO-COUNSELLING, there are three typical forms of helping contract (Heron 1998a):

• **free attention contract** The counsellor gives free attention only. No other interventions.

• **normal contract** The counsellor intervenes when the client appears to have lost her way, to be blocking, to be 'in pattern', to be missing her own cues. There is a co-operative balance between client self-direction and counsellor suggestions. Occasional interventions.

• **intensive contract** The counsellor works intensively with client cues, making as many interventions as seem necessary to enable her to deepen and sustain her process. This may include leading a client in to working areas being omitted or avoided. Frequent interventions.

control control is often used in a pejorative sense in personal development. It might refer, for example, to one person exercising POWER over another (a 'controlling parent') or to a person's apparent need for their intellect to be in charge of their behaviour. The notion of 'self-control' often denotes a social need for people to contain and restrict their emotions, i.e. controlling emotions rather than letting them 'out'. Control may also be opposed by those who object to others influencing their behaviour. Paradoxically, this can become very controlling of others' ability to express their needs and feelings.

The positive connotations of control are less commonly expressed, although people could not walk or function at all without appropriate physiological control. Heron (e.g. 1990: 66) emphasizes control of emotional expression as a core aspect of EMOTIONAL COMPETENCE. Here, control refers to the capacity to exercise choice and will over the expression and discharge of emotion, as distinct from either suppression or COMPULSIVE expression.

convergent–divergent two contrasting but complementary styles of thinking, originating in the work of Jacob Getzels and Philip Jackson in the USA.

A convergent style prefers to reach definite conclusions or answers from data available. Convergent thinkers are analytical, preferring problems that have certain answers, even if those answers are difficult to reach. A divergent style is more exploratory, preferring to branch out, explore relationships and follow links. It is 'creative' rather than 'analytical'.

This work was pursued in Great Britain by the educator Liam Hudson (1967), who linked the styles to preferences for arts (divergent style) and science (convergence). Hudson became increasingly sceptical of the distinction itself and its value. For example, he suggested that both styles are necessary and complementary components of CREATIVITY, rather than creativity being the province of divergers. He questioned the implication that divergence was therefore somehow more valuable, and he concluded that the styles were 'closer to a public role than a private reality' (Hampden-Turner 1981: 106).

Convergent and divergent are also the labels of two of Kolb's LEARNING STYLES.

Co-operative Inquiry a form of research inquiry developed by Peter Reason (Reason 1994) and John Heron (Heron 1996), representing a move towards a 'new paradigm' (see Rowan 1988: 184) of research suitable for human experience.

Co-operative Inquiry emphasizes collaboration and action, and is based on a participatory worldview. It is likely to be of interest to those who wish to pursue personal and professional development through collaborative research. The website of John Heron's International Centre for Co-operative Inquiry (see Resources) has many useful papers.

coping behaviour this term describes the strategies and behaviours that people use to survive traumatic events psychologically, and to function as effectively as possible (see Kleber 1992). TRAUMAS and other kinds of unhappiness affect people consciously and unconsciously. Coping may involve forgetting the traumas, denying their reality, or dissociating from their emotional impacts. Often what may seem like strange behaviour, such as mildly OBSESSIVE or COMPULSIVE acts, may actually be a part of an individual's coping. It is very important for therapists and counsellors who treat traumatized individuals to recognize people's coping strategies, and enable them to develop others.

Coping behaviours have been studied by the delegates of the International Committee of the Red Cross who, in various countries, visit political and other prisoners who have been tortured. It finds that for healthy coping behaviour to develop, it is important for such people to be able to make some meaning of their awful experiences, to integrate them into the fabric of the whole of their lives, and to feel that they have the support and VALIDATION of other people.

counselling a process in which counsellors enable clients to explore present circumstances which are being experienced as problematic (see Feltman and Horton 2000). There is no definite distinction between counselling and PSYCHOTHERAPY. The former is sometimes characterized as more likely to be issue-specific, and less concerned with exploring the client's PSYCHE.

There are many different schools of counselling (see, for example, INTEGRATIVE COUNSELLING). In the main, counsellors aim to give clients a safe 'space' in which to explore. This can enable people to acquire COPING skills, learn to view their situations from different perspectives, explore troublesome feelings, or simply to talk freely and safely with a counsellor who is supportive and non-judgemental. Appropriate counselling interventions in cases such as rape, TRAUMA, bereavement, divorce, abortion, tragic accidents, stress, and surviving abuse appear to increase the chances of a recovery. As with psychotherapy, counselling can be one to one, or carried out in groups. CO-COUNSELLING is a form of peer counselling.

Carl Rogers (1951) is one of the best known founders of modern approaches to counselling. He believed that the most important aspect of counselling was allowing clients to explore their own feelings in a non-directive way. This is no longer viewed as the only approach; people may be encouraged to explore their perceptions of their situations from many different points of view. Some practitioners would give the political dimensions of a client's situation at least as much importance as the psychological aspects.

In the UK the professional body is the British Association for Counselling (see Resources). This has various divisions, including the Association for Workplace Counselling.

counter-dependence usually denotes a stage of development in human relationships, for example, in groups (see also GROUP STAGES). This model is described by Boud (1988) in relation to student autonomy:

- DEPENDENCE (the group is dependent on the leader)
- counter-dependence (the group rebels against the leader)
- independence (the group works independently, apart from the leader)
- INTERDEPENDENCE (the group and the leader form an adult, reciprocal relationship).

A related usage is emerging in the field of business (e.g. Kets de Vries 1993), where counter-dependence is seen as a negative choice that is associated with a 'win-lose' attitude. This usage seems close to what is called a POLARITY RESPONSE.

counter-transference see TRANSFERENCE.

couple therapy therapy for a couple, which involves both partners seeing the therapist together and often individually as well (e.g. Hooper and Dryden 1991). The therapist will typically be working with the couple's RELATIONSHIP, rather than with two individuals.

The most widely known form of couples work is that of Relate (formerly the Marriage Guidance Council) – see Resources. This is described as couple counselling rather than therapy.

creativity creativity is generally valued in personal development; for example, it entails a capacity for self-expression and problem-solving. Creativity may also be seen as a characteristic of a SELF-ACTUALIZING person.

Rollo May, influenced by EXISTENTIALISM and HUMANISTIC PSYCHOLOGY, wrote a classic book, *The Courage to Create* (1976), in which he says: 'When we define creativity, we must make the distinction between its pseudo-forms, on the one hand – that is, creativity as a superficial aestheticism. And, on the other, its authentic form – that is, the process of *bringing something into being*. The crucial distinction is between art as artificiality (as in "artifice" or "artful") and genuine art' (May 1976: 37).

Creativity also has an existential significance in the sense that each person creates their own REALITY. This concept is addressed well by John Rowan (1998: 110).

Creative methods have a significant role in many modes of personal development. For example, creative writing (e.g. Hunt and Sampson 1998), including BIOGRAPHY, poetry, short stories, and so on, is a medium for self-expression and personal development. In experiential workshops, exercises such as that of writing one's own obituary encourage a person to review their life and gain a different perspective on the present. See also FLOW STATE; LATERAL THINKING; SYNECTICS.

Among writers on creativity are Peter Russell (see Resources), and Robert Fritz (1994).

creeping death in a group, the practice of going round the circle with each participant saying something in turn (e.g. in response to a theme or question). The phrase refers to the 'turn' which slowly advances towards each individual, who is often anxiously preparing what he or she is going to say rather than listening to others' contributions. Thus, the practice can also kill off spontaneity. Creeping death can be avoided in all kinds of ways, for example, by agreeing that each person may speak if and when they feel moved to do so.

critical education theory 'Critical theory' has become prominent in fields such as management and education. It is a perspective that aims to question taken-for-granted assumptions that may be embedded within the processes as well as the content of education (Giroux 1981).

Reynolds points out that many apparently progressive educators and educational ideas (for example, Malcolm Knowles through his work on LEARNING CONTRACTS and his emphasis on student-centred learning) have had a concern 'to counter the intrusion into education of hierarchy and author-

itarianism with methods based on more humanistic values' (Reynolds 1997b: 313). While this HUMANISTIC, CLIENT-CENTRED approach (in which we might include personal development workshops) is liberating in some respects, Reynolds argues that a humanistic perspective can isolate 'educational experience from its history and context. As a consequence, the social, political and cultural forces which make up the formative context of learning are reduced to mere background' (1997b: 319).

critical incident a critical incident is a distinct episode of experience (i.e. at a specific time and place, and the action having an identified beginning, middle and end), which may be examined for a range of purposes, including professional development and selection interviewing.

Managers and educators, for example, might be asked within a training course to identify a critical incident from their experience in order to analyse and improve an area of COMPETENCE.

Tripp (1993) emphasizes that critical incidents are not objectively identifiable, but are value judgements and interpretations of the significance of an event. Tripp shows how critical incidents can be used as a professional development method in teaching, including the way incidents can be analysed at different levels (pragmatic, ideological, etc.).

The principle of the use of critical incidents in selection interviewing is that the best predictor of an applicant's future performance is behavioural evidence of their past performance in similar contexts.

Critical incident debriefing is common in areas such as stress or disaster counselling. Here there is a clear connotation that a 'critical incident' is traumatic in nature. This is not the case in the more general, educational or developmental use of the term, where the criticality of an incident is more usually defined by its relevance or significance for the practitioner, or for the educational topic being explored.

critical reflection a process of identifying and examining values and assumptions that may be implicit in one's thinking. It involves stepping outside an existing frame of reference and questioning the nature of the frame of reference itself.

For example, learning might involve activity (experience). Then the learner might make notes in a journal about what happened (reflection) before interpreting their experience through a conceptual framework or theory (such as TRANSACTIONAL ANALYSIS). Critical reflection would involve examining this TA framework. What assumptions, for example, does it make about the nature of the person, or society, or the relationship between the two? How might it embody cultural and historical assumptions, perhaps arising from its own origins (in the case of TA, for example, as a development from PSYCHOANALYSIS)?

Stephen Brookfield (1987) suggests four components of the critical thinking process:

- **'Identifying and challenging assumptions:** Much of our thinking and behaviour is based on unexamined assumptions which we take for granted and of which we may hardly be aware. One aim of critical thinking is to unearth these hidden assumptions, to check their validity or plausibility, and to modify them if they are found wanting.
- **Creating contextual awareness:** This involves becoming aware of how the social, political and historical circumstances of the times in which we live conditions our ideas and assumptions. The way we think and act is not simply a natural and inevitable given but is a product of historical and social circumstances.
- **Identifying alternatives:** Contextual awareness opens up the possibility of identifying or imagining different contexts in which things are done differently. Alternatives are examined to see if they can be adopted.
- **Developing reflective scepticism:** Awareness of alternatives encourages a sceptical attitude towards fixed and final beliefs, ultimate explanations and universal truths. Accepted ideas and practices are not regarded as inevitable, necessary or above questioning. Critical thinkers are unwilling to accept that authoritative pronouncements are automatically beyond rational justification and challenge.' (Brookfield 1987, cited in Thomas 1993: 10.)

cult this refers to a group of people who hold strong beliefs, which may be unorthodox, in common (Hassan 1990, 2000). They may claim that they alone have access to knowledge leading to spiritual or cosmic insights. Some argue, however, that concern focuses disproportionately on marginal or unorthodox groups rather than mainstream 'cults' represented by religious and economic institutions.

Cults are often run by particularly CHARISMATIC leaders or small groups, who ensure the purity of the cult's doctrines and the obedience of its followers. There are over a thousand different cults, some of which may be offshoots of traditional religions. Others appear to arise anew through the influence and inspiration of particular teachers or gurus.

A characteristic of cults is that followers are subjected to external controls ranging from the benign to the brutal, such as the enforced mass suicide of hundreds in Jonestown, Guyana. Another characteristic is that senior members exert strong controls over the beliefs, behaviour, thoughts, emotions and finances of others. Cults usually attract people by promising more or less secret knowledge or insights necessary to save themselves and/or the world. Such groups may maintain themselves through strong social bonds, and keep their members through fear of what will happen if they leave. Often members are asked to donate a significant part of their income to the organization.

Most countries now have organizations that help ex-members emotionally and psychologically to leave their cult if they wish to.

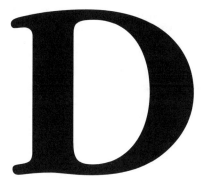

death death is decided when the living biological form(s) ceases to exist in relation to the physical environment.

The universally experienced phenomenon of death does not seem to make the acceptance of it any easier, particularly in Western cultures. Death and the process of dying are often subject to many social taboos with fewer people witnessing death until it happens to their immediate family. Therefore death becomes alien to modern life. This is reflected not only in the experience of biological death, but also in common difficulties with endings of various kinds (e.g. of relationships, and of groups).

Theosophy has a particular interpretation of death, seeing it as a necessary study to understand the concept of BEING which we are only aware of through our self-consciousness. However, the state of non-being (death) is likened to 'being' in latency, that is, dormant or resting, and as the pulse of life is ceaseless (they espouse) after a period of non-being, a new period of activity stirs and the process of re-becoming starts (Farthing 1974). This is the concept of re-incarnation. Many Eastern philosophies such as BUDDHISM and Hinduism accept the concept of death and reincarnation (Evans-Wentz 1960), as did Christianity in the early years.

Freud identified what he thought of as a 'death instinct', or Thanatos. He came to see human behaviour as an expression at a personal level of the struggle between life (Eros) and death.

The process and experience of dying, and of bereavement, was the subject of a classic study by Elisabeth Kübler-Ross (1970); see also Murray Parkes (1996).

In personal development work, concepts of death are likened to shedding a false mask or PERSONA, seeing this as illusory and becoming more in touch with nature and the seasons as a reminder of the transient nature of existence. The reality of death is the most pressing evidence for many of polarity (e.g. birth and death, BEING and non-being, past and future, good and bad, giving and receiving). 'The tension between them is the very substance of life. Energy flows from the positive pole to the negative one and power is generated. Creative living is about allowing the current between the two poles' (van Deurzen 1987: 61). Many counsellors and therapists are trained to recognize talk of death as dysfunctional and dangerous, however 'such fear of recognizing our limitations and our mortality comes from a fear of life rather than a fear of death' (1987: 20). A useful source is Keleman (1989).

A 'near-death experience' is a close but not terminal encounter with death that has transformative potential, often enabling a person to appreciate and value their life much more and to see themselves in a wider context.

defences the origin of psychological defences is intrapsychic and interpersonal ANXIETY brought about by the actual or perceived threat of attack, either physical or psychological. Defences operate within the individual and when a group of individuals are anxious the phenomenon manifests as negative group, community and culture defences (see e.g. Morgan 1997: 223).

Defensiveness is understood as a self-protective mechanism, useful to a degree when the person feels under threat, but limiting and dysfunctional when continued into adult life and where there is seemingly no threat to the person. The defences take the form of passive behaviours, in increasing hierarchy of seriousness from the mildest form of withdrawal (into oneself and from others); to over-adaptation (to others' needs or wishes); to agitation, which can be quite severe; and finally to either incapacitation (catatonia) or violence. Other forms are forced laughter, denial in the form of DISCOUNTING and intellectualization.

Psychological defences are less likely to be self-reported as they are usually unconscious, but they may be inferred from the behaviour of the individual. Defensiveness can have a de-stressing effect for the individual as a strategy against anxiety and fear of rejection.

Freudian and Kleinian psychological defences involve interpretation of very early childhood trauma and FIXATION at a critical developmental stage, which Heron (1992) calls archaic anxiety. Severe defensiveness may result in DEPRESSION, and suppression or denial of feelings.

Some people cannot tolerate serious anxiety and develop behaviour patterns that structure the anxiety before it reaches conscious awareness. These PSYCHOSOMATIC symptoms are displaced psychological defence mechanisms, a way of avoiding anxiety.

deflection to deflect is to turn away from, or turn aside, a perceived direct line of attack or an attempt at personal contact. Deflection is a form of interruption to the GESTALT CYCLE (Clarkson 1989: 51).

Light beams and radio waves deflect off some surfaces rather than penetrating them. In the same way, a person may put up a psychologically protective shield to keep others out. This defensive shield can take many forms, such as attacking first, avoidance and blaming others. The intention is not to let the other person's neediness or emotions penetrate into the individual's psyche.

degenerate intervention in relation to verbal interventions in facilitation (see SIX CATEGORY INTERVENTION ANALYSIS), a degenerate intervention is one that fails in its intention in one or more ways, whether because the practitioner is incompetent, lacks personal development, or training, or experience, or awareness, or some combination of these (Heron 1990). This never implies deliberate, malicious or PERVERTED facilitation, which is an ethical issue.

The four kinds of degenerative interventions are unsolicited, manipulative, compulsive, and unskilled:

- **unsolicited:** 'The grossest kind of unsolicited intervention is when there is no formal practitioner–client relationship at all, and one person simply appoints himself as "practitioner" to another, and without being asked, starts to inform, advise, interpret, confront, or elicit, in ways that are interfering and disrespectful of the autonomy and good sense of the other. These occur too frequently in ordinary social relations' (Heron 1990: 144).
- **manipulative:** When the facilitator is motivated by self-interest and makes interventions regardless of the client's interests. The intended

outcome is for the benefit of the facilitator, not the client or participant.

- **compulsive:** This type is DISTRESS driven. Such interventions may come from the hurt child of the facilitator, which has not been worked through in personal development, or from CONFLUENCE with institutional pressures. The distress is PROJECTED out unawarely unto others. So COMPULSIVE helping is an example; 'training in the helping professions does not include any training in EMOTIONAL COMPETENCE' (Heron 1990: 146).

- **unskilled:** 'There is clearly a class of degenerate or mismanaged interventions which are neither unsolicited, nor manipulative, nor compulsive. They are simply incompetent; because the practitioner has never had any interactive skills training, has no grasp of a wide-ranging repertoire, and is stuck with an ad hoc array of interventions that is too limited in its scope and too variable in its quality or suitability' (Heron 1990: 147).

denial while the common use of this word means to declare something as untrue, its specific meaning in personal development (i.e. saying he or she is 'in denial') is the denial of some aspect of self that is perceived to be too vulnerable, or too traumatized or too unacceptable to the person's self-image.

This usage has its roots in Freud's psychoanalysis theory as one of the psychological DEFENCE mechanisms. Denial is usually of a painful experience and its associated attributes or elements, which may be buried in the unconscious, so that the person is unaware of the denial.

dependence the need to have others close to oneself is a normal attribute of the young child. Part of the maturation process is a gradual separation from significant caregivers, particularly par-

ents. Dependence is a feature of ANXIETY in the child due to a disturbed child–parent relationship when the child's need for the parent is in conflict with the hostility the child feels towards a parent who is intimidating and rejecting. This form of dependency weakens the normal separation process and the child may continue to struggle with hostility versus clingingness in other relationships even in adult life.

Dependency is one of Wilfred Bion's (1961) three 'basic assumptions' in groups (see FIGHT–FLIGHT).

depression a transient mood or chronic emotional state characterized by hopelessness, despair, sadness, a sense of meaninglessness, low SELF-ESTEEM, high self-depreciation and apathy with a reduced ability to enjoy life (Tilney 1998). Depression differs from simple GRIEF, bereavement, or mourning, which are appropriate emotional responses to the loss of loved persons or objects. Depression can also be seen as the tip of the iceberg of unresolved DISTRESS in a non-cathartic society.

There are two main types of depression: reactive and endogenous. Reactive depression is the most common and is often the result of external social and environmental factors, such as chronic grief for the loss of a close relative or friend. Endogenous depression is when depression seems to arise from internal sources, more recently attributed to biochemical imbalances.

People with depression tend to feel hollow and empty inside. Depression, according to Hillman (1997) a symptom of a soul in despair, is probably the most common psychiatric complaint (it is more common in women than in men) and has been described by physicians from at least the time of Hippocrates, who called it melancholia.

development development refers generally to processes of personal or professional 'improvement'. In this wide sense it is almost interchangeable with LEARNING and CHANGE.

43

A more specific usage refers to models of developmental stages, often relating to human development from birth. The classic example is Piaget's theory, which identifies distinct stages of psychological development (there is a specific field of developmental psychology). Freudian theory is of PSYCHO-SEXUAL phases, developed by Erik Erikson into a model of the LIFE CYCLE. Another example is Loevinger's model, on which Fisher and Torbert's STAGES OF DEVELOPMENT are based.

Such models tend to imply that development is arrested or interrupted if a stage has not been completed; and/or that there is virtue in progressing as far, or as high, as possible towards what may be an idealized state of being.

Many theories of the person incorporate a particular model of development and/or healthy functioning. The model in use is not always explicit, and whether articulated or not may well carry cultural or ideological assumptions about what it is to be human. For example, Rowan (1993: 36) refers to racist and sexist assumptions that can be found within Jung's work. Management training is likely also to reflect views about the preferred goals of development.

devil's advocate to play devil's advocate is to be a 'friendly adversary', challenging and testing opinions, judgements, ideas or plans (giving them a 'rattle and shake'), to help them become more robust or watertight (Heron 1999: 127). The devil's advocate position entails permission to question and to air doubt, and so is a procedure that may help to avoid GROUP THINK.

dialectics from Hegel, the philosopher, referring to a process through which an idea (thesis) begets its opposite (antithesis). The tension and relationship between these eventually create a synthesis.

In personal development, denotes the way in which people grow through experiencing and resolving conflicts and dilemmas, in contrast to a linear view of development as the incremental acquisition of knowledge and skills.

dialogue in GESTALT, an approach that describes the interaction between two people where there is a desire to genuinely meet the other person. It was developed by Richard Hycner (1993) and others as an approach to therapy that is based on Martin Buber's concept of I–THOU. The focus is on relationship and the healing for the client that can take place through a form of contact that is described as the 'between'.

The underlying assumptions of dialogue are that human beings are inherently relational as 'all living is meeting' (Buber 1958); that we become fully human and discover our true self through relationship to others; and that we have the capacity and urge to establish meaningful relationships with others. The dialogical relationship describes the interaction or meeting that occurs between two people where they are open, in the moment, to genuine meeting with each other.

The concepts of dialogue and dialogic relationship have been criticized because experiencing our true self in meeting with other human beings would seem to exclude the possibilities of developing self through our environment. Also, the extent to which dialogue can be equated to the Gestalt concept of the contact BOUNDARY is open to question.

dimensions of facilitator style a model of FACILITATION developed by John Heron (1999; first edition published in 1977 within the Human Potential Research Project, as it was then called, at the University of Surrey).

The model offers a critical analysis of styles of facilitating learning, most particularly experiential learning with groups, although it can be used in one-to-one facilitation as well.

The model describes three different political modes of decision-making, which reflect the intentions and purpose of the facilitator. These modes of decision-making and power balance are Hierarchy, Cooperation and Autonomy (of the learners). The political modes reflect the intentions and purpose of the facilitator, about what she or he is seeking to achieve, with regard to various forms of learning in the group (Heron 1999).

Within those modes there are six dimensions, thus offering a matrix of eighteen forms of facilitation. The six dimensions are: planning, meaning, confronting, feeling, structuring and valuing.

Application of the model has been successful in higher and further education, medical and other professional groups as well as in consultancy and management training.

direction in CO-COUNSELLING: 'A direction is a statement or word that releases discharge on a chronic pattern; to "hold a direction" is to work by repeating the direction to release discharge; the direction levers off the pattern to let discharge out. For the more experienced client, but beginners need to start building up the skill' (Heron 1998a).

discharge to release DISTRESS, often leading to insight. The principle is that distress held in the body inhibits full human functioning. The ability to discharge distress is a core skill of CO-COUNSELLING. *See also* CATHARSIS.

disclosure the action of sharing with others aspects of our internal world. Disclosure can have many forms, such as self-assessing own attitudes and competence before soliciting feedback from others, facilitators and peers in an educational forum (*see* SELF AND PEER ASSESSMENT) to an individual sharing their internal (phenomenological) worldview with others, that is, how they feel, what they think or what opinions they hold.

The aim of disclosure is usually to be transparent (Jourard 1971), better understood, AUTHENTIC and CONGRUENT with external behaviour and inner feelings and thinking. Research shows that people need to feel a strong sense of trust, and an environment of empathy and understanding, to self-disclose (Gregory 1996). Fears of being ridiculed, punished, repeating previous bad experiences of not being taken seriously and being gossiped about will inhibit such trust.

discounting in TRANSACTIONAL ANALYSIS, an unconscious minimizing or ignoring of some aspect of self, others or the external situation. Discounting is an internal DEFENCE mechanism, inferred through behaviour rather than observed directly (Schiff and Schiff 1975). The function of discounting seems to be the maintenance of limited and distorted self-image and belief systems, however destructive.

There are three areas to which discounting may be applied (self, other and the external world); three types of phenomenon that can be discounted (stimuli, problems and options); and four modes of discounting (existence, significance, change possibility, and personal ability to activate change).

To discount at the level of existence is to minimize or ignore that a problem or situation exists. This ignoring allows the person not to act to change the situation. For example, a mother may hear her new baby cry and decide that the baby is just exercising his lungs.

Discounting at the level of significance implies either exaggeration or minimizing the significance. A heavy drinker might minimize by saying, 'I only have one bottle of whisky a day and as long as I can keep working then I am all right.'

Discounting at the change possibility level is reflected in generalizations. The drinker might recognize that drinking a bottle of whisky a day is a serious problem, but generalize by saying, 'Everybody does this'; 'All my friends do it'; or 'It runs in the family, it's probably genetic.'

Finally, discounting at the level of personal ability implies that it is the person's belief in his or her own inability to act that is causing the problem to persist. Like all the others this level of discount involves a passive stance, illustrated by statements such as 'I can't possibly change' or 'It's too late for me, I'm too old, too far gone.'

Mellor and Sigmund (1975) developed a discount matrix to show the relationship of all the modes and levels of discounting.

discovery method the discovery 'method' is not a method as such, but a general principle that people learn most potently (or at all) through discovering and experiencing for themselves rather than accepting or absorbing pre-existing knowledge. The principle can be translated into methods used in educational settings. It is related to EXPERIENTIAL LEARNING and PROBLEM-BASED LEARNING.

The discovery principle is sometimes contrasted specifically with the view that learners are 'empty vessels' into which knowledge can be poured. For a discussion of discovery in relation to problem-based learning see Margetson (1997).

displacement a psychological DEFENCE mechanism that involves 'shifting impulses aroused by one person or situation to a safer target' (Morgan 1997: 222); or, the externalization of hostile and conflictual feelings onto others in the environment. It is a form of projection of parts of the self 'onto a recipient which allows the projector to feel estranged from, threatened by, bewildered by, or out of touch with the recipient' (Ogden 1991: 14).

distress an experience of great sorrow, troubles or pain. Usually associated with the frustration or denial of personal needs which then causes emotional distress.

For Heron (1992) an experience of OPPRESSION will result in distress and a splitting off from the emotional and spontaneous aspects of self, creating a false self through IDENTIFICATION with the oppressors. This is a coping strategy for managing and living with the oppressors, who are likely to be parents and significant others in the child's formative years.

In CO-COUNSELLING it is the 'wounded Child' (Heron 1992: 56), manifesting as COMPULSIVE behaviour, that needs to heal his/her archaic primary, secondary and even tertiary distress. Heron talks of primary distress as our birth trauma, which is unavoidable but creates potentially maladaptive behaviour as a compensatory mechanism. Primary distress is likely to occur when the three basic human needs are not met through natural life events: the need to love and be loved; the need to understand and be understood; and the need to choose and be chosen. Natural life events mean that we must eventually separate even from a good parent, not always understand or feel understood and not always feel that we have been chosen or that we can choose. Secondary distress is interpersonal: it is caused by other people who through negligence or malevolence seek to put their needs before ours and sometimes intentionally abuse us. Tertiary distress arises when there is tension between the individual's need and family, group and societal needs.

double bind the double bind is a pathogenic communication pattern discovered by Gregory Bateson (1973). In essence, it creates the experience of being 'Damned if you do, damned if you don't.'

Bateson defines the double bind as 'communication in the context of an emotionally important relationship in which there is unacknowledged contradiction between messages at different LOGICAL LEVELS' (Bateson and Bateson 1988: 207). Watzlawick (1990: 19–38) describes the structure of the double bind.

Bateson observed this mode of communication in the families of schizophrenics. He believed that communication was always multi-level, including non-verbal messages. The non-verbal or PRESUPPOSITIONAL levels normally contain information about how the verbal message is to be understood. In the double bind the non-verbal messages are confusing, so that interpreting the communication becomes uncertain. Bateson cites the case of a mother visiting her schizophrenic son, who goes to embrace her. She recoils, and when her son then becomes uncertain about what to do next, she castigates him for being afraid to show his feelings.

drama triangle the Drama Triangle (Karpman 1968) is a method of analysing psychological GAMES in TRANSACTIONAL ANALYSIS using three ROLES of Victim, Persecutor and Rescuer.

It was influenced by role theory as a mapping of the unconscious destructive communication between two or more people. However, these three roles are not social roles, but EXISTENTIAL, unconscious psychological positions that need to be continuously kept alive by drama.

Because the behavioural manifestations of the roles are very like real life positions, in TA the psychological roles are differentiated by capitalizing the first letter. A real victim is a person who is mugged. A psychological Victim is someone who believes that they are helpless and too vulnerable to solve their own problems.

The fundamental internal frame of reference for each role is that of DISCOUNTING, with inauthentic feelings and faulty thinking. The Victim discounts her personal AUTONOMY in a way that is age and ability inappropriate. The Persecutor agrees with the Victim's discounts, and often operates from a grandiose stance, believing himself or herself to be the best person to take control of situations and other people who cannot psychologically manage this for themselves. The Rescuer is equally discounting of the Victim's ability to look after him or herself and has a need to look after others less able than themselves in order to feel OK about themselves. So all roles are interdependent and have the flavour of CO-DEPENDENCY.

The drama triangle, like other psychological games, can be played at first, second or third degree level, where the third degree can result in serious physical and psychological abuse between the Persecutor and Victim, or self-harm in the Victim. During the unfolding of the game individuals can move around the triangle, so that a Victim can turn and persecute the Rescuer, or the Victim can persecute from the Victim position.

dreams Sigmund Freud described dreams as the 'royal road to the unconscious', proposing that the analysis and interpretation of dreams were a central part of the analytical process. They were also the indicators along the way to psychological maturation.

Dreaming sleep is essential to health. Views differ as to whether dreams are a mere by-product of neurological activity during sleep, or are of great significance and potential to the dreamer. Freud believed that the symbolic content of dreams was of a mostly sexual nature, and revealed the repressed contents of the UNCONSCIOUS. In this he differed markedly from Jung, who saw a dream as 'a little hidden door in the innermost and most secret recess of the psyche', providing rich and essential information from the unconscious of both individuals and the collective.

The Jungian tradition (Jung 1968, 1982) holds that the material of dreams is distinct from waking material, being SYMBOLIC and ARCHETYPAL. Dreams are the language of the unconscious, which for Jung was distinct from the rationality of consciousness and ego. For Jung dreams were an essential part of the self-regulation of the PSYCHE, seeking to express itself to the light of day. Working with dreams is central to the Jungian approach, as they can be diagnostically valuable, and shed light into the inner situation of the dreamer. Jung has described the analysis and interpretation of dreams as an attempt to read an unknown text unique to each individual, as they also reveal insights into the dreamer's moral and philosophical convictions.

Dreams are used in various modes of therapy, and there are many ways of working with dreams – see Shohet (1985).

drivers in TRANSACTIONAL ANALYSIS, Drivers, and driver behaviour, refer to concentrated unconscious psychological attention or energy manifesting as repetitive patterns of thinking, feeling and behaving, which are the person's response to parental and other significant people's injunctions how to be and behave in relation to self and others.

Distressed behaviour can be described as an expression of one of the following five Drivers: Be Perfect, Be Strong, Please Others, Try Hard, and Hurry Up. Some authors believe that Please Others is the primary Driver and the other four are different behavioural strategies the child has learned from others within the family circle as a way of achieving the Please Others Driver (Kahler and Capers 1974).

The following is a short description of each driver belief (from Stewart 1989: 116):

- Be Perfect: I am only OK if I get everything right (therefore I have got to cover every detail before I can finish anything)
- Be Strong: I am only OK if I disown my feelings and wants
- Try Hard: I am only OK if I keep on trying hard (this means that I won't actually complete what I am trying to do, because if I did it, I wouldn't be 'trying to' anymore)
- Please Others: I am only OK if I please other people
- Hurry Up: I am only OK if I hurry up

The Drivers are also called counterinjunctions as they are considered the child's best way of surviving continuous distressing family and cultural oppressive prescriptions in an effort to gain conditional acceptance.

Driver behaviour is described as a 'gateway into SCRIPT' (Stewart 1996: 10).

dyad a pair; sometimes two people or individuals usually thought of as a pair (e.g. mother and daughter; therapist and client). Dyads are the principal format used in CO-COUNSELLING and in ENLIGHTENMENT INTENSIVES.

East–West refers to the crossover or cross-fertilization of (usually) ancient wisdoms from the East with contemporary Western society or thought. Classic examples include Capra (1992), Heider (1986), Pirsig (1974), Watts (1961) and Welwood (1983). This became something of a fashion and books titled *The TAO or Zen of (. . . this, that and everything)* are commonplace.

ecological psychology 'Ecopsychology' is the name most often used to represent the synthesis of the psychological and the ecological. At present it is more a line of enquiry than a single psychotherapeutic methodology.

Its fundamental premise is that the separation of the world into the human and non-human ultimately 'shrinks' our imagination of what it is to be human. Theodore Roszak, possibly the best known of all ecopsychologists, puts forward a hypothesis (Roszak 1992) that an ecological unconscious lies at the core of the human psyche, which is a resource for restoring us to environmental harmony. He himself acknowledges that such a proposition is speculative, no more so, however, than Jung's concept of the COLLECTIVE UNCONSCIOUS.

Many ideas and traditions have fed into Ecopsychology. Perhaps the main strands are Deep Ecology (Naess 1989); EcoFeminism (Gomer, in Roszak et al. 1995); systems theory (Bateson 1979); and therapeutic methodologies, such as Wilderness experiences or Joanna Macy's collective mourning ritual 'The Council of All Beings' (in Roszak et al. 1995).

Ecopsychology expands the concept of psychology from the intra- and inter-human to include the extra-human. This allows a revisioning of the concept of 'sanity'. In fact the central question that Ecopsychology poses is, 'How sane are we (in the industrialized West) if we abuse a system that we are embodied within?'

ecology ecology, in NLP, is principally a criterion for whether a change is appropriate for the person to make: what will be the consequences for the 'whole person' – for the mind–body system, their relationships in the world and so on – and will there be any unwanted by-products? This notion is derived from Gregory Bateson's work, where ecology is defined as 'the science of interrelations and interdependence between organisms and their environments' (Bateson and Bateson 1988: 207).

Ecology as a criterion is especially important in NLP when working at levels of belief or identity (see NEUROLOGICAL LEVELS). We cannot predict through any rational calculation all the consequences of such a change; any belief is likely to be related as if in a three-dimensional web to other beliefs, capabilities, behaviours and so on. Changing one part of the web can affect much else in the person's experience – it is not like replacing a component in a car with a new version of the same part.

A search for how ecological a change may be for the person will consider, among other things, the SECONDARY GAINS of the existing belief. For example, if I seek to change a belief that 'life is a struggle', will I consider the benefits I have gained to date from 'struggling', and whether I have alternative ways to maintain whatever success I have achieved? A related issue, important and common in personal development workshops, is of the consequences for the ecology of a relationship if one partner pursues their personal growth and undergoes changes.

ego the concept of ego can refer to the PSYCHE (the mind) or total personality. More commonly, as in Freudian theory, the ego is seen as one part of a three-part system of psychic organs: the ID (with instinctual drives); the SUPEREGO (the INTROJECTED controlling function obeying what is socially and morally right to do); and the ego, which attends to external social reality and which seeks compromise between the conflictual interests of the id and superego.

Developmentally, awakening of SELF-AWARENESS can be seen as the emergence of the ego, between the ages of one and three years old. Freudian use of the term implies the ego has a function of dealing with the outside world over the internal struggle with instinctual drives.

In Jungian psychology, the ego as the organ of awareness (Singer 1994) functions as the centre of consciousness. The ego complex is the constellation of ideas the individual draws together about self to form a powerful self-concept. Ego development depends on the integration into the ego of as much of the content that is formerly unknown and residing in the unconscious. Two categories of knowledge need to be integrated: knowledge of the world and how it works; and wisdom, which is essentially understanding human nature, including one's own nature as an individual. So ego development depends on the expansion of awareness for the unconscious to the conscious. This is not the same as 'SELF development', which in Jungian psychology would be viewed as a union of the conscious with the unconscious.

In TRANSACTIONAL ANALYSIS, which is an ego psychology (i.e. a theory or model in which the concepts of the ego and ego development are central), ego refers to the psychic organ with its thinking, feeling and behaving (see EGO STATE).

'Egocentric' means self-centred, or habitually perceiving oneself as the centre of existence. See also NARCISSISM.

ego state ego state theory forms the foundation of structural analysis (personality development) in TRANSACTIONAL ANALYSIS. There is also an ego state functional analysis model which describes how people relate and communicate with each other from different ego states.

Berne, the founder of TA, describes ego states as 'a phenomenologically coherent system of feelings related to a given subject, and operationally as a set of coherent behaviour patterns' (1961: 17). Implied in this definition is that ego states are 'psychic organs' within which there is alignment of behaviour, thinking and feeling identified with that state.

As part of structural analysis, Berne identified three main types of ego state based on the manner in which a person manages and stores experiences. Past experiences are stored in the CHILD ego states, experiences with powerful others and AUTHORITY figures are stored as PARENT ego states and HERE AND NOW reality types of experience are ADULT ego states (Tilney 1998: 34). The capital letters denote that the Parent, Adult and Child are PHENOMENOLOGICAL realities that can be cathected (re-stimulated into operation) and different from the chronological and social role of parent, adult and child.

In functional analysis, the Adult ego state is a coherent system of behaviours, thinking and feeling that manages the present reality or experiences of the person. Adult ego state development is dependent on the cognitive skills of the growing child and his or her ability to analyse and assimilate personal and social present reality. There is a strong link with Piaget's theory of cognitive development. The aim of most psychotherapy and counselling, and some organizational training, is to develop the Adult ego state.

In structural analysis, the Parent ego state is the psychic organ that contains INTROJECTED material, beliefs, values, and injunctions about how one ought to behave. It is held in Transactional Analysis that the Parent is not an abstract, an example of Freud's notion of SUPEREGO, but rather a real person, such as a father or mother, 'who now exists or once existed, who has legal names and civic identities' (Berne 1961: 32). In functional analysis, the Parent ego state is inferred through Nurturing Parent behaviour or Critical (Controlling) Parent behaviour.

In structural analysis there are many Child ego states containing experiences from different developmental stages (Stewart and Joines 1987; Tilney 1998). It is believed that the whole experience – thinking, emotions, sensations and behaviour – is preserved so that the person can re-experience complete units of life events from different developmental ages and times. Functionally, the Child ego state is divided into Free Child and Adaptive Child.

The Nurturing and Critical Parent ego states and Free and Adapted Child ego states can be functionally positive or negative. When the individual is said to be in Child, he or she will be REGRESSED. When in the Parent ego state, the person will often report the sensation and insight of 'behaving like my mother' or other such authority figure. The function of the Adult, when not contaminated by either Child or Parent content, is experienced as the 'true self', behaving in an AUTHENTIC manner.

emancipatory education emancipatory education is education aimed at freeing learners from social, cultural, political or other forms of OPPRESSION.

A key name in this tradition is that of Paolo Freire, the Brazilian educator, whose book *The Pedagogy of the Oppressed* (1972) is an acknowledged classic.

The notion of emancipation derives from the work of Habermas, who identified three forms of learning – technical, communicative and emancipatory. Jarvis et al. (1998: 62) identify Habermas's notion of emancipation as influential on Mezirow's 'perspective transformation' (see TRANSFORMATIVE LEARNING), and say that emancipatory learning 'involves identifying and challenging distorted meaning perspectives . . . through a process of critical self-reflection'.

emotion a psychological and experiential state, such as joy, sorrow, anger, or fear. There is no definitive view of what emotion is in psychological or physiological terms, although there is consensus that emotions play a very significant role in human and social functioning. See also FEELING.

In personal development, emotion is generally considered important because of the emotionally repressive or inhibiting nature of Western society, and the neglect of the education of the AFFECT.

Social conditioning and the selective emphasis of formal educational agendas may be seen as impediments to healthy emotional functioning and growth (*see* EMOTIONAL COMPETENCE and EMOTIONAL INTELLIGENCE). For example, Mulligan says 'Besides the difficulties which this lopsided emotional development creates in the area of interpersonal relating, experiential learners are without their early warning system which can tell them that their needs are not being met. This often results in states of mental indigestion, confusion, and even physical exhaustion or worry which are counter-productive from a learning point of view' (Mulligan and Griffin 1992: 182).

emotional competence John Heron says that a person who has developed emotional competence 'is able to manage their emotions awarely in terms of the basic skills of CONTROL, EXPRESSION, CATHARSIS and TRANSMUTATION . . .' (1992: 131). Roger Harrison (1995: 37) refers to emotional competence as 'being open about feelings, expressing vulnerability and uncertainty, supporting, caring and the like'.

In humanistic education in general there is a strong interest in the education of the AFFECT – embracing emotional experience, and not confining education to the intellect.

Denis Postle (1993: 39–41) presents and discusses the notion of emotional competence and how this relates to practical and conceptual learning. He proposes ten criteria for emotional competence, such that an emotionally competent person:

1. has ready access to their emotions and feelings; (a) can express feelings freely, where and when appropriate; (b) can hold on to feelings for later expression; and (c) can tolerate the expression of feelings, including distress, in other people
2. has discovered the main elements of their traumatic early experience and appreciates how they influence adult behaviour
3. actively seeks to identify and own PROJECTION and DISPLACEMENT, TRANS-

FERENCE and counter-transference
4. will have an adequate appreciation of the contribution of OPPRESSION both covert and overt to feelings and emotions
5. can supportively confront unaware behaviour in others
6. can cathartically release strong emotions
7. can TRANSMUTE tense emotion through choosing to make a shift in consciousness
8. takes responsibility for commitment to developing and sustaining their emotional competence
9. will have an adequate repertoire of skills for dealing with feelings and emotions arising from a need for cooperation or negotiation
10. has a self-reflexive approach to monitoring the quality of their attention, relations with others and general health.

Recently the idea of EMOTIONAL INTELLIGENCE has been popularized through the work of Goleman (1996). This has come from a different source (Howard Gardner's notion of multiple INTELLIGENCES) but is addressing the same territory and has similar implications for personal development.

emotional intelligence emotional intelligence refers to the capacity for five main domains of emotional functioning:

- knowing one's emotions (SELF-AWARENESS)
- managing emotions
- motivating oneself
- recognizing emotions in others
- handling relationships.

Popularized by Goleman (1996), the term originates in the work of Peter Salovey, a Yale psychologist. Salovey has aimed to extend the work of Howard Gardner, who posited seven main human INTELLIGENCES as a critique of the narrow focus of IQ. Goleman's book usefully includes reference to relevant psychological and neurophysiological research.

Emotional intelligence (or 'EQ' as it has become known) is closely related to the humanistic psychology notion of EMOTIONAL COMPETENCE. See also SPIRITUAL INTELLIGENCE (SQ).

empathy empathy can refer to two distinctive experiences; emotional empathy and resonance.

Developmentally, emotional empathy is described as the 'emotional contagion and communion' that occurs between the infant and early significant persons. Out of this communion, which is a need for security and self-expression, ANXIETY is born (May 1996: 167). From PRIMAL needs for emotional communication, we develop the ability to imagine ourselves in another's place and to understand the other's feelings, desires, ideas, and actions.

Most people think of empathy as altruistic: however, there is a legitimate self-interest in emotionally-driven empathy. There is a PROJECTION of one's own needs onto the other, or IDENTIFICATION with the other (INTROJECTION) for which one can then express empathy.

Empathy is also a FEELING state, a resonance with what is other. Here, empathy often (but not exclusively) refers to aesthetic experience, feeling a deep connection with poetry, music, walking in nature and feeling at one with it, and feeling at one with cosmic energy.

In some ways emotional empathy mirrors the bonding and ATTACHMENT of the infant in the therapeutic interpersonal dynamic while resonance is a PSYCHIC and metaphysical empathy.

The use of empathy is an important part of the counselling technique developed by the American psychologist Carl Rogers (*see also* RAPPORT).

empowerment empowerment has become something of a slogan, especially in the business world. There is much talk of 'empowering' people, yet this entails the quite odd idea that some external AUTHORITY is capable of enabling others to become 'empowered'. Rather like LEARNING, empowerment may be spoken of as if it were a universal good. This contemporary rhetoric usually begs analysis also of the restrictions likely to be placed on empowerment in organizations – many employees have found that acting in an empowered way attracts sanctions.

Empowerment is related to notions of AUTONOMY and self-directedness. Christine Hogan, a humanistic educator and facilitator from Australia, has written about empowerment from a personal development perspective. She cites a definition of empowerment by Hamelink: 'a process in which people achieve the capacity to control decisions affecting their lives. Empowerment enables people to define themselves and to construct their own identities. Empowerment can be the outcome of an intentional strategy which is neither initiated externally by empowering agents or solicited by disempowered people.' (Hamelink 1994: 132–33, cited in Hogan 2000: 12.)

Hogan describes the model of an 'empowerment cycle' (2000: 20), a process of reflection and development that involves five stages over time:

- recall depowering/empowering experiences
- discuss reasons for depowerment/ empowerment
- identify one problem or project
- identify useful power bases
- develop and implement action plans.

encounter group encounter usually refers to the methods of Will Schutz (1971). (A different form of encounter, called 'basic encounter', operating on PERSON-CENTRED principles, was developed by Carl Rogers – see Bozarth 1986.) However, John Rowan (1998: 9) attributes the origin of encounter to Moreno, founder of PSYCHODRAMA.

Schutz's practice originated at the Esalen Institute at Big Sur, California (see Resources), where he was a faculty member. Esalen Institute ran inter-racial encounter groups between 1967 and 1970. In 1969, Esalen launched a study of alternative approaches to psychosis, which included encounter groups, with support from the National Institute of Mental Health and the California Department of Health.

Schutz developed the idea of 'open encounter', a format for personal growth. An encounter group, fundamentally, operates by facilitating encounters between participants in the HERE AND NOW. It is often associated with a confrontational style of relating, encouraging people to voice their irritation, anger, disappointment and so on with others in the room, and to become AUTHENTIC.

Encounter groups are, according to Schutz and others, capable of achieving great intimacy and releasing joy; at the same time they can be anxiety-provoking and potentially destructive for those who feel insecure in groups. See also SENSITIVITY TRAINING.

energizing raising or increasing the level of AROUSAL. Facilitators and trainers will often use short energizing activities to change the level of attention and arousal in a workshop. These almost always involve physical activity.

An example is where participants stand in a circle. Each gives themselves a brief massage by brushing themselves down with their hands, as if brushing off anxiety or tension, starting with the head and moving downwards to the feet.

energy in personal development, energy can refer to Freud's concept of mental energy (also called cathexis); physical (body) energy, particularly arising from the work of Wilhelm Reich (see, for example, BIOENERGETICS), or as used in approaches to healing such as acupuncture; or to the energetic qualities of CONSCIOUSNESS.

Many sources, both ancient and modern, purport the existence of some form of 'life force', often associated with consciousness or, more widely, with all living matter. There is much similarity with QUANTUM views of the universe. In a general sense energy is a metaphor for properties of fields of human interaction, representing the qualities of relationships between people and the context in which they meet (see, for example, Wheatley 1992).

'Subtle energy' refers to that which, it is claimed, can be perceived psychically rather than through the usual sensory channels, because it is at a very refined level of vibration (see, for example, Brennan 1988).

enlightenment for many writers in humanistic and transpersonal psychology, enlightenment is a transcendent experience of cosmic consciousness.

Enlightenment is the goal of Zen BUDDHISM; the Zen master contributes to the pupil's gradual enlightenment through, for example, posing koans ('What is the sound of one hand clapping?') that confront the limits of language, rationality and human understanding.

Enlightenment can refer generally to the purpose of MEDITATION. Levine refers to this sense of enlightenment as 'synonymous with the ability simply to be present, to be in the moment with no attachments anywhere else, with our whole life right here, right now' (Levine 1993: 75).

Enlightenment Intensive an 'Enlightenment Intensive' (Noyes 1998) is a residential group retreat in which participants work contemplatively and in dyads (pairs) to focus on the question 'Who Am I?'; and on related questions ('What Am I? What Is Life? What Is Another? What is Love?').

Enlightenment Intensives were devised by an American, Charles Berner, in the 1960s. Berner 'had noticed that people who tend not to make much progress in personal growth are those who do not truly know who they are (i.e. they are identified with their egos or personalities).

So he wondered how ordinary Westerners might be able to experience actual self-realization in a relatively short period of time. The inspiration for EIs – combining the Zen *sesshin* format with the yogic question 'Who am I?' and modern communication techniques – came while he was on a retreat in 1968, and the first, experimental EI was held in the Californian desert soon afterwards. Berner went on to run 99 Intensives in all over a ten-year period; he also trained several others to lead EIs in the same manner.' (From an Enlightenment Intensives website – see Resources). The Enlightenment Intensive movement claims to have no affiliations and no hierarchy.

John Rowan (1993: 148–49) comments on this format and its potential for discovery of the 'real SELF'.

enneagram the enneagram is a model of personality that consists of nine principal types (*ennea* is Greek for nine). It is primarily a tool for understanding one's own personality drive. Each type has a dominant energy that is both our greatest strength and potentially our greatest weakness, and the basis of how we relate to other types. The origins of the enneagram are not clear. The enneagram symbol and related teachings are attributed, for example, to the Kabbalah and to SUFISM, although it is probable that descriptions of the personality types themselves are modern additions. Gurdjieff is identified as bringing the enneagram to Western attention around the beginning of the 20th century. See, for example, Palmer (1995), Riso and Hudson (1999).

According to the International Enneagram Association (see Resources): 'The Enneagram symbol is a nine-pointed, star-like figure. The nine lines comprise a perfect triangle and a twisted hexagon contained within a circle. There is intrinsic meaning in the relationship between the parts of the figure and the whole. It forms the basis for an exploration of human evolution, including the evolution of consciousness and self-development.'

The Enneagram Monthly website (see Resources) summarizes each type as follows:

Type 1: A perfectionist, driven to do the 'right' thing. Often critical of self as well as others, with a strongly developed sense of responsibility. Prone to repressed anger.

Type 2: A helper, needing to be needed. Will go the extra mile to please others at the cost of taking care of self. Gives and is proud of it, but strings are often attached.

Type 3: An achiever, efficient, goal-driven and focused on being a 'winner'. Concern with appearances – style over substance – can crowd out friends, family and self-awareness.

Type 4: An individualist, craving self-expression and emotional depth. Sensitive to beauty and meaning, but prone to melancholy, feelings of inadequacy, and envy.

Type 5: An observer, perceptive and capable of synthesizing information in new ways. Protective of privacy and personal resources and prone to emotional detachment.

Type 6: A team-player – or a rebel – vigilant for threats from the environment. Loyal and engaging, but full of contradictions which create self-doubt and indecisiveness.

Type 7: An enthusiast with a perpetual surplus of plans and ideas, eager for experiences and/or material goods. Habitual optimism may cover a fear of boredom and pain.

Type 8: A leader, driven to control self and environment, capable of both domination and protectiveness. Vulnerabilities and a tender heart are hidden beneath a tough exterior.

Type 9: A peacemaker, good at seeing all points of view and easily distracted from personal needs and priorities. Avoids direct confrontation but can be passive and immovable.

espoused theory Argyris (1994) contrasts 'espoused theory', a person's verbal or reported account of how they behave, with their 'theory-in-use', or the principles the same person could be observed to use in practice.

Argyris says that typically there will be discrepancies between espoused theory and theory-in-use. This is reminiscent of the idea that 'actions speak louder than words', or the question of whether someone practises what they preach. A leader might espouse a democratic style of management, but do employees experience the leader's actual behaviour as democratic?

He argues that the theories-in-use of almost everybody conform to what he calls 'Model 1' behaviour: 'The primary behavioural strategies in Model 1 are to control unilaterally the relevant environment and tasks and to protect oneself and others. Characteristic ways of implementing this strategy include making unillustrated attributions and evaluations, advocating in ways that discourage inquiry, treating one's own views as obviously correct, making covert attributions and evaluations, and face-saving' (1994: 218).

This boils down to four main principles:

• achieve the purpose as the actor defines it
• win, do not lose
• suppress negative feelings
• emphasize rationality.

Essentially, this results in a culture that is antithetical to learning because it is geared to preventing inquiry.

est est stands for 'Erhard Seminar Trainings'. This was a large group-based personal development method founded by Werner Erhard in California in 1971. It draws from a highly eclectic variety of spiritual and psychological development theories and models, apparently the personal selection of Erhard (see, for example, Rawlinson 1997).

Today it is hard to appreciate the enormous impact of Erhard and est on the consciousness movement of the 1970s and 1980s. The seminar was billed as 'two weekends that would change your life'. Groups of 250 people at a time paid a substantial fee (then $250) for a highly disciplined (some would say authoritarian) seminar. They paid, in est parlance, to 'Get It'. That 'It' (the est ENLIGHTENMENT) was that 'Life works perfectly, you are responsible for everything that has ever happened to you, and you are perfect, even though you may experience barriers to perceiving and expressing that perfection.' (For one participant's account see Pressman 1993.)

By the end of 1975, 70 000 people had taken part in trainings in the USA, and by the 1990s the movement would claim nearly a million 'graduates' worldwide. Critics called it brainwashing. They pointed to the lack of formal qualifications held by Erhard and his trainers, the financial secrecy of est and the hard sell way in which est graduates were encouraged, indeed pestered, to enrol their friends and family (see CULT). Erhard made as many enemies as he did friends. On 3 March 1991, the US news programme *60 Minutes* ran an expose on Erhard which was watched by over 2 million people.

Today, est and related practices continue under a variety of new names, such as the Landmark Forum.

ethics ethics is the application of moral philosophy, which is the 'philosophical inquiry about norms and values, about ideas of right and wrong, good and bad, what should and what should not be done' (Raphael 1994: 8).

Ethical theories vary, and are often based on subjective notions such as 'the will of God' or 'the good of society'. For example, Kantian ethics advocate respect for others with each individual person having equal rights. Utilitarianism advocates happiness for the greatest number of people and would over-ride individual need for the greater good – however, it is impossible to follow actions to their ultimate conclusion, so whether the greatest happiness for the many is achieved cannot be known.

Ethics as moral principles are recruited to create social and professional codes of conduct. Some ethical codes are imperative and become enshrined in law – just as the law is not the same in all countries, so ethical practice is not identical in all professions.

Ethical practice is therefore context-bound. This is highlighted when it comes to forming professional standards of good practice. Achieving consensus on issues of, for example, professional boundaries in practitioner–client relationships, or financial and other business agreements, can be a minefield. Some believe that appeals to ethics are used as a pretext for imposing standardization and control – there are significant debates about accreditation amongst many groups of practitioners (see, for example, the G.O.R.I.L.L.A. website in Resources). However, most would probably subscribe to the intention of protecting clients from unscrupulous practitioners.

existentialism a philosophical approach associated with Sartre, Camus and other 20th-century figures, concentrating on the nature of human existence.

Existentialism emphasizes a non-mystical view of human existence. It suggests that our daily living reality is all that exists, and that the human condition entails choice about how to be. In Sartre's work there is an emphasis, for example, on coming to terms with the pain and boredom of existence.

In personal development, an existential approach emphasizes the taking of responsibility for the choices one makes. This is an important influence on GESTALT.

Influential figures in existential thought relevant to personal development are Rollo May (see ANXIETY and CREATIVITY); Viktor Frankl; and Ronnie Laing.

Frankl spent many years in Nazi concentration camps, and through this experience concluded that the search for meaning and purpose was the most important human drive (Frankl 1994). Later he based an approach to psychotherapy, which he called 'logotherapy', on this principle. There is a Viktor Frankl Institute in Vienna (see Resources).

Laing (e.g. 1990a, 1990b, original versions both written in the 1960s) was a Scottish radical psychiatrist. The underlying intent of this movement was to challenge notions of madness as illness, and of what is 'normal' or 'abnormal', in order to understand better the experience of 'madness' and promote a more humanistic treatment of psychiatric patients.

expectations literally, what a person expects to find or to receive. People operate at times without questioning their expectations, or as if they have a right to have their expectations fulfilled. They can feel disappointed and affronted when this does not happen. Fritz Perls, founder of GESTALT psychotherapy, would assert that he had no responsibility for meeting others' expectations.

For comment on ways in which others' expectations may affect a person's performance see SELF-FULFILLING PROPHECY.

experience in everyday terms, experience refers to the person's encounter with the world – how each of us perceives, senses and makes meaning. This itself points to some of the complexity of the term – are we talking about PERCEPTION *and* sense-making? Are we assuming that perception is unmediated by language, social conventions, and so on? Experience is difficult to define, and its nature is problematic.

Boud et al. (1993) have a useful

brief discussion of the term, and among other things they say: 'In our view, the idea of experience has within it judgement, thought and connectedness with other experience – it is not isolated sensing. Even in its most elementary form, it involves perception and it implies consciousness; it always comes with meaning . . . This suggests that experience is a meaningful encounter. It is not just an observation, a passive undergoing of something, but an active engagement with the environment, of which the learner is an important part' (1993: 6).

In personal development, the intent of drawing attention to experience is perhaps summed up as a concern that:

• each person's way of perceiving and being in the world is of value, and valid for them, but subject to testing and challenge from others

• epistemologically, KNOWLEDGE has an important experiential dimension – conceptual knowledge, and knowing in a cognitive mode, is only part of the picture, even though these modes may be treated as the most important in, for example, formal education.

Critiques of the notion of experience would include the risk that the individual is being valued over the social; and that the social and political influences on perception and meaning making are overlooked.

experiential learning experiential learning refers to LEARNING from (personal) experience. This is still a relatively unorthodox approach in formal education. An experiential learning perspective views learning as a more complex process involving theory and practice, action and reflection. It also gives more emphasis to the AFFECTIVE dimension of learning.

Boud et al. say that: 'Most of what is written about learning is from the perspective of teachers or researchers who assume that there is a body of knowledge to be taught and learned. What is

missing is the role and relevance of learning from experience no matter where it occurs. Learning involves much more than an interaction with an extant body of knowledge; learning is all around us, it shapes and helps create our lives – who we are, what we do. It involves dealing with complex and intractable problems, it requires personal commitment, it utilizes interaction with others, it engages our emotions and feelings, all of which are inseparable from the influence of context and culture' (Boud et al. 1993: 1).

Boud et al. (1993: 8–16) also list five propositions about learning from experience:

1. Experience is the foundation of, and the stimulus for, learning.
2. Learners actively construct their experience,
3. Learning is a holistic process.
4. Learning is socially and culturally constructed.
5. Learning is influenced by the socio-emotional context in which it occurs.

experiential learning cycle a model of EXPERIENTIAL LEARNING developed by David Kolb (1984). Kolb, building on Dewey's ideas about learning, and also influenced by Lewin, Piaget and Vygotsky, suggested that learning is a continual, adaptive process. Knowledge is being created and recreated all the time, and is not something that has an independent existence.

Following Lewin, he conceived of learning as a four-stage cycle. **Concrete experience** is action in the world or an encounter. This generates information, the basis for **reflective observation**; from reflecting on experience we create hypotheses, tentative beliefs or mental models, labelled **abstract conceptualizations**. We then prepare to test these out through **active experimentation**. Kolb emphasized the significance of the dynamic tension between opposite poles on the cycle. He also developed a LEARNING STYLE inventory to identify individual preferences

This experiential learning cycle has been very influential in, for example, education and management development, although it is typically used in a much simplified and even stereotypical form that neglects the depth and variation to be found in Kolb (1984). For example, following Lewin and others, Kolb saw the opposite 'poles' of the cycle as important DIALECTICAL tensions (e.g. that between concrete experience and abstract conceptualization). The ways in which these dialectics are resolved or handled greatly influences the type and level of learning that ensues.

The model has been criticized for being stronger conceptually than as an accurate representation of the way people actually learn through experience.

expression expression can refer to a facial expression (an example of BODY LANGUAGE) or to expressiveness.

The latter is valued in personal development as a characteristic of the healthy person. In particular, having a full range of emotional expression means a person is in touch with and able to communicate their feelings – a characteristic of EMOTIONAL COMPETENCE.

Creative expressiveness is a capacity for self-expression through artistic and imaginal media, such as poetry, painting, dance and music.

extrovert a person who habitually directs attention toward the outer world. The modern psychological term derives from a term (i.e. extraversion) already in use before Jung popularized it in his typology (see Jung 1971).

The extroversion–introversion polarity is important in Jung's work (see Fordham 1966: 29). These are two modes of response to the environment. The extrovert instinctively moves toward, and focuses his or her interest upon, the possibilities of the external reality, while the INTROVERT instinctively withdraws from the inherent threat of the external world and focuses on his or her own responses (or inner world).

Both of these types are natural and healthy, without moral implication; however, there is a social tendency to value extroversion more highly. Within the psyche a balance is maintained. If the dominant attitude is extroverted then the unconscious attitude will be introverted, and vice versa. The attitude type combines with the PSYCHO-LOGICAL FUNCTIONS to create further complexity.

Many believe that introverts are more energized by the internal world and extroverts by the external world, but this fails to honour the complexity of the psychological situation. For the extrovert the experiences of the external world do not in themselves stimulate a great deal of excitement, but the extrovert may flee from the troublesome inner world (with its scary demons) towards the relative tranquillity of the outer world. Therefore it is for the sake of psychic harmony that the extrovert directs his or her focus towards the external world.

Extroverts readily form attachments and, classically, are outgoing, sociable, gregarious, talkative, expressive, open and accessible. As extroverts concentrate on the outer world, they require continual stimulation from it and without social contacts may become bored, listless and lonely.

eye contact literally, the meeting of one person's gaze by another. Eye contact is a form of NON-VERBAL COMMUNICATION. John Heron worked with 'the PHENOMENOLOGY of the gaze'. In this he considered eye contact through the mutual gaze to be a primal experience, a deeply significant human encounter. As the saying goes, 'the eyes are the windows of the soul'.

'Good' eye contact is assumed to be an element both of interpersonal contact, and of RAPPORT, though not to be followed slavishly: it should not be forgotten that the circumstances under which eye contact is acceptable or desirable vary from culture to culture. For example, people doing presentations, or being interviewed, are generally advised to make (positive) eye contact with their audience or interviewer.

'Poor' eye contact – such as a reluctance to look the other in the eye – can be taken to mean that a person is anxious, insecure, or lacking in SELF-ESTEEM.

facilitation facilitation literally means 'easing'. A facilitator helps to create conditions within which other human beings can, so far as is possible, select and direct their own learning and development.

The art of facilitation is best demonstrated within experiential groupwork where participants agree to be actively and awarely involved in their own learning. In this sense facilitation is very different from lecturing and instructing although on occasion it may include elements of both. The basic premise is that learning is SELF-DIRECTED, holistic and grounded in personal experience.

John Heron has developed two well-known models of skills and strategies of facilitation, SIX CATEGORY INTERVENTION ANALYSIS and DIMENSIONS OF FACILITATOR STYLE, a group-based facilitation model.

Facilitation of others' learning implies a differential POWER relationship, which needs to be made explicit.

facilitator a facilitator is a person who is appointed to facilitate others to learn. The contractual relationship is usually explicit, both with the organization sponsoring the learning event and with the participants. Without such agreement the facilitation is unsolicited (see DEGENERATE facilitation).

The skills of the facilitator need to span expertise in the knowledge base (professional, technical, and academic), a sophisticated understanding of GROUP DYNAMICS, in-depth knowledge of human learning processes and excellent communication skills. The facilitator also needs to be comfortable to work experientially with the whole person of the participant, their intuition, imagination, emotions, spirituality, behaviour, and cognition.

Facilitator training was made popular in the 1980s when the Human Potential Research Group offered courses to many different professional groups (nurses, social workers, doctors, police and organizational trainers). Criteria of excellence for facilitators can be found in Heron (1999).

While facilitators mainly see themselves as educators, they are such in the broadest sense of the word. Their roles include being organizational consultants, spiritual mentors, counsellors, psychotherapists, trainers, group leaders, retreat directors, mediators, human resource professionals, social and probationary officers, and many others.

failure failure can lead to a lowering of SELF-ESTEEM and a sense of shame. But failure is a socially constructed experience – a person can only fail in relation to some standard or expectation. In personal development it would be important to explore how the person is judging themselves to have failed;

whether they are INTROJECTING other people's judgements; and whether they are seeing failure as a feature of their IDENTITY ('I am a failure') rather than as a specific, behavioural event ('I failed at that task').

Kipling talked about treating triumph and disaster as twin impostors (in his poem *If*). One of the PRESUPPOSITIONS in NLP is 'No failure, only feedback'. This is the principle that unsuccessful attempts to reach a target give us information that can help us with subsequent attempts (see also T.O.T.E.).

fear people often talk of wanting to overcome their fears. This may run the risk of defining fear as negative, and forgetting that in circumstances of danger instinctual fear is an ally that keeps us safe. But fear is also a learned, ANXIETY response, and can inhibit our choices. Even then, self-help authors such as Jeffers (1996) suggest attending to and acknowledging feelings of fear, rather than treating it as an obstacle. The maxim 'There is nothing to fear but fear itself' is oft-quoted. Facing one's fears is also a theme in shamanic sources such as Castañeda's books (see URBAN SHAMANISM).

feedback feedback has a technical meaning as a core concept of the field of cybernetics (an 'interdisciplinary science focusing on the study of information, communication and control', Morgan 1997: 83). Cybernetics is a key influence on NLP. The concept of feedback is also relevant as an important interpersonal skill set, i.e. in giving and receiving feedback from others.

Bateson and Bateson define the technical, cybernetic meaning as follows: "Negative" feedback is . . . a report of the outcome of previous functioning . . . used to adjust the mechanism governing future functioning, allowing for corrections that are apparently goal directed. In "positive" feedback (or schismogenesis), the effect of the feedback message is to move the system further in the direction of its previous movement, thus increasing instability rather than returning to stability or HOMEOSTASIS' (Bateson and Bateson 1988: 208).

It is worth emphasizing that in the cybernetic sense, 'negative' feedback is not bad, nor is 'positive' feedback good. In the interpersonal domain, however, we usually expect that negative feedback will be unpleasant.

The link with interpersonal skills is that feedback is information intended to help a person to develop. Various sources list guidelines or rules for giving and receiving feedback (such as that it is specific, timely and actionable). Handled unskilfully, feedback may do more harm than good (for example, the person who interjects with 'Let me give you some feedback . . .' and launches into unsolicited criticism).

In management, 360° feedback has been in vogue for some years. The positive intention of this is to ensure that managers are sensitive to their impact upon, and the views of, those other than their boss. Used well this can be a powerful developmental experience – as with many other personal developmental methods, effective and ethical facilitation is likely to be important. Used as a mechanistic process without regard to relational and human dimensions, it can result in 360° fallout. A quick search on the Internet reveals many sites offering computer- or web-based 360° feedback programmes or services; worryingly, the emphasis typically seems to be on the efficiency of the technology and rarely, if ever, on the personal and interpersonal dimensions.

feeling sometimes used synonymously with EMOTION, and sometimes distinguished. See also EMOTIONAL COMPETENCE; EMOTIONAL INTELLIGENCE; AFFECT. In personal development work, the idea of being 'in touch with' one's feelings is prominent. It is a curiosity of everyday language that 'I feel' more often refers to a thought than to a feeling.

There is no absolute definition of what 'feeling' is, and there is varying usage according to the model or perspective being taken. For example, feeling refers in Jungian psychology (see PSYCHOLOGICAL FUNCTIONS), to a preference over thinking as a mode of judging (making decisions or drawing conclusions from perceptions). In NLP, it is regarded as part of the kinaesthetic REPRESENTATIONAL SYSTEM and, by extension, the felt quality of one's internal STATE.

Heron has a particular usage of feeling, which he differentiates from emotion: '. . . by 'feeling' I refer, with special usage, to the capacity of the psyche to participate in wider unities of being, to become at one with the different content of the whole field of experience, to indwell what is present through attunement and resonance, and to know its own distinctiveness while unified with the differentiate other. This is the domain of empathy, indwelling, participation, presence, resonance and the like' (Heron 1992: 16).

felt sense the term coined by Eugene Gendlin (1978, 1996) to describe a cluster of thoughts, feelings, memories, body sensations, desires, dreams and so on that together constitute 'everything' about an issue in our life.

A felt sense has to be allowed to form as it is not a discrete entity that already exists. It is formed and experienced in a state of consciousness called FOCUSING.

In summary, according to Gendlin (1996: 24) a felt sense has eight characteristics:

1. A felt sense forms at the border zone between conscious and unconscious.
2. The felt sense has at first only an unclear quality (although unique and unmistakable).
3. The felt sense is experienced bodily.

4. The felt sense is experienced as a whole, a single datum that is internally complex.
5. The felt sense moves through steps. It shifts and opens step by step.
6. A step brings one closer to being that self which is not any content.
7. The process step has its own growth direction.
8. Theoretical explanations of a step can be devised only retrospectively.

feminism feminist critiques have been important in many spheres for revealing patriarchal biases, and enabling women to define experience more effectively in their own terms. This is certainly true in the somewhat male-dominated field of personal development. It would not be at all wise to assume that the espoused values of humanistic personal development – for example, for AUTHENTICITY and the fulfilment of each person's potential – make it immune from GENDER or other forms of OPPRESSION.

Feminist approaches (see Rowan 1998: 161–66) have produced forms or modes of personal development that address women's needs (e.g. Ernst and Goodison 1981; Worell and Remer 1992) as well as critiques of major theories (e.g. Wehr 1988).

field theory field theory appears in the work of GESTALT psychologists, with versions developed by Kurt Lewin and Fritz Perls (Clarkson and Mackewn 1993: 40). It is based on the principle that any moment, or any event, is understandable only in relation to the environment, or field of experience and meaning, in which it is located. Thus 'The field is all the coexisting, mutually interdependent factors of a person and his environment' (Clarkson and Mackewn 1993: 42). The Gestalt therapist aims to attend to the whole field, for example, drawing attention to an apparently innocuous gesture in order to discover how the field changes when this gesture is made figural (see FIGURE AND GROUND).

fight–flight Wilfred Bion (1961) wrote a classic account of dynamics in groups, based on rehabilitation in a military psychiatric hospital. He identified three 'basic assumptions' that groups are likely to make, each of which will prevent the group from addressing its task.

The three basic assumptions are dependency (in which a leader is expected to provide the group's nourishment and protection); 'pairing' (characterized by Messianic feelings of hope, which participants ensure unconsciously is never fulfilled); and fight–flight (in which the group seeks either to fight something – such as an 'enemy', whether real or imagined – or to run away from it).

Bion contrasted these basic assumption modes with seven characteristics of healthy group functioning or, as he expressed it, 'good group spirit' (1961: 25).

figure and ground a core notion of GESTALT psychotherapy that originates in Gestalt psychology (Clarkson 1989: 6–7). The field of a person's potential awareness at any moment is vast. What a person pays attention to is figural – it comes to the foreground as being most prominent, or has most attraction or urgency. The remainder of their awareness is the 'ground' – the background or backcloth. Figure and ground exist together, though, and any figural thought or emotion needs to be viewed in relation to its ground.

A classic illustration is the picture that can be seen either as a vase, or as two faces in silhouette. One or other form becomes figural – they cannot both be seen simultaneously.

firewalking a recent trend – Rowan (1983) refers to it as a fad – has been to offer firewalking as a developmental experience. Contemporary practice appears to have re-emerged particularly through Tony Robbins, through whom there are associations with NLP.

The basis appears to be that if you can walk across a bed of hot coals – a dangerous activity that many might believe they are not capable of – you are likely to expand significantly the range of what you believe you can do, and overcome fears and self-imposed limitations.

Like many apparently NEW AGE practices, firewalking has ancient roots in several cultures. For example, according to Danforth (1990), the Anastenaria is 'a northern Greek ritual in which people who are possessed by Saint Constantine dance dramatically over red-hot coals . . . The Anastenaria and the songs accompanying it allow people to express and resolve conflict-laden family relationships that may lead to certain kinds of illnesses . . . women use the ritual to gain a sense of power and control over their lives without actually challenging the ideology of male dominance that pervades Greek culture.'

To what extent contemporary practices retain any sense of the sacred nature or cultural roots of the process is open to question. Firewalking seems touted often as a macho 'barrier-busting' form of instant transformation and there appears a risk of mistaking the euphoria resulting from a seemingly impossible achievement with a lasting increase in confidence. Clearly this is a practice that would require both the skills and the ethics of facilitators to be thoroughly reliable.

first and second order change first and second order changes are concepts used in BRIEF THERAPY (see Watzlawick et al. 1974).

A first order change is one where there is a change within a system, but the overall system does not change. In psychotherapy, a first order change would be said to occur when a symptom is eliminated but the overall problem remains, perhaps in another form, or as symptom substitution. Thus a problem may be created by the solutions that people seek. A second order change is one that effects change in the whole of the system, because it reframes what at the first level was a problem. It involves insights which alter a person's perception of the problem in such a way that it no longer exists in that form.

For instance, the use of medication to alleviate emotional symptoms is of a first order change. If we then acquire a different and more generative meaning to our lives, then both depression and medication may no longer be relevant within the new conceptual framework (second order change).

The proponents of Brief Therapy believe that second order changes are the only lasting changes, because they occur at a higher LOGICAL LEVEL. Interventions aimed at creating second order changes may appear paradoxical and arational.

fishbowl a fishbowl exercise typically involves a selection of participants in some activity (such as ROLE-PLAY) in the centre of the room, with other participants observing or witnessing in an outer circle. Those engaging in the activity are the 'goldfish'.

This format has the advantage that those looking in on the goldfish can also engage in the activity. First, they can observe and be charged with giving feedback to participants. Second, there can be provision for a 'tag' system whereby an observer changes places with a goldfish.

Another option is to use this as a dialogical format, with an inner circle and an outer circle. This can be an alternative to a presentation. Those in the outer circle are attuned more to listening, and need to make a conscious decision to move in order to enter the dialogue. Those in the inner circle are typically less anxious about airing their questions, and can address concerns in a more conversational way. The facilitator can attend during the process to the limited number of participants in the inner circle. The metaphor of the goldfish bowl is somewhat cold, hard and wet for this process – at Surrey we call it a 'campfire'.

fixated a psychoanalytic term referring to a person's development being fixed or stuck at a particular stage; or to their attention and energy being fixed rigidly on a particular thought or issue.

flow state flow state is a term coined by Mihaly Csikszentmihalyi (1990) to describe an optimal state of consciousness where we become completely absorbed in what we are doing – where the task takes us over and we become one with it. This flow state is effortless and linked with exceptional performance. (See also PEAK EXPERIENCE).

The ideal relationship between individual skills and level of challenge is shown in graphical form as the 'flow channel' where an individual's responsibility and size of job increases following the natural development of her/his capability. It also reveals the boredom and frustration that can result when an individual is working at a level below their capacity, and conversely the anxiety that is produced when their work is more than they can handle.

This research has been used as a basis for the design of personal development tools like Personal Flow Profiling (Adroit International), which helps an individual become more aware of the conditions necessary for her/him to get into flow, thus making it more likely to occur. It has also influenced the career planning aspects of management development: for example, it has been used by Gillian Stamp at Brunel University (UK) in her Career Path Appreciation process (Stamp 1993).

Focusing Focusing (Gendlin 1978, 1996) is an experiential process claimed to be the (client) skill that enables therapy to be effective. It is reckoned that 15–20 per cent of Western-educated people have this skill naturally, and it can be learnt. Focusing is taught, and practised in groups or partnerships, with the ultimate aim of becoming self-reliant.

Focusing works through the ability consciously to feel feelings physiologically and allow them to symbolize themselves accurately. It rests on the discovery that 'meaning' is not only thought, but also felt, or experienced, in the body. The bodymind, which has its own intentionality, knows something in a felt way (see FELT SENSE), but this felt-meaning is incomplete. It moves toward completion through interaction with a symbol, a process that is not subject to rational control.

The roots of Focusing were in America, where Carl Rogers and his doctoral student and later colleague Eugene Gendlin were studying what made therapy successful. Early in his career, Rogers, one of the founding fathers of the HUMANISTIC movement, stumbled upon a crucial observation: 'When I accept myself as I am, then I change.' Gendlin was investigating the phenomenon whereby therapy clients could become better and better at understanding the roots of their prob-

lems without being able to change – the principle that 'Knowing is not the process of changing.'

free association the action of verbally expressing streams of consciousness as they arise in the psyche without censorship.

Freud stipulated that the UNCONSCIOUS psyche needs a medium for expression and mainly uses metaphor, expressive art, dreams, free association, myth and ritual (Singer 1998). In psychoanalysis the belief is that there is conflict between the EGO and the ID, which motivates us in ways we are unaware of. By the systematic use of free association the complexity of unconscious material is encouraged to surface to awareness. This can help bring about resolution of infantile conflicts.

In TRANSACTIONAL ANALYSIS, free association 'allows the Child EGO STATE to talk freely while the Parent and the Adult ego states of the patient witness and hear what the Child has to say' (Berne 1961: 163). This is a powerful method for the healing of emotional traumas, aiding integration of the split parts of the personality.

games can refer to educational activities used in workshops, or to the use of a game format in personal development (for example, the TRANSFORMATION GAME).

Specifically in TRANSACTIONAL ANALYSIS, games are psychological manoeuvres by which the individual seeks affirmations (STROKES) through ulterior (indirect and unconscious) transactions (Berne 1961).

Each person has learned through experience that asking for positive affirmations (recognition for existing, and doing OK in the world) has resulted in rejection, ranging from minor to major, so has learned to be recognized negatively. It is like the saying, 'A bad press is better than no press.' Games in this case are called 'psychological games' as they exist for the sole purpose of meeting the psychological needs of the individual. They are also considered to work at the level of the UNCONSCIOUS.

'Playing games' is a way people pass time (see PASTIMING) and seek to get their needs met. In adult life, games are a re-play of strategies from childhood that may no longer be appropriate. We hold on to these strategies and play them out unconsciously as we perceive them to be the only way of getting our childhood psychological needs met.

Psychological games are interpersonal. Two or more people need to be involved for the game to be sustained. They may be communicating one message at a social level while an altogether different type of communication is being transmitted at the psychological level. The latter level is more profound and more likely to influence the response (also often at an unconscious psychological level) from the other person.

Games are best understood when analysed within the framework of process communication developed by Berne and made popular in his book *Games People Play* (1968). In all psychological games there is a payoff for both partners.

gender there have been few attempts to evolve a credible psychology of gender. Early theorists ignored gender issues, while in the main, the practitioners were men and the patients women. With the advent of FEMINISM in the 1970s the gender perspective began to change. However, since the needed theories of social construction concentrated on the enfranchisement of women and homosexuals, the study of difference did not advance. The impetus to make everyone the same was primary, since social equality was yet to be achieved.

The question remains as to what differences between males and females predate cultural influences. Interesting work is currently being done on this.

The post-Jungians, notably Woodman (1993), Pinkola Estes (1992), Meade (1993) and Bly (1990), researching mythology and anthropology, acclaim the social and psychological wisdom of pre-industrial indigenous people, whose young people underwent RITES OF PASSAGE in order to join their adult sister- and brotherhoods as vital resources for life.

Researchers from the Tavistock Institute (see Resources), Hudson and Jacot (1991), propose a fundamental difference in the imagination of males and females due to their experience of similarity and difference in relation to their mothers. Coming from BIOENERGETICS, Willem Poppeliers (1998) suggests that men and women have a fundamentally different bodily and sexual energetic organization. There are further ideas in the recently popular *Men Are From Mars, Women Are From Venus* (Gray 1993), though some (e.g. the Centre for Gender Psychology – see Resources) question whether this engages sufficiently in the struggle that arises from difference, and thus misses out on the creative alchemy which can result.

Gestalt Gestalt literally means 'whole'. Gestalt psychology developed as a branch of cognitive psychology, with particular interest in the way that people make patterns in their experience. Gestalt psychologists believed that such pattern-making was usually below conscious awareness, and more significant than rational, conscious decision-making. For example, someone looking at a circular line on paper that does not quite join up with itself is likely to see it as a circle even though there is a gap. According to Gestalt psychology too, we are more likely to remember details of an incomplete Gestalt – as if some part of our consciousness remains restless until the Gestalt is complete.

Fritz Perls, the founder of Gestalt psychotherapy, had a background in Gestalt psychology and in psychoana-

lysis. The relationship and lineage between Gestalt counselling/psychotherapy (Clarkson 1989) and Gestalt psychology is a matter of controversy.

Gestalt psychotherapy emphasizes human experience more than the production of knowledge about experience, and aims to promote AUTHENTIC existence free of the constraining influences of a repressive society. It is essentially an EXISTENTIAL and PHENOMENOLOGICAL approach.

Fritz Perls is sometimes criticized for having taken this to an anti-intellectual extreme, and having contributed to a cult of the individual (see, for example, Perls 1969). His 'Gestalt prayer' seems at once to be a celebration of liberated existence and a two-fingered salute to any idea of social responsibility. An excellent retrospective appraisal of Perls's contribution is provided by Clarkson and Mackewn (1993: Chapter 4), which distances Gestalt therapy from the widely publicized work of Fritz Perls during the 1960s.

Gestalt training, in therapy and in other modes of professional practice (for example, in organizational consulting), remains very popular.

Gestalt cycle the Gestalt cycle is a model of human experience, purported to represent a universal pattern and rhythm of creation and destruction.

The notion and form of the cycle originated in the work of Fritz Perls (Clarkson and Mackewn 1993: 50) and has been developed by various others in the field (e.g. by Zinker 1977, as a teaching aid in the Gestalt Institute of Cleveland).

Typically it consists of seven stages. While there is no definitive form, or start or end point, and no rigid demarcation between stages (this would be antithetical to the notion of being a continuous cycle), a typical sequence (Clarkson 1989) is:

1. Withdrawal/rest

2. Sensation
3. Awareness
4. Mobilization
5. Action
6. (Final) contact
7. Satisfaction – where satisfaction represents completion of a Gestalt.

Healthy human functioning involves the capacity to progress through these stages continually. This applies to both individuals and groups.

The model attends to forms of 'BOUNDARY disturbance' or interruption at each stage, and thus may be used in a diagnostic tool. Five types of interrupt (broadly equivalent to psychological DEFENCES in psychodynamic terms) are PROJECTION, INTROJECTION, DEFLECTION, RETROFLECTION and CONFLUENCE. These are not inherently problematic.

grief grief is an intensely painful emotion associated with the normal, healthy process of mourning loss or bereavement. Grief is an emotion that may be blocked for many people (see CATHARSIS). There are specialisms in grief counselling and therapy that are designed to facilitate the mourning process – see, for example, Worden (1991).

Kübler-Ross's (1970) bereavement model is an example of the stages a person may go through when grieving and coming to an acceptance of loss. Heron identified one of the three primary needs of the person as to love and be loved. When the first of these is denied the emotional release is grief, 'the suffering of frustrated love' (Heron 1992: 126).

ground rules rules or norms that a group negotiates, or agrees to, as guidelines for behaviour. Often used as an activity early in the life of a new group, which helps with orientation and takes care of basic safety needs. In a new group many people find it helpful to state their needs and discuss what will be expected of them.

Ground rules can address norms of behaviour (e.g. that there will be no physical violence), practical arrangements (e.g. times of refreshments breaks) and understandings related to the purpose of the group (e.g. that it is legitimate for participants to offer each other feedback on their behaviour). Heron (1999: 262) refers to ground rules that relate to discipline, decision-making, and growth (i.e. to intensify personal learning and awareness). He lists (1999: 155) a possible set of ground rules for a peer support group.

Sometimes trainers or facilitators introduce pre-determined sets of ground rules. This is a more hierarchical form of FACILITATION that, if imposed rather than used as a basis for negotiated agreement, can miss out on the value of a ground rules discussion for GROUP STAGES of forming and norming.

Ground rules, once negotiated, are not normally set in stone, and may be revisited periodically.

grounded being grounded means being focused with a balance of attention into self and to the outside world as necessary. It is like keeping your feet firmly on the ground while raising your sights to the heavens.

Feeling grounded implies a psychological alignment of mind, body and spirit towards one's purpose. The term often implies building ideas on the basis of solid (grounded) experience.

The phrase is a colloquialism for a person who has developed sufficient self-awareness to own their own gifts and failings and not PROJECT them out onto others. It means being EMOTIONALLY COMPETENT and not being so swamped by emotional pain, rage or fear as to lose sight of the meaning and learning that experience has to offer.

group cycle within any one session or meeting a group will go through different phases (See also GROUP STAGES). Randall and Southgate (1980), who were influenced by Wilhelm Reich's work, say that in effective groups, these stages form a creative cycle:

- **nurturing** creates a supportive atmosphere and establishes good working relationships
- **energizing** involves people in and focuses energy upon the task
- **peak** is a sense of exhilaration as the group can see the task being achieved
- **relaxing** allows celebration of achievement, summary and ending.

But in a destructive group:

- **nurturing** might become smothering or a distraction from the task
- **energizing** could be aggressive, raising fear rather than productive energy; or energy may be locked into boredom
- **peak** (if it happens) could be an explosion of hostility
- **relaxing** may be retreat – followed by post mortems on how awful meetings are.

Most often we find intermediate groups. These have a mixture of the characteristics of creative and destructive groups.

group dynamics   the events or patterns of events that characterize the behavioural, psychological and (often) unconscious life of groups.

Robert de Board (1978), quoting the work of Cartwright and Zander, lists seven approaches to the theory of group dynamics. He cites (1978: 14) Cartwright and Zander's conclusion that these theories hold four assumptions in common:

1. groups are inevitable and ubiquitous
2. groups mobilize powerful forces which produce effects of utmost importance to individuals
3. groups may produce both good and bad consequences
4. a correct understanding of group dynamics – obtainable from research – permits the possibility that desirable consequences from groups can be deliberately enhanced.

One classic theory of group dynamics is that of Wilfred Bion (1961), based on his work in a military psychiatric hospital (see FIGHT–FLIGHT). A comprehensive account of group dynamics, including group defensiveness, can be found in Heron 1999 (Chapter 4). See also GROUPWORK.

group hygiene   group hygiene is the principle that some unspoken conflicts go 'underground' in the group dynamic and remain as repressed hurt, anger and resentment. This repressed negativity is believed to obstruct positive working energy and cooperation as those hurt displace their frustrations and resentments onto the group task. The belief is that by articulating the interpersonal conflict and working at resolving the issues, the people involved will feel heard and that their feelings are being taken account of and valued. Group relationships will then become current and authentic and the group will become more effective.

group roles   in Schein's (1969) model of process consultancy, a range of behaviours is needed for a group to be effective. Task behaviours are concerned with performance and productivity, while maintenance behaviours are concerned with relationships and people. Examples of task and maintenance behaviours are:

- **task roles:** initiating, seeking information or opinion, giving information or opinion, clarifying, summarizing, evaluating
- **maintenance roles:** encouraging, gatekeeping, standard setting, supporting, expressing group feeling, compromising.

As Clark (1994) says, the overwhelming majority of teams in organizations concern themselves only with the task. But neglect of maintenance needs will almost certainly lead to destructiveness.

Meredith Belbin's work on team roles (Belbin 1996) provides another well-known model.

group stages   the notion that groups evolve or develop through a series of reasonably distinct phases. There are many models of this type (see, for example, COMMUNITY BUILDING), perhaps the best known being that put forward by Tuckman (1965). The stages that Tuckman suggested groups progress through are:

- **forming:** members meet and first form as a group; they get to know each other and establish what their group task is
- **storming:** differences and potential conflicts surface – members find out about, and express, mismatches in their expectations, or dislikes of other members, and/or compete for status
- **norming:** the group arrives at shared norms – these can be implicit or explicit
- **performing:** the group carries out its task.

The stages reflect development in both interpersonal (group structure) and task dimensions.

This model was based on a review of 55 articles about small group development. In other words, there was no direct empirical basis for the model, although it aims to represent the empirical work surveyed. Tuckman and Jensen (1977) later reviewed research and articles that developed or tested the original model, though they found that little empirical testing had been done.

On the basis of this survey they proposed a fifth stage, that of 'adjourning', which some refer to as 'mourning'. This happens when the task is done, and perhaps the need for the group's existence has been satisfied, allowing the group to end and deal with issues of loss.

group think the phenomenon whereby a group operates with less intelligence than that of its members, through excessive collusion, ignoring information that does not match the group's consensus view, suppressing dissent, or attacking those who challenge.

The term was invented by Irving Janis (1972), based on study of American foreign policy fiascos such as the 'Bay of Pigs'. Janis was advocating a better understanding of the role of group dynamics in such decision-making processes. The concept highlights some negative aspects of group cohesion and loyalty, and particularly the tendency for individuals' thoughts and creativity to become blocked in group settings.

groupwork personal development activity that takes place in a group, with attendant GROUP DYNAMICS.

Groups are a prime medium in which personal development is pursued. Most training courses and workshops operate in a group format, whether or not the dynamics of the group are given explicit attention. Some methods (for example, PSYCHODRAMA, T-GROUPS and ENCOUNTER GROUPS) make deliberate use of group dynamics as a vehicle for personal development.

Groupwork is so common in personal development that practitioners should normally have developed competence in group FACILITATION.

growth movement the 'growth movement' emerged in the 1960s, particularly associated with HUMANISTIC PSYCHOLOGY and the drive to realize individual human potential. In effect the phrase refers generically to the PERSONAL DEVELOPMENT 'industry' – workshops, practitioners, associations, interest groups, networks and communities. It is less common nowadays, partly because the metaphor 'growth' was recognized as having an unfortunate double meaning (i.e. a cancer is also referred to as a growth).

Part of a flourishing of creativity across many fields, the growth movement was influenced by or contemporaneous with a loosening of class boundaries, sexual liberation, feminist perspectives, political action, radical education and psychotherapy, pop culture, awareness of environmental issues and ecology, and emerging interest in spiritual development. The growth movement can also be seen as preconventional, a rebellious urge to change an unfair and repressive society.

The growth movement has fostered a wider sense of permission for people to be themselves, and to engage in personal development. There has been a huge, creative variety of methods and practices, as noted in other entries in this volume. At the same time the emphasis on self has a potentially NARCISSISTIC, egocentric flavour (see 'MEGENERATION'), and innovation became undermined by a failure to deal effectively with internal structural and political issues.

guided fantasy/imagery guided fantasy is a method for enabling people to access their creative imagination and for enabling non-verbal knowledge (or inner experience) to be brought to conscious awareness (Samuels and Samuels 1975). It has been defined in various other ways, for example, 'creative visualization' (Gawain 1995), 'interactive daydreaming' or 'active imagination'.

Techniques for deliberately accessing, engaging and training the imagination for the purpose of facilitating personal growth have been known since recorded history, and are the foundation of many forms of Eastern MEDITATION practices. In Western psychology, two of the earliest researchers and writers to explore this area were Carl Jung (1964) and Roberto Assagioli (1965), and much has been written by them and their followers about the role of symbol and imagination in this field. Guided fantasy is a frequently-used technique in many types of therapy and counselling, for example, PSYCHOSYNTHESIS.

Guided fantasy can have many different applications. Its basic modus operandi is that the person is encouraged to become relaxed, and given some basic, fairly general information about a situation, place or journey, leaving scope for them to supply the detail from their own imagination. The guide or facilitator prompts them from time to time with further very open-ended suggestions or questions, and as the corresponding detail is added by the subject's imagination, or symbolic memory, the whole experience deepens. Subsequently the person may be encouraged to draw, paint, act, talk about or model the detail of their imaginative experience. This can bring fresh insight, altered mood or different perspective to the topic they are exploring.

guilt guilt is a complex emotion. Some argue that it is essentially shame. Fritz Perls saw guilt as projected RESENTMENT. Dryden (1999: 12), from a RATIONAL-EMOTIVE perspective, distinguishes between remorse (which he says is the healthier of the two) and guilt, saying that 'guilt occurs when the person condemns himself as bad, wicked or rotten for acting badly. Here, the person feels badly both about the act and his "self" because he holds the belief: "I must not act badly and if I do it's awful and I am a rotten person!"'

hang-up an emotional problem; a bug-bear, pet hate, or topic or issue that a person finds difficult or annoying (for example, 'He has a hang-up about people who push into queues'). The origin of the phrase is not clear, but probably refers metaphorically to something on which a person becomes hooked or snagged.

health 'health' derives from the same root as the word 'whole'. Personal and societal health and well-being are the ultimate goals of personal development work. HUMANISTIC PSYCHOLOGY is growth and health-orientated, rather than remedial. In other words it is concerned with realization of potential, in domains of mind, body, emotion and spirit, rather than correction or cure of disease. Health is therefore closely related to SELF-ESTEEM and EMOTIONAL COMPETENCE among other things.

This is reflected in various writers' conceptions of health. For example, Maslow (1970: 33) said, 'Health is not simply the absence of disease or even the opposite of it.' Fritz Perls's view of psychologically healthy people was that they are 'self-regulating individuals, able to support themselves while accepting mutual interdependency with other people' (Clarkson and Mackewn 1993: 67).

here and now GESTALT therapy emphasizes living in the present, with attention on the here and now. This was probably a counter to the tendency in psychoanalysis to dwell almost exclusively on the past. In Fritz Perls's view, people typically spent too much energy thinking about the past and worrying about the future, neglecting to be fully in the present. It is not a total rejection of the significance of the past, but (in common with NLP) the past is seen as an inherent part of the present 'FIELD'.

Rollo May expressed a similar view from his EXISTENTIAL perspective: 'The first thing necessary for a constructive dealing with time is to learn to live in the reality of the present moment. For psychologically speaking, this present moment is all we have. The past and future have meaning because they are part of the present: a past event has existence now because you are thinking of it at this present moment, or because it influences you so that you, as a living being in the present, are that much different. The future has reality because one can bring it into his mind in the present. Past was the present at one time, and the future will be the present at some coming moment. To try to live in the 'when' of the future or the 'then' of the past always involves an artificiality, a separating one's self from reality; for in actuality one exists in the present. The past has meaning as it lights up the present, and the future as it makes the present richer and more profound' (May 1953: 227).

heroic quest rather than seeing each person as developing towards some standard idea of level or ideal state, we can see each person's life as a quest or journey.

The notion of the heroic quest is present in MYTHS throughout the world. Joseph Campbell identified the pattern of the 'hero myth' and noted that '. . . the imagery of schizophrenic fantasy perfectly matches that of the mythological hero journey' (Campbell 1985: 161).

Campbell identified the following stages to this journey:

- break-away or departure from the local social order
- long, deep retreat inward (into the psyche) and backward (in time)
- a chaotic series of encounters – then encounters of a centring kind
- return journey and rebirth.

He characterized these as three main stages of separation, initiation and return (Campbell 1985: 162).

The heroic quest embodies the idea of gaining self-knowledge through journeying into the unknown, and facing and overcoming ordeals. The outward journey of the hero myth is paralleled by the inward journey of psychic development. Several ancient symbol systems are thought to represent this journey; for example, the CHAKRAS (Myss 1997); the TAROT; and the TREE OF LIFE. The idea of the heroic quest has been applied to management development by Cairnes (1998).

heuristic a heuristic device is a map or model that does not purport to be true, but which enables a learner to explore and discover. It may be a rule of thumb that allows for exploration through trial and error, or a model such as Maslow's HIERARCHY OF NEEDS.

This understanding of heuristics as an inquiry process allows it to be used successfully as a qualitative research methodology when investigating the inner world of individuals. It is a process of internal searching to give meaning to human experience. Moustakas (1990) is the most prolific researcher and writer of heuristic research.

hidden agenda there are different individual and group needs vying for attention and submerged and even suppressed under the surface of group tasks. A hidden agenda is an unspoken psychological or political agenda that will divert energy and attention away from the task if it is not accounted for and where possible addressed.

Hidden agendas can be positive as well as negative. Some people go to evening classes ostensibly to learn to cook or speak another language, while an underlying psychological need is to meet potential friends or a life partner. If the teacher does not allow interaction in the group such needs are stifled and individuals are likely to become uncooperative or leave the group.

Equally the hidden agenda might be negative, involving power struggles between group members. Raising awareness to possible hidden agendas is an aspect of GROUP HYGIENE.

hidden curriculum the hidden curriculum expresses the idea that every educational experience has an overt curriculum, i.e. the stated learning aims, activities and so on, and a hidden curriculum, or what is taught tacitly. Thus learners are taught norms of behaviour and are socialized into the practices and expectations of the particular educational setting. Typically, issues of POWER and politics are prominent in the hidden curriculum.

Benson Snyder, an American educator and psychiatrist, created the term through concerns about the quality of human experience in educational settings. He suggested that 'a hidden curriculum determines, to a significant degree, what becomes the basis for all participants' sense of worth and SELF-ESTEEM. It is this hidden curriculum, more than the formal curriculum, that influences the adaptation of students and faculty' (Snyder 1971: xii–xiii). Snyder warned of the dangers of (as he saw it) effectively teaching learners that success comes through conforming to institutional norms and expectations.

While his study was of an American university campus, the concept of the hidden curriculum has since been cited in relation to a variety of educational settings, including workplaces (e.g. Marsick and Watkins 1989) and management training courses.

hierarchy of needs a model of human motivation devised by Abraham Maslow, classifying human needs into various types. It is organized hierarchically, such that people will satisfy lower-level needs before seeking to satisfy higher-level needs.

Maslow's hierarchy of needs is probably the most familiar model in the whole field of personal development – although as Watson (1996) shows in the field of management education, it is not only poorly understood but also promulgated as established theory rather than as the speculative map of human development that Maslow originally seems to have intended. In management education it is presented primarily as an example of HUMAN RELATIONS thinking.

The typical version found in textbooks and training courses has five types of need. Arranged 'top down', these are:

- SELF-ACTUALIZATION (e.g. fulfilment)
- esteem (e.g. recognition, status)
- LOVE (e.g. social contact, belonging, acceptance)
- safety (e.g. security, protection)
- physiological (e.g. food, drink, shelter).

Maslow first published this perspective on human MOTIVATION in the 1940s (Maslow 1943). It is not clear how many levels in total Maslow intended to portray. For example, Buchanan and Huczynski (1997: 72) settle on seven levels of need, with two additional, 'higher' needs (for freedom of inquiry

and expression; and for the need to know and understand).

According to the Association for Humanistic Psychology (see Resources), Maslow's 'rather speculative theory has now been confirmed through the research of people like Kohlberg, Alderfer and Jane Loevinger in many different countries of the world'. The consensus from the field of management, however, is that as a theory of motivation it has not been supported by empirical research. There is a question, of course, of whether it is appropriate to assess or claim empirical validity for an HEURISTIC model. There is no doubt that Maslow's hierarchy of needs has spread far and wide and has been highly influential.

higher purpose a person's ultimate or cosmic goal, their reason for being.

We can experience higher purpose as contact with the divine or a relationship with God. But the experience of higher purpose does not necessarily need to be understood within a religious context. The composer Michael Tippett believed that being open to the channels through which he composed his music was his life's purpose.

Sometimes our higher purpose can be understood as a need to fulfil our own creativity and potential, and many believe that healthy individuals need such goals to strive towards. People who have a sense of their own higher purpose may experience this as actively belonging to something that is greater than themselves, of which they are a necessary and intimate part.

Many schools of psychotherapy or modes of development aim to put people in touch with their innermost goals and to develop their abilities to transcend themselves. Jung believed that to cure a person's neurosis, it was necessary for them to become aware of their own unique higher purpose. He understood this as a religious quest. In BUDDHISM, higher purpose is the attainment of an absolutely purified state that liberates the individual from the cycle of birth and death. In systemic counselling, it is held that our SPIRITU-ALITY is a necessary part of ourselves as living systems, and vital to health and healing, essential as a way to make meaning of our whole lives.

higher self the concept of the Higher Self presupposes that there are levels of organization and identity beyond those of EGO or even SOUL. The tradition of belief in a Higher Self can be traced in its European origins to the Gnostics, Cathars, and Alchemists, and in the Orient to the Hindu or Vedantic notion of the Atman.

In the early part of this century the concept was brought to life by Gurdjieff, Alice Bailey and the Theosophists. In psychology, Roberto Assagioli's PSYCHOSYNTHESIS posited the Personal Self, or 'I', as a reflection of the Higher Self, which held the supreme position in his map of consciousness, ASSAGIOLI'S EGG.

In these traditions the Higher Self is distinguished by its difference from the Lower or Small Self, being unattached to the consciousness and concerns of everyday life, and the struggle to form an acceptable self-image. The Higher Self is considered the spiritual self or Divine Self, closely linked to the experience of universal consciousness. The lower self is the existential experience of self as pure self-consciousness, the discovery of the 'I'. The Higher Self is usually said to transcend death, and sometimes to be the source of several different souls, so that different incarnations may be thought of as emanations of a sole spirit (Davidson 1997).

NEW AGE philosophy relies heavily on the notion of the Higher Self, which is said to have a specific intention for each incarnation. Discovering its purpose and task is thereby a means of reframing the obstacles of life, and finding meaning. This view has been given considerable exposure by the bestselling cult novelist, James Redfield (1994).

holistic whole, or concerned with wholeness. Particularly refers to practitioners who deal with the 'whole person' (e.g. mind, body, emotion and spirit). 'Jan Smuts developed the concept of holism, which extends to a radical acceptance of BODYMIND unity which is not based on any notion of causality . . . An holistic approach to the person embraces and affirms complexity, inclusion and diversity and resists reductionism' (Clarkson 1989: 8).

Modern Western thinking is influenced by the Cartesian-Newtonian view of the world that encourages the fragmentation of phenomena. By contrast, holistic approaches portray a different reality that unifies mind, body, spirit and universe, and acknowledges the wide range of parallel activities occurring simultaneously and the interactions occurring between them.

Various writers have used different metaphors and models to communicate these concepts: unbroken wholeness reminiscent of a hologram that contains the image of the whole in every fragment (Bohm 1980); open systems with a constant interchange with the environment (Bertalanffy 1975); and co-evolution.

Individuals who espouse a holistic perspective in their work accommodate the reality of complex interactions and their shared purpose, rather than changing specific elements to achieve results that do not acknowledge the effects on the whole. For example, when a practitioner works conventionally to solve someone's problem, he/she will consider the immediate circumstances of the individual and the interactions directly associated with the focus situation. By contrast, a holistic practitioner will have cognizance of the HOMEOSTATIC influences in the existing situation and a much wider range of interactions and effects. While both practitioners are able to offer solutions to the original problem, the foresight inherent in the holistic practitioner's exploration is intended to be alert to potential adverse consequences of the proposed strategy.

homeostasis refers to 'self-regulation and the ability to maintain a steady state. Biological organisms seek a regularity of form and distinctness from the environment while maintaining a continuous exchange with that environment. This form and distinctness is achieved through homeostatic processes that relate and control system operation on the basis of what is now called "negative FEEDBACK", where deviations from some standard or norm initiate actions to correct the deviation. Thus, when our body temperature rises above normal limits, certain bodily functions operate to try to counteract the rise (e.g. we begin to perspire and breathe heavily). Social systems also require such homeostatic control process if they are to acquire enduring form' (Morgan 1997: 40).

This concept helps us to understand why efforts to produce change can sometimes have little real impact. In an organization the intervention of a consultant may be treated by the 'system' as a disturbance to homeostasis. The system can attempt to regain homeostasis by 'recruiting' the consultant to its existing patterns of behaviour. The consultant may notice RESISTANCE – difficulty with gaining commitment, a sense of feeling responsible for the organization's problems, and so on. This is not usually a conscious effort by members of the organization.

The same may apply at individual level. Watzlawick et al. (1974) would call this an example of FIRST ORDER CHANGE.

human potential the self-creating capacity of the person. The Human Potential Movement developed in the 1960s, with a focus on self-development and the development of a more liberating life style (see GROWTH MOVEMENT).

Human Relations a school of thought in management that is associated with treating human relations within organizations as a crucial factor impinging on productivity.

The origin of the Human Relations School of thought is typically associated with the work of Elton Mayo. Mayo and colleagues studied the 'bank wiring room' of the Hawthorne Electric Company in the late 1920s and early 1930s, experimenting to determine the effect of environmental conditions (such as lighting) on productivity.

In essence, the famed finding was that variation in productivity could not be accounted for without taking social interaction into account. More specifically, the experiments found that variations in productivity did not correlate with variations in controlled environmental conditions; and apparently worsening conditions still resulted in increases in productivity. The explanation put forward was that the interest shown in the people in the bank wiring room by the researchers, and the forming of a cohesive work group, were responsible for the increase in productivity.

These experiments are often cited as the dawning of a more enlightened era of management, especially compared with that represented by F.W. Taylor and Scientific Management. However, this view is criticized by authors such as Huczynski (1993) and Collins (1998), who argue that the purpose of these experiments, and the use to which the results were put, were instrumental. In other words, the Human Relations School was not HUMANISTIC, it was simply sensitized to the importance of the human factor in the productivity equation. Collins suggests that the research methods used by Mayo and colleagues were 'dubious', and that 'the contrast between Human Relations thinking and scientific management is rather more imagined than real' (1998: 18).

Huczynski suggests that later, through writers such as Abraham

Maslow, a more genuinely humanistic approach emerged: Huczynski terms this 'Neo-Human Relations'.

An implication for personal development is that the espousal of Human Relations, especially in organizational settings, does not necessarily imply an intrinsic concern for the personal development and well-being of the employee.

humanistic the central principle of HUMANISTIC PSYCHOLOGY is to treat people as people. This contrasts with the alienation of PSYCHOANALYSIS, where human contact between analyst and analysand is seen as a potential contaminant of the therapy, and the reductionist tendencies of BEHAVIOURISM.

The term 'humanistic' therefore usually refers to the theories and practices of the Humanistic Psychology movement. It is different in substance or nuance from:

- humanism (which refers, among other things, to a pragmatic, non-supernatural philosophy)
- HUMAN RELATIONS (a school of thought in the field of management)
- humanitarianism (which usually refers to a philanthropic principle).

Rowan (1998) gives a good introduction to the typical qualities of humanistic counselling and psychotherapy. According to the Association for Humanistic Psychology website (see Resources), the core values that humanistic practitioners share are:

- a belief in the worth of persons and dedication to the development of human potential
- an understanding of life as a process, and that change is inevitable
- an appreciation of the spiritual and intuitive
- a commitment to ecological integrity
- a recognition of the profound problems affecting our world and a responsibility to hope, and constructive change.

Humanistic Psychology a branch of psychology that had its roots in objections to psychoanalysis and behaviourism, hence it is sometimes called 'third force' psychology.

The shapers of Humanistic Psychology were people like Kurt Lewin, Abraham Maslow, often called the Father of Humanistic Psychology, and Carl Rogers (another Father!).

In its early days, some academics protested against the tendency to link psychology with science. For example, William James was interested in studying the subjective experience of people without mechanistic reductionism. They called for an expansive, understanding psychology that emphasized the uniqueness of individuals. Aspects of the German psychology, GESTALT, emphasizing the need for holism in visual perception, were incorporated. The highest value of Humanistic Psychology was, and still is, a respect for the uniqueness of the person.

Many of the modern founders of this movement were academics and psychoanalysts exiled to the USA from war-torn Europe in the 1930s and 1940s. Humanistic Psychology was in one sense a reaction and a response to oppressive pedagogical, professional and political regimes.

The history of the Humanistic Psychology movement is well documented by John Rowan in his book *Ordinary Ecstasy* (originally 1976, revised edition due to be published by Brunner-Routledge in 2001). The Association for Humanistic Psychology (AHP) was founded in 1962. According to the AHP (see Resources), approaches embraced by humanistic therapists include BIOENERGETICS, FOCUSING, ENCOUNTER, RATIONAL-EMOTIVE THERAPY, ARCHETYPAL PSYCHOLOGY, PSYCHO-SYNTHESIS, GESTALT, EXISTENTIAL analysis, and NEURO-LINGUISTIC PROGRAMMING among others.

hyperventilation a rapid breathing that can lead to light-headedness and dizziness, but which also is used intentionally in some forms of MEDITATION and therapy, for example, in RE-BIRTHING.

According to Heron (1998b), hyper-ventilation 'becomes defensive if it is excessively fast or too slow. There is a frequency which opens up the emotionality of the whole psycho-physical system, if it is sustained long enough. It can be used to lead the client into discharge from scratch, by working on basic CHARACTER ARMOUR. Or it can be used to follow a mobile body cue, especially a sudden deepening of the breath. To prevent tetany and excessive dizziness, have the client do it in many cycles, with pauses in-between. When carried on for a sufficient period of time, this is a very direct and powerful route to PRIMAL and perinatal experiences, which may also be interwoven with TRANSPERSONAL encounters.'

hypnotherapy hypnotherapy refers to the use of hypnosis as a medium for therapeutic work (see Peiffer 1996; James 2000). Generally it works by creating an ALTERED STATE of consciousness, or relaxation, on which the limiting nature of the conscious mind may be bypassed.

There are different schools of thought and practice, and a wide range of practices from those with a more clinical emphasis on remedies for psychological or emotional problems to those with a more developmental approach.

One style of hypnotherapy is that developed by Milton Erickson, who influenced much NLP (see Zeig and Munion 1999).

I Ching the *I Ching* or *Book of Changes* is an ancient Chinese text (see also TAOISM). Some attribute parts of the text to Confucius; however, this is in dispute. Carl Jung was an enthusiastic user of the *I Ching*, and wrote a foreword to the classic European edition by Richard Wilhelm.

Richard Wilhelm's (translated) introduction to his edition of the *I Ching* states: 'The Book of Changes . . . is unquestionably one of the most important books in the world's literature. Its origin goes back to mythical antiquity, and it has occupied the attention of the most eminent scholars of China down to the present day. Nearly all that is greatest and most significant in the three thousand years of Chinese cultural history has either taken its inspiration from this book, or has exerted an influence on the interpretation of its text . . . Small wonder then that both of the two branches of Chinese philosophy, Confucianism and Taoism, have their common roots here' (Wilhelm 1968).

The *I Ching* is a cosmology, representing the varying patterns of existence in the form of 64 hexagrams. The book is used in contemplation and divination. Traditionally, either yarrow stalks or coins are cast to form the six lines of each hexagram. Each line is either solid (yang) or broken (yin), and any line can be 'moving' (about to change from yang to yin, or vice versa) or 'still'. The moving lines indicate a subsequent hexagram indicating the way the present situation is likely to unfold.

A very accessible, practical and contemporary guide to the *I Ching* is Wing's *I Ching Workbook* (1979).

ice-breaker an exercise in a workshop or training course designed to 'break the ice', in other words to help participants overcome the ANXIETY and social difficulty at the beginning of the event. For example, participants may be asked to spend a few minutes in pairs telling each other something about themselves. Depending on the nature of the event, the 'ice' may be seen as something to avoid or to break through as swiftly as possible, or perhaps as a vehicle for drawing attention to the HERE AND NOW.

id according to PSYCHOANALYTIC theory (see Marcuse 1987), the id is the oldest and largest layer of the UNCONSCIOUS, the domain of the primary instincts. The id has no connection with the conscious, social individual; rather it is free from the forms and principles of conscious living. It is neither affected by time nor troubled by contradictions; it knows no values, no good or evil, no morality. It does not aim at self-preservation: all it strives for is satisfaction of its instinctual needs, in accordance with the pleasure principle (see also LIBIDO).

idealization a concept originating in the work of Melanie Klein (de Board 1978: 30). Refers to making another person, concept or aspect of the world into an ideal; attributing special, unrealistic powers or qualities to another person, with the effect that the other is seen as powerful and the self as powerless.

Idealization is a form of PROJECTION, which parents and leaders often receive. It functions as a defence against intimacy.

identification a Freudian term referring to the process through which one person identifies with and wants to be like another person. That other person is INTROJECTED into the EGO (de Board 1978: 18).

Over-identification denotes a form of CONFLUENCE, whereby the person's identity is merged with that of the object of identification. Any slight to the object is taken personally; and similarly the success of the object is felt personally too.

Projective identification occurs when one person expresses thoughts, or has feelings, that belong to or originate from another. In groups, this can lead to one member becoming the vehicle through which difficult emotions are expressed (see also PROJECTION).

identity a person's sense or understanding of who they are.

Many authors on personal development approach the issue of identity from a psychological perspective, emphasizing the person's own sense of self. There are important other perspectives (such as the ideas of George Herbert Mead) that emphasize the way individual identity is socially defined. See, for example, Glover (1989).

We can only define ourselves in relation to others. A sense of identity requires the existence of another by whom we are known, and a conjunction of this other person's recognition with our own self-recognition. If there were no 'I' and no 'other' the world would be unified and identity-less.

An identity crisis refers to a person's sense of not knowing who they are, or a deep questioning of their identity.

See also LIFE CYCLE; NEUROLOGICAL LEVELS; SEXUALITY.

ideology the set of beliefs, values and assumptions which underlie a society's organization. Ideological beliefs are reflected in, for example, religions, political parties, and social and economic institutions.

Any view of personal development is culture-bound and will embody ideological elements. Thus it may be seen as no coincidence that personal growth, positive thinking, and achievement motivation are characteristic of the USA, where notions of the 'land of the free', individual rights and independence are part of the cultural apparatus. These ideological beliefs may be seen as characterizing NLP, for example. Any personal development theory or modality will, in some way, reflect ideological views about the social order, and what society could or should be like.

imagery people have the ability to create and process images. Visual imagery plays an important role in remembering, dreaming, fantasizing and planning. It is also one of the inner sources through which art and music are produced. Without our ability to think in images, there would be no architecture, photography, poetry, literature, or even simple day-to-day planning ahead. It is as if we need to produce images internally, and to manipulate them in order to think about even the most mundane tasks. Our nervous system enables us to rehearse and test out practical ideas through using images. Whether consciously or unconsciously produced, imagery is as important to human functioning as breathing and eating. It is used in various ways in personal development (see GUIDED FANTASY; IMAGINAL; VISUALIZATION).

imaginal the imaginal world is 'the world we enter when we make up stories or see visions, or hear internal music, and so on' (Rowan 1993: 53). The imaginal is a rich inner world of IMAGERY, SYMBOLS and MYTHS, of which many modes of personal development (for example, ARCHETYPAL PSYCHOLOGY; PSYCHOSYNTHESIS) encourage exploration.

Jung (1964) believed that the imagery produced by DREAMS and fantasies could be of great significance in gaining new insights and understanding. Such imagery originated from the deepest parts of the human PSYCHE. It may carry symbolic information about an individual's present condition. Sometimes the images may have ARCHETYPAL qualities, resembling themes of old and powerful myths, such as the Mandala image.

imagination a faculty that enables a person to conceive of what does not exist (see IMAGERY), and/or to enter the realm of the IMAGINAL, utilized in many modes of personal development (see e.g. Dilts 1998b). Mulligan (Mulligan and Griffin 1992: 184–85) says, 'Imagining is the key to the future and to what has not yet been realized. It is the precursor to creativity and action. It can reproduce or recreate past and present and envisage how things might be. It helps us transcend current experience of reality and combine the possible with the impossible.' See also VISUALIZATION.

impostor phenomenon the impostor phenomenon is a psychological syndrome or pattern introduced by Clance and Imes (1978) to denote a feeling of intellectual phoniness. They found this to be prevalent amongst a sample of high-achieving women. Despite outstanding academic or professional achievements, they felt they had somehow managed to fool the world, experienced a fear that they were not as competent as they appear to be and attributed their success to factors such as luck, interpersonal skills and hard work, rather than ability. Whilst the impostor phenomenon was considered to be associated primarily with women, later research indicated that men experience the phenomenon as much as women (Clance and O'Toole 1988; see also Clance 1985).

inclusion William Schutz (see ENCOUNTER GROUP) identified inclusion, control and affection as core human needs, and also as stages of a repeating cycle of group interaction. Schutz also developed the FIRO B, a PSYCHOMETRIC test that assesses the person on these three dimensions.

individuation one of Jung's most complex ideas. The process of individuation is the emergence of the development of the SELF as a mature individual, divested of the false wrappings of the PERSONA and the powers of the EGO, and a harmonious integration between conscious and unconscious. Individuation is not individualism. As well as the development of a unique individuality, it presupposes a wholehearted engagement with society (see Jung 1974; Edinger 1992).

Jung considered individuation to be an urge in every individual to achieve his or her full potential. Individuation is the task of the second half of life. Jung's views echo those of Teilhard de Chardin (1959) and Martin Buber (1958), who stressed the importance of others as essential to an individual's spiritual development.

The process of individuation is broadly as follows (e.g. Pettifor 1995). The PSYCHE begins as an unconscious unity. From this emerges EGO consciousness, the focal point of identity. But the ego finds that elements of the total psyche make it feel uncomfortable, so consciousness of them is repressed; they are disowned, sink into the personal SHADOW, and are PROJECTED on to others. The ego thus becomes alienated and the person suffers from a sense of meaningless and emptiness.

Around mid-life, internal dissatisfactions precipitate a growth towards SELF-AWARENESS that begins with the withdrawal of projections and the integration of complexes from the shadow. After integrating the shadow comes the meeting with the contrasexual image and, with it, the SOUL, the true inner being (see ANIMA and ANIMUS). By maintaining a conscious relationship with this inner figure, we learn to relate to our unconscious, allowing its manifestations to speak to us but not dominate or overwhelm us.

This view proposes that personal crises, illnesses and psychological disturbances are not of themselves pathological, but important indicators of obstacles in the journey of individuation and potentially fruitful confrontations with the individual's unconscious rather than symptoms to be suppressed.

informal and incidental learning Marsick and Watkins have advocated the significance of informal learning (EXPERIENTIAL, and non-institutional) and incidental learning (an unintentional by-product of other activity) in contrast to formally delivered learning (training and education). They have looked both at the type of work environment that supports informal and incidental learning, and at qualities of individuals that enhance their capacity to learn in the workplace.

Incidental learning is defined as 'a by-product of some other activity, such as task accomplishment, interpersonal interaction, sensing the organizational culture, or trial-and-error experimentation' (Marsick and Watkins 1989: 6–7). Examples cited by Marsick and Watkins include learning from 'mistakes, assumptions beliefs, attributions, internalized meaning constructions about the actions of others, [and the] HIDDEN CURRICULUM in formal learning' (1989: 7).

inhibitions an inhibition is something that blocks or interrupts a spontaneous response. An inhibited person may be one who is over-cautious for fear of transgressing social norms or upsetting other people.

Inhibition is also a technical term in the ALEXANDER TECHNIQUE, where it refers to the practice of interrupting the body's learned bad habits.

inner child in Jungian work, refers to the eternal CHILD within each person, which always needs affection, attention and guidance. The inner child helps us achieve our fullest expression as adults by connecting with a central core of our being. It is representative of our preconscious experiences as a vulnerable, instinctual, intuitive being in the world.

Some writers use the image of the inner child more literally than others when exploring this phenomenon. Jung, the originator of the phrase, uses it to describe an ARCHETYPAL facet of personality that is in-built at birth: 'a preconscious childhood aspect of the collective psyche' (Jung 1995: 33), emphasizing the aspects that have been forgotten in our childhood. The 'inner child' is different from the Transactional Analysis concept of the Child EGO STATE.

An alternative approach is to extend the description to incorporate what has been learnt through the experience of a child-like SUB-PERSONALITY that represents the 'soft, vulnerable and feelings-orientated "gut" instinct' (Paul 1992: 13). Authors such as Miller (1990) and Parks (1994), use the concept of the inner child to refer to the part of a person affected by childhood trauma (such as sexual abuse) that severed their emotional link with the adult world and then resulted in guilt, fear and feelings of inadequacy.

Regardless of which perspective of the inner child is adopted, it represents an unconscious, denied or repressed part of the person that, when synthesized or integrated with other aspects of personality, results in more complete or less distorted recognition of the needs of the whole person. A pack of 'inner child' cards (Lerner et al. 1992) is available for use in personal development.

inner game an approach to personal development and management COACHING developed by Timothy Gallwey (1986, 1999). The 'inner game' focuses on the mind of the performer, and is intended to remove or minimize self-imposed barriers to success – such as limiting BELIEFS or unhelpful INTERNAL DIALOGUE. The aim is to attain a Zen-like, focused but peaceful attention that enables effortless performance.

inner world people have an astonishingly complex inner world, which they use to make sense of experience. For Jung, and for some philosophers, the inner world of the human psyche is the only reality we can actually know.

Recently, cognitive psychology has become interested in aspects of our inner world, and recognizes that without an internal REPRESENTATION of our experiences of reality, we would not be able to function. Our nervous systems re-create our worlds in terms of sights, sounds, feelings, tastes and smells so that we can reflect, dream, fantasize, plan ahead or remember. Everyone's inner world is unique to them. Language plays a vital role in people's inner worlds, especially in INTERNAL DIALOGUE.

Some believe that we are programmed to assign events to categories. In many so-called mental illnesses, people cannot make sense of their experience because their ability to assign events to useful categories is impaired. Our inner worlds also give us information about what we value, what is to be avoided, who we are, and the meaning we make out of our life experiences. BELIEFS and values are powerful guiding principles of this internal life.

insecurity in personal development, insecurity has many facets both within the person and in their relationships with others or objects. Insecurity can have emotional, cognitive, physiological and EXISTENTIAL overtones. It implies undesirable uncertainty, to the point of agitation, about the reliability, constancy, predictability, solidity and permanence of people (including self) and objects deemed essential to a person's sense of identity and belonging.

From Erikson's developmental theory (see LIFE CYCLE) psychological security through all stages of development will be jeopardized if human relationships in the first stage (trust versus mistrust) are problematic. The final developmental stage is considered successful if the person can let go of security. Here, ego integration is not dependent on attachment to restricted concepts of self or others.

A sense of vulnerability or insecurity in the human condition, and the attendant ANXIETY, may trigger psychological DEFENCES including addictive behaviour. When living life fully is seen as too much of an effort and a risk, the person gradually disengages, burying him- or herself in alcohol, overwork, isolation, CO-DEPENDENCE and even despair. The emphasis in personal development can be to search for meaning, or more significantly to come to a place of peace about one's imperfect, finite existence, knowing that 'full and lasting security is fundamentally an illusion' (Assagioli 1994: 31).

instinct in neurophysiological terms an instinct is an unconscious reflex, which reacts to external stimuli without prior cognitive apprehension. So instinctive behaviour seems to be a primal reaction to danger. The adrenergic system of FIGHT–FLIGHT is an example of this. Freud's model of the personality includes the ID, a deeply unconscious source of instinctive drives.

integration usually refers to integration of different parts of the SELF, towards being more whole (see INDIVIDUATION).

In PSYCHOSYNTHESIS the 'synthesis' is an integration or a synergy of the various psychological functions. The human WILL is considered to be the unifying energy that works towards unity in diversity at the personal level. This seems to be a necessary prerequisite to unification of the personal centre of consciousness, the 'I' or ego, with the TRANSPERSONAL self, for spiritual or transpersonal psychosynthesis (Assagioli 1994).

Integration also refers to the personal need to consolidate learning or insight from, or the impact of, personal development work, incorporating this into our lives.

integrative counselling integrative counselling and psychotherapy is a form of therapy which draws on more than one psychotherapeutic approach, with an emphasis on the elements common to all therapies and particularly on the therapeutic relationship as the medium for change (see Palmer and Woolfe 2000). The word 'integrative' refers both to the therapeutic aim of facilitating integration of all aspects of the person, and to the method used by the therapist.

The European Association for Integrative Psychotherapy (EAIP – see Resources) defines as integrative, 'any methodology and integrative orientation in psychotherapy which exemplifies, or is developing towards, a conceptually coherent, principled, theoretical combination of two or more specific approaches, and/or represents a model of integration in its own right . . . A central tenet of Integrative Psychotherapy is that no single form of therapy is best or even adequate in all situations' (EAIP Statement of Philosophy, 1993).

Goldfried and Newman suggest that one of the earliest attempts at integration was in an address by T.M. French in 1932, 'in which he drew certain parallels between Psychoanalysis and Pavlovian conditioning' (Goldfried and Newman 1992: 47). They go on to describe how the following decades saw a number of

other works focusing on the commonalities between different approaches, culminating in over 200 publications in the 1980s, and the formation in 1983 of the Society for the Exploration of Psychotherapy Integration (SEPI). Since then integrative therapy has continued to grow, and today it is an accredited orientation to counselling and psychotherapy in the UK.

integrity to have integrity means to live and work according to one's values and beliefs. It also refers to trustworthiness, and/or consistency (e.g. a person practising what they preach or 'walking their talk').

intelligence intelligence is typically associated with IQ, a measure originating in the 19th century to assess competence in cognitive, intellectual skills such as verbal reasoning and mental arithmetic. But this is a quite narrow notion of intelligence. For example, it values propositional KNOWLEDGE above other forms, in addition to other flaws (Gardner et al. 1996).

American psychologist Howard Gardner (1993) critiqued this notion and, in tune with many views that predate IQ, proposed a wider concept. This is encapsulated in his model of seven intelligences (e.g. Gardner et al. 1996: 205–11). These are:

1. **linguistic:** 'exemplified by poets, who are keenly attuned to the sound and rich meanings of the language they use'
2. **musical:** reflecting the patterned elements of music as well as the power of musical expression
3. **logical-mathematical:** 'involves using and appreciating abstract relations'
4. **spatial:** 'the ability to perceive visual or spatial information, to transform and modify this information, and to recreate visual images'
5. **bodily-kinesthetic:** 'along with dancers and rock climbers, bodily-kinesthetic intelligence is exemplified by gymnasts and other athletes and jugglers'

6. **intrapersonal**: 'processes that enable people to distinguish among their own feelings . . . At its highest level, discriminations among one's feelings, intentions and motivations yield a deep self-knowledge of the sort elders draw on when making a crucial decision or when advising others in their community'

7. **interpersonal**: 'core capacities to recognize and make distinctions among *others*' feelings, beliefs and intentions . . . This intelligence is broadly called on by therapists, parents and dedicated teachers'.

Personal development is particularly concerned with intrapersonal and interpersonal intelligences, as reflected in Goleman's concept of EMOTIONAL INTELLIGENCE. Another recent, related concept is that of SPIRITUAL INTELLIGENCE.

intention this is both a philosophical statement and a psychological construct. The philosophical meaning of intention is linked to INTENTIONALITY.

Intention is a quality of CONSCIOUSNESS. Consciousness is always consciousness about something; it is relational. If you are conscious that you are worried, you are worried about something. You may not know what that something is, however; your attention will focus on identifying it. So whatever sense you make of the world is intentionally derived.

The psychological construct of intention is about purpose (conscious or unconscious) to effect an OUTCOME or a change in environment, through communication or other form of intervention. Intention is related to an 'outcomes model' described in different communication theories such as NLP, TRANSACTIONAL ANALYSIS, and SIX CATEGORY INTERVENTION ANALYSIS. In the latter, for example, emphasis is given to the intended outcome as a means to assess the effectiveness of an intervention.

intentionality a philosophical term from PHENOMENOLOGY to indicate the basis of all mental experiences. According to Husserl (Spinelli 1989) all our meaning-based constructs of the world lie in our fundamental relationship with that world. Intentionality means to 'stretch forth'; the mind reaches out towards stimuli which make up the real world in order to translate them into its realm of meaningful experience.

interdependent mutually dependent, as distinct from either DEPENDENT or independent. In SYSTEMS THINKING, all elements of a system influence each other in patterns of interdependence. Thompson (1967) has noted three forms of interdependence found in systems; pooled, sequential and reciprocal.

internal dialogue an essential part of a person's inner world. Most people have the experience of 'talking to themselves in their heads'. Inner dialogue is thought to help us to plan, to think, to remember, and is also the creator of fantasy and poetry. It can help us solve problems, and run through future plans and solutions internally before trying them on the external world.

Sometimes internal dialogue can be a source of distress. People may find they have angry or critical 'voices' over which they have little control. These can even affect the individual's physiology, such as raising blood pressure and heart rate. They can be a sign of depression and in extreme cases, where it seems impossible to switch the dialogue off, it can be one of the symptoms of post-traumatic stress disorder.

Some internal voices may belong to 'critical parents' or significant others, and cause distress if they are judgemental and negative.

Many MEDITATION techniques aim at stilling the internal dialogue. Some find it useful to be able to recognize when their internal dialogue is serving them well, and when it is in danger of becoming destructive. Modes of therapy such as NLP may focus on the qualities (see SUB-MODALITIES) of a person's internal dialogue, help them to change unhelpful tonalities and words, and find more generative ones.

internal state see STATE.

internalize to take within the self; or to attribute something (e.g. a quality, success, failure) to oneself.

interpersonal literally, between people, as distinct from INTRAPERSONAL. Gardner's framework of multiple INTELLIGENCE includes an 'interpersonal intelligence' based on the capacity to discern other people's feelings.

interpersonal skills a generic term for various skills of communicating with, and relating to, other people. Interpersonal skills might include, for example: LISTENING skills; leadership skills; ASSERTIVENESS; interviewing skills; COUNSELLING skills; negotiation skills; conflict resolution; presentation skills; FACILITATION skills; and so on. SIX CATEGORY INTERVENTION ANALYSIS is a helpful model of interpersonal skills.

intervention a verbal or behavioural act, usually intended to facilitate a client or interaction towards a desired outcome. See SIX CATEGORY INTERVENTION ANALYSIS.

intimacy generally denotes a quality of closeness, trust and deep involvement between people.

Erik Erikson's LIFE CYCLE model includes 'intimacy vs. isolation' as the sixth stage, experienced in young adulthood. According to Erikson, the major developmental task here is forging strong new interpersonal relationships, thereby exploring one's capacity for intimacy. A person who emerges from the preceding stage (ego identity vs. role confusion) with a strong identity will move into intimacy with others with little or no fear of engulfment or loss of identity. Intimacy in this sense implies an ability to have a mature sexual relationship, ability and willingness to forge identity with another, and to develop concrete affiliations and partnerships even though they may call for significant challenge and sacrifice.

In TRANSACTIONAL ANALYSIS, within the theory of PASTIMING, intimate communication is authentic behaviour which responds appropriately to the immediate situation. There are 'no secret messages, that is, the social level and the psychological level of communication are congruent' (Stewart and Joines 1987: 93). Intimate communication is powerful enough to complete the transaction, leaving people satisfied that the issue has been honestly explored and resolved where possible without manipulation, or other unproductive feelings or behaviour. Such intimate behaviour carries the highest risk of interpersonal misunderstanding and other forms of apparent rejection; however, the numbers of STROKES both positive and negative are very high, so the reward for engaging in intimate communication is high. When people cannot engage in intimate (authentic) communication they will often resort to (psychological) GAMES as the indirect way of obtaining strokes, usually of a negative type.

intrapersonal within the person, i.e. concerning the inner (or intrapsychic) functioning of the person, rather than the interpersonal ('between people') domain.

'Intrapersonal intelligence' is one of Howard Gardner's seven INTELLIGENCES. This concerns a person's sense of being and familiarity with his or her INNER WORLD; their sense of identity, and capacity for understanding their own feelings and values. Intrapersonal intelligence may be associated with INTROVERSION, in Jung's sense.

See also EMOTIONAL INTELLIGENCE.

introject literally, to throw inwards. A psychodynamic concept indicating an external idea or message, especially a SHOULD, that has been 'swallowed' by a person, which they then assume belongs to them and is part of their identity (e.g. Clarkson 1989: 52). A typical introject is a parent's opinion that may have been repeatedly expressed, and which the child grows up believing (e.g. 'You are so clumsy'; 'Boys don't cry').

introvert one who, having an inherently high level of arousal, habitually withdraws attention from the outer world in order to reduce excessive stimulation. In 20th century psychology, the German equivalent of the term was first used by Jung (see Jung 1971) to mean an introverted person, and from his usage the word has come to be employed popularly for a reserved, retiring or reflective person. For details on the extroversion–introversion polarity, see EXTROVERT.

For the introvert, external stimuli create an overload of internal response. The optimum level of stimulation is easily exceeded and an introvert's inner response to the outer world may be so extreme as to make him or her emotionally vulnerable. Introverts have to beware of inappropriate or imprudent behaviour, for example, of abandoning themselves to what the outer world is prompting, which is often disproportionate to its real significance for them.

The introvert attempts to reduce the level of ambient stimulation by fleeing from the troublesome outer world towards the safety and relative tranquillity of his or her own inner world. Because of this direction of interest, introverts are conscious of what is going on inside of themselves, of thoughts, feelings, fantasies and so on. This subjective world is the primary one and introverts tend to judge and define the external world according to their own viewpoint.

Introverts can get worn out by prolonged social interaction and need quiet time alone to recover their energy and equilibrium. Solitude offers them a haven where they can be with their thoughts and they generally prefer privacy and quiet. They reflect before acting and generally appear hesitant, thoughtful, retiring, private,

reserved, complicated, even reclusive. However, they can be excellent listeners (unlike extroverts), and sometimes evince intense passion with very deep (but usually unexpressed) feelings.

intuition a cognitive but arational faculty that works outside conscious awareness. There are differing views on the nature of intuition. Some see it as a quasi-mystical ability, whilst others believe it to be much closer to rational thought. John Rowan (1993: 14–19) summarizes six different types or usages of intuition, spanning prepersonal, personal and transpersonal levels of development.

Traditionally intuition meant the ability to discern or perceive the true nature of objects, people or events, without an awareness of the conceptual processes involved. Jung, in his development of his theory of types, distinguished intuition as a way of knowing that was distinct and opposite to sensing. In the Jungian tradition, intuition has come to be understood as the ability to access unconscious information about situations very rapidly. It is also the ability to see possibilities, significance and inner meanings.

People who show a marked preference for this mode of perception are known as intuitors, people who are believed to be initiators, inventors or great artistic and cultural innovators. MYERS AND BRIGGS claim that such people are more imaginative and creative.

Some warn against the overvaluing of intuition, urging that it should be balanced with greater attention to detail and the external world. The inspirations that come through intuition are not always benevolent. Intuitors are also said to be characterized by having a small capacity for living in the present, are often restless, and dislike tasks that involve sensing. They may be fickle and lacking in persistence, and need to balance their insights with sound judgement.

issues park in experiential groups, issues often arise that are important but to which participants do not wish to attend immediately. An 'issues park' is, for example, a sheet of flip chart paper on the wall on which anyone can write such an issue. This record stays in the group's awareness and the issue can be dealt with later if desired.

I–Thou Martin Buber (1958) identified the polarities of 'I–Thou' and 'I–It' as the two forms of meeting that human beings can experience in relation to each other and the world in general. An 'I–Thou' meeting is characterized by a genuine interest in the other person. It values the 'otherness' of the person whose humanity is perceived as being an end rather than the person merely being a means to an end. In an 'I–It' meeting, the other person is seen as an object and is utilized primarily as a means to an end. In reality, we experience a rhythmic alteration between the two. 'I–Thou' moments have the potential for healing. The focus of the 'I–It' moment is the need to get things done. 'I–It' is only problematic when it dominates existence. Buber described the three essential elements of an 'I–Thou' meeting as PRESENCE; INCLUSION and confirmation; and genuine and unreserved communication. We can only be open to the possibility of an 'I–Thou' moment as it requires mutuality between two people; when it comes and when it goes cannot be controlled by one person.

J

Johari Window the Johari Window (e.g. Hanson 1973) is a widely known model for soliciting and giving FEEDBACK in personal growth and experiential training groups. The model illustrates how people can hold information about self and about others and what happens when that information is kept secret or shared. It is used for increasing personal and interpersonal awareness (Gregory 1994).

The model was developed by two psychologists, Luft and Ingram (1967) which they called the Johari Window (a conflation of their first names, Joe and Harry). The 'window' is a two-by-two matrix with dimensions of self-disclosure, and seeking feedback. This creates four sections or panes, with the internal sectional dividers being flexible, so that the window panes can move in all directions depending on the degree of disclosure and amount of feedback.

These four panes are as follows:

- **the Public Arena:** this is shared information, what is observable socially and what is shared about personal biography. People will disclose more the more they trust that information will be received and treated respectfully.
- **the Blind Spot:** contains information about the individual of which they are not aware, that is, they are blind. In groupwork, the group acts as a mirror, reflecting back to us behaviour we have become unconscious of over the years.
- **the Facade or Hidden Arena:** represents the private subjective world of the individual. The reasons for keeping personal knowledge private may be more to do with preference than with a need to withhold information through lack of trust. To hold private knowledge about self in a group may be a way of keeping a sense of individuality, or separateness, not getting too swamped in 'group identity'. However, a person's silence might also be because the individual has unresolved issues about trust or that the trust in the group is not perceived to be strong enough.
- **the Unknown Arena:** refers to information about the person not yet known to the person and unknown to others. This is the preconscious area, which is out of conscious awareness, but which can be accessed through the process of DISCLOSURE and feedback. (Hanson 1973: 116; descriptions taken from Gregory 1994).

joy an uplifting emotional state of gladness, abundance and delight. Many authors and researchers have written at length on joy and how to increase one's experience of joy. These include C.S. Lewis (1977); Joy (1979); and Maslow (1964).

The experience of unalloyed spontaneous joy is frequently linked with God (Lewis 1977) and surrender to the awe, or mystery or unconditional love of God in the moment. For example: '. . . this joy must not be the goal toward which you strive. It will be vouchsafed you if you strive to "give joy to God." Your personal joy will rise up when you want nothing but the joy of God – nothing but joy in itself' (Buber, in Vardey 1995: 532).

Others concentrate more on prac-tices and techniques which when adopted increase the likelihood of experiencing joy. High on the list are ways of forgetting oneself, and over-coming self-consciousness: 'One can and one does learn from such (mystic or peak) experiences that, e.g. joy, ecstasy and rapture do in fact exist and that they are in principle available for the experiencer, even if they never have been before' (Maslow, in Vardey 1995: 526).

The HUMAN POTENTIAL movement focuses less on the experience of joy in relation to God, but rather recognizes joy as the outcome of realizing one's potential and feeling fully accepted by, and open to, other people and nature.

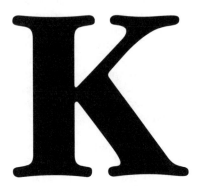

Kabbalah, the see TREE OF LIFE.

karma the term *karma* comes from the Sanskrit and literally means 'doing' or 'making' action. When used in the philosophical sense, the term can best be translated into English by the word 'consequence'.

Karma is an ancient doctrine which asserts a universal moral law similar to the physical law of causality. Any act impacts on its environment causing a reaction that is inevitably felt by the source point, much as a pebble thrown into a pond will cause ripples which eventually meet the bank and send ripples back to the source point. The Law of Karma affirms that the actions our Soul has sown in past lives determine the experiences we draw to us in this lifetime. Our response to and learning from the situations that confront us determine our future reincarnations.

According to many Eastern traditions (for example, the Upanishads), our ultimate goal is to be free from karma and the cycles of birth and rebirth (*samsara*) and to reach a state of release (*moksha*) or enlightenment. In this context suffering and disease can be seen as a purification for past lives that challenge the sufferer to overcome all attachment to *maya* (the illusion of our present reality where karma is played out).

Many world religions teach the need for mindfulness in the process of releasing ourselves from our individual and collective karmic debts.

kinesiology kinesiology is literally the study of human movement. In the sphere of personal development (rather than health/medicine), the main interest is in more specialized forms that work on the BODYMIND principle. Examples include 'Touch for Health' and 'Educational Kinesiology' (see BRAIN GYM). There are several more.

These forms generally use muscle testing (see, for example, La Tourelle and Courtenay 1997) or similar signals from the body to indicate the needs of the mind-body system, which may be outside or contrary to the awareness of the conscious mind. In muscle testing, the client holds out an arm; the practitioner asks a question (to which the client does not respond verbally); and the practitioner presses down on the arm to test the 'bodymind' response. Typically, the muscles holding up the arm go weak if the answer is negative, and remain strong or resistant if the answer is positive.

knowledge the issue of the nature of knowledge is a vast field. Common-sense usage has it that knowledge is the content we learn at school, or in formal education, but this is a narrow perspective. For the context of personal development, a useful framework is John Heron's (1989) model of MANIFOLD LEARNING. This suggests that experience is the most primary form of knowing; that our experience is typically translated next into presentational knowing (using images, metaphors, etc.); that conceptual or propositional knowing is a further stage; and that altogether these create the possibility of practical knowing, that is, of using knowledge in action. Heron's model therefore emphasizes the validity and importance of experiential, imaginal and practical knowing in addition to that most usually valued, propositional knowledge (see also TACIT KNOWLEDGE).

The study of knowledge or, more accurately, of the processes by which humans know, is called epistemology. This involves views about the nature of reality and its relationship with consciousness. Again, a common-sense view holds these to be separate. An alternative is the participatory worldview espoused by writers such as Reason and Heron: 'Participation is a way of knowing in which knower and known are distinct but not separate, in an unfolding unitive field of being . . . Orthodox scientific approaches to research honour participation neither as a way of knowing nor as a political system. They use a divisive epistemology that separates the knower from the known, and an authoritarian political system in which researchers make all decisions about content, methodology, and findings so that their subjects are treated as passive objects of observation. Since scientific research is such a powerful force in our lives it is shocking that its techniques largely ignore the epistemological and political significance of participation' (Reason and Heron 1995).

kundalini *kundalini* is a Sanskrit word meaning coiled, winding, or spiral. The Hindu goddess of the same name is strongly connected to the ancient energy system of the CHAKRAS. This energy of higher consciousness is often visualized as a coiled serpent. The symbol of the unfolding serpent has long been associated with healing and is still present in the Caduceus, our modern symbol of healing. 'Mankind does indeed contain all the higher levels of consciousness as a true potential known in general terms as kundalini energy which is said to lie dormant, asleep in the unconscious of all men and women' (Wilber 1983: 33).

In most individuals, kundalini lies dormant at the base of the spine, at the root or *muladhara* chakra centre. Once this energy is activated, usually through meditational exercises, it begins to unwind. It is thought to travel in a figure-of-eight-like path, rising up through meridians of energies to which the chakras are connected. This activates each of the centres and creates a series of transformative awakenings. The arrival of kundalini at the crown centre, the *sahasrara*, is said to bring profound change of consciousness leading to ENLIGHTENMENT. There are many warnings about allowing the kundalini to rise too quickly, and the difficulties that may occur (Grof and Grof 1989).

large group awareness training the use of large groups (scores or perhaps hundreds of people at a time), often in several days of intense workshops, as a vehicle for personal development, as used in EST and related modalities. Concerns are about the extent to which the dynamics of such large groups are understood, or perhaps even exploited, by practitioners. There appears to be little research into the effects or effectiveness of this type of format. On the basis of anecdotal evidence, participants may experience anything from a life-changing transformation to near-breakdown.

lateral thinking a term coined by Edward de Bono (1990) to refer to non-linear, non-logical thinking, the purpose of which is to make creative associations. According to de Bono's website, it indicates:

- seeking to solve problems by apparently illogical means
- a process and willingness to look at things in a different way
- a relatively new type of thinking that complements analytical and critical thinking not part of our mainstream education – yet
- a fast, effective tool used to help individuals, companies and teams solve tough problems and create new ideas, new products, new processes and new services
- a term that is used interchangeably with CREATIVITY.

leadership the words 'leadership' and 'management' are often used as if synonymous, but they are not. While some aspects of management benefit from positive leadership behaviours, by no means all of them do. Not all organizational leaders occupy managerial positions. Neither is positive leadership behaviour limited to formal organizations. Leadership is, therefore, a diffuse quality where what the leader *does* is continually informed by what he or she knows, feels, values and understands. The notion of leadership style is relevant to those facilitating personal development groups, as well as to the development of organizational leaders themselves.

Many writers have attempted to classify variations in leadership behaviour in terms of style or situational demands. Tannenbaum and Schmidt (1958) proposed a continuum of decision styles or leadership behaviours running from total leadership autocracy at one end to total group autonomy at the other. A number of other writers have developed models that are similarly based on the choice of more or less appropriate leadership styles (Blake and Mouton 1964, Hersey and Blanchard 1969, and Reddin 1970, for example).

Leadership action based on rational managerial decision-making that would be quite appropriate in a stable bureaucracy is much less so in circumstances in which boundaries, rules and traditions are simultaneously being called into question. In such circumstances it is argued that organizations require leadership of the kind that Weber (1947) labelled CHARISMATIC. James McGregor Burns (1978) describes such leadership as *transformational*, involving confidence in the leader's ability to show the way forward by focusing on goals which he or she perceives with a clarity not yet shared by others in the organization. Rational, strategic or performance-focused leadership, in contrast, is described as *transactional*. Transformational or charismatic leadership is less a matter of rational choice than a passionate self-expression.

Another recent concept is that of *servant leadership*: 'The servant-leader is servant first. It begins with the natural feeling that one wants to serve. Then conscious choice brings one to aspire to lead. The best test is: do those served grow as persons; do they, while being served, become healthier, wiser, freer, more autonomous, more likely themselves to become servants' (Greenleaf 1970, cited in Spears 1998: 1).

learned helplessness refers to the state certain individuals induce in themselves when feeling trapped in situations that provoke high levels of ANXIETY (Seligman 1975). Learned helplessness arises from the belief that there is no relationship between the person's actions and the consequences, so the individual feels that they cannot influence their external environment in their favour. Motivation to influence change is diminished and the psychological effect is low SELF-ESTEEM. This decreased sense of self-worth can lead to DEPRESSION.

This construct is not unlike Rotter's (1966) external LOCUS OF CONTROL, although the latter is a more enduring personality trait and not reliant on stressful situations. However, people who are 'externals', that is, those who believe that their destiny depends on events outside of themselves, such as luck, fate or change, are likely to be more prone to learned helplessness.

learning there is no agreed definition of learning, and there are very many theories and models (see, for example, Jarvis et al. 1998). The concept is closely related to and sometimes used synonymously with terms such as CHANGE and DEVELOPMENT.

Learning can refer both to a process (the events and actions through which a person learns) and to the product of the process (the 'learning outcome'). It is also worth noting that the English language is unusual, apparently, in having different words for 'teaching' and 'learning'.

Theories of learning can be seen as belonging to four main (overlapping) types (e.g. Jarvis 1995): BEHAVIOURIST, cognitive, EXPERIENTIAL and social. A cognitive perspective is interested in the mental processes through which knowledge is acquired. This emphasizes memory, information processing and the structure of thought. A social learning perspective emphasizes the extent to which people's behaviour and beliefs are socially influenced or orientated rather than purely individual.

A model of learning commonly found in personal development and training is that of a four-stage progression (also portrayed as a cycle) from unconscious incompetence through conscious incompetence and conscious competence to unconscious competence. It appears not to be derived from Kirkpatrick's (1971) four levels of training, as some believe, and indeed has no authenticated source of which we are aware, though it has been suggested that it derives from a Middle Eastern saying:

He who knows, and knows he knows,
He is a wise man, seek him.
He who knows and knows not he knows,

He is asleep, wake him.
He who knows not, and knows he
knows not,
He is a child, teach him.
He who knows not, and knows not
he knows not,
He is a fool, shun him.

However, the provenance of the model is obscure. This is not to say that it is not useful or intuitively valid, but it is remarkable that it is used and cited so often without reference to source or questioning of its authority.

learning contract a means of clarifying and specifying learning outcomes, methods, and criteria for success, used in formal education and in WORKPLACE LEARNING.

The principle is to formulate an agreement between the learner and others, such as peers or tutors, about intended learning. It is similar to an action plan or self-development plan. Negotiating and agreeing the contract with others focuses effort, generates commitment, and enables assessment against explicit, agreed criteria.

According to Knowles (1986), forming and using a learning contract involves the following seven stages:

1. diagnosing needs by reviewing current development and identifying developmental goals
2. stating intentions and specifying outcome(s)
3. planning proposed actions, including the involvement of other people and the resources needed
4. deciding how you will know you have achieved your outcomes, by what criteria you will be assessed, and what forms of evidence you will produce
5. asking peers/tutor to 'rattle and shake' plans so that they are robust, and thus agreeing the contract with them
6. carrying out the plan
7. reviewing and assessing the results.

learning style learning style refers to a preferred way of LEARNING (such as

Gordon Pask's 'holist' and 'serialist' styles; or 'deep' and 'surface' approaches – see Marton et al. 1997), or to a relative preference for some aspects of the learning process over others.

Learning style is often associated with Kolb's EXPERIENTIAL LEARNING CYCLE. Kolb (1984: 77) identified four preferences or styles relating to different stages of the cycle, which he called:

- convergent (abstract conceptualization and active experimentation)
- divergent (reflective observation and concrete experience)
- assimilation (abstract conceptualization and reflective observation)
- accommodation (concrete experience and active experimentation).

Convergent and divergent styles are opposites, as are assimilation and accommodation.

A related model and instrument (the Learning Styles Questionnaire), which is generally accepted as better validated in relation to the way managers learn in practice, was developed by Peter Honey and Alan Mumford (1992) in the UK. Their styles are labelled Activist, Pragmatist, Reflector and Theorist.

Reynolds (1997a) critiques the concept of learning styles for placing undue emphasis on supposed, but empirically unsupported, differences in individual learning style. He also argues that the notion of learning style is culture-bound.

learning to learn 'learning to learn' is purported to be a higher-order process than LEARNING. Bateson and Bateson define this (they use the term 'deutero-learning') as 'learning in which the learning capacity of the system is modified . . . a higher logical type than learning in which the organism is changed without an alteration in learning capacity' (1988: 209).

In management and education (e.g. Mumford 1995), there is often an emphasis on becoming aware of one's own LEARNING STYLE (although aware-ness in itself does not constitute an alteration in learning capacity). Learning to learn is promoted as a core skill for employees in 'learning organiz-ations' and appears on the UK higher education agenda.

However, contemporary usage emphasizes the learning of study skills for work or educational programmes more than the REFLEXIVITY that Bateson and Bateson appear to have intended. Enhancing behavioural skills of study-ing per se does not necessarily consti-tute learning at a higher LOGICAL LEVEL.

left-brain/right-brain the idea that the two hemispheres of the brain have dif-ferent functions. Originating in 'split brain' research (by, for example, Roger Sperry 1964) with people who had their corpus callosum (the connection between the left and right hemi-spheres) cut, the idea was popularized by authors such as Robert Ornstein (1972).

The typical associations are that the left-brain is logical, sequential, rational, analytical and objective; the right-brain is intuitive, holistic, synthesizing and subjective.

The somewhat simplistic and romantic nature of the distinction – particularly underestimating the extent to which the hemispheres are comple-mentary and interdependent – has been seriously challenged by recent researchers. For example, McCrone (1998, 1999) reports on research that seems to confirm that there is a dif-ferentiation of style of processing between the hemispheres.

If treated as a metaphor rather than as a matter of scientific truth, the left-brain/right-brain model is a useful aid to 'thinking about thinking', even if it does not explain the workings of the brain. It is useful in the same way as other metaphors such as, for example, Guy Claxton's *d-mode* and *undermind* thinking (1997: 7). Claxton, while drawing on a range of well-researched

psychological studies, does not make any claim for scientific validity of the concept.

levels of learning Gregory Bateson (1973) produced a seminal paper on the notion of logical levels of LEARNING. In it he introduced the notion that learning is not homogeneous. Building on Russell and Whitehead's theory of logical typing, Bateson suggested that we can think of a number of qualita-tively different levels of learning. He called these Levels 0 through to III.

The essence of the difference is that learning 0 involves no change; learning I is what we typically think of as 'learn-ing', such as learning new behaviour; learning II is what we mean by LEARN-ING TO LEARN; learning III is more akin to a PARADIGM shift.

This type of model can help make sense, for example, of experiences such as training managers in new skills with-out necessarily achieving any resulting change in organizational performance.

Bateson's work has been influential on a number of people working with change and learning in organizations, particularly Chris Argyris and his notion of SINGLE- AND DOUBLE-LOOP LEARNING. Another application is through Paul Watzlawick's notion of FIRST AND SECOND ORDER CHANGE.

libido literally, in Latin, lust. Freud intro-duced the term into modern psycho-logical usage. He saw the libido as an instinctive, unconscious, sexual drive that lay behind conscious action. Freud is thought now to have over-empha-sized the importance of sex in human development.

life cycle Erik Erikson, a German who later became an American citizen, developed Freud's work on stages of human development to produce his 'life cycle'. In addition to his psychoan-alytic training and his personal experi-ence of identity change (for example, he was Erik Homberger – his step-father's name – until adopting the name 'Erikson' after moving to America), he studied the development of identity in several contexts, including the Sioux and the Yurok in America.

According to Erikson (1977, 1994), a person's IDENTITY develops to maturity through eight stages, each involving a crisis that has to be encountered and resolved. Problems in later life may come from lack of resolution of these crises, in which case therapy helps the client to revisit and address the relevant stage.

The eight successive crises, starting with the earliest, are:

- basic trust vs. mistrust (infant)
- autonomy vs. shame and doubt (toddler)
- initiative vs. guilt (pre-school)
- industry vs. inferiority (school)
- ego identity vs. role confusion (adolescent)
- intimacy vs. isolation (young adult)
- generativity vs. stagnation (middle adult)
- integrity vs. despair (old adult).

The model bears much resemblance to the seven ages of man depicted in Shakespeare's 'As You Like It'.

It seems important to understand that these terms are ego values, with preference for the positive pole of the construct. Erikson summarizes these crises as alternative basic attitudes which pervade consciousness and unconsciousness. 'They are ways of *experiencing, of behaving and are unconscious inner states* determinable by test and analysis' (adapted from Erikson 1977: 226).

life position an (existential) Life Position is a TRANSACTIONAL ANALYSIS concept referring to a decision about self in relation to self, others and the world. For example, a person may conclude:

- people are wonderful – or – people are no damn good – including self
- people will help me – or – people are out to get me
- people can't be trusted – or – people are basically honest.

These decisions are characterized in TA as: 'I'm OK' or 'I'm not OK', and 'You're OK' or 'You're not OK'. In combination, they form the four basic life positions (see Stewart and Joines 1987):

The First Position: 'I'm OK, You're OK.' A mentally healthy position. If realistic, people with this position about themselves and others can solve their problems constructively. Their expectations are likely to be valid.

The Second Position: 'I'm OK, You're Not OK.' The position of persons who feel victimized or persecuted. They blame others for their miseries. Delinquents and criminals often have this position and take on PARANOID behaviour, which in extreme cases may lead to homicide.

The Third or Introject Position: 'I'm Not OK, You're OK.' A common position of persons who feel powerless when they compare themselves to others. This position leads them to withdraw, to experience depression, and in severe cases, to become suicidal.

The Fourth or Futility Position: 'I'm Not OK, You're Not OK.' The position of the person who loses interest in living, who exhibits SCHIZOID behaviour, and, in extreme cases, will commit suicide and/or homicide.

lifelong learning a term that reflects global societal shifts and developments in education. It emphasizes literally that learning happens throughout life and not just through formal education.

In principle, this supports the idea of personal development. Jarvis et al. say: '. . . lifelong learning stands for various new and emerging emphases: learners rather than teachers, programmes rather than curricula, integration rather than specialization, consumer sovereignty rather than institutional provision, and so on' (1998: 11).

A Lifelong Learning Act was passed in the USA in 1976. The term has since acquired global currency, and has been adopted in UK government policy.

Researchers such as Coffield (1999) argue that education appears thereby to have been re-defined as an instrument of economy, and that the rhetoric of lifelong learning needs critique.

listening 'Listening is more than just hearing. Hearing is the reception of auditory information. Listening is an intellectual and emotional process that decodes physical, emotional and intellectual input in a search for meaning and understanding. Effective listening occurs when the listener correctly understands the sender's meaning' (Mulligan 1988: 94). However, Mulligan argues that only a small proportion of oral communication is listened to effectively.

Listening involves, for example, attending, following and supporting, and reflective and active listening. It is a proactive rather than a passive skill, and a highly significant part of the COMMUNICATION process, but it is often neglected in programmes of training, education and professional development.

Reflective listening is a verbal equivalent of MIRRORING, a skill of paraphrasing what one has heard and feeding this back to the other person. Done well, this helps the speaker to feel that they have been heard and may encourage them to elaborate further.

Active listening is closely related. It requires that the listener demonstrates understanding of what is being said. The listener may use BODY LANGUAGE or paraphrasing, reflecting back, or other ways of checking understanding. It involves interaction between the speaker and listener, rather than a passive approach to listening.

locus of control Rotter's (1966) concept of internal and external locus of control refers to the extent to which a person believes their experience to be controlled by them (internal) or by external influences (see Lefcourt 1982; also LEARNED HELPLESSNESS).

logical levels or typing a theory formulated by Bertrand Russell that distinguishes between levels of abstraction.

'The notion of logical types is used by Bateson as a way of charting the classification inherent in all perceiving, thinking, learning, and communicating. A class is a different logical type, a higher level of abstraction, than the members it classifies: the class of "all books" is not itself a book; the name of a thing is itself not a thing, but a classification of it . . .' (Flemons 1991: 5–6).

The significance is that if we treat all aspects of thought and communication as being at the same logical level, then we encounter paradox and confusion. 'The classic example of the Cretan who announced that "All Cretans lie" demonstrates how a self-referential statement can oscillate between being a statement and a frame of reference about itself as a statement' (Keeney 1983: 29).

The theory of logical types underlies Bateson's LEVELS OF LEARNING, Argyris's concept of SINGLE- AND DOUBLE-LOOP LEARNING, and the principle of LEARNING TO LEARN. See also NEUROLOGICAL LEVELS.

logotherapy see EXISTENTIALISM.

love love is an experience of deep intimacy between people, and/or a sense of connection and unity with the divine; a life-enhancing human experience which humanistic work aims to enhance. Loving feelings are accentuated by SELF-ESTEEM, calmness and trust, and an absence of fear or doubt. Maslow (1968) referred to this as B-motivation and B-love (where B denotes BEING). Erich Fromm suggested that love is 'the answer to the problem of human existence' (1975: 14).

Love has been defined in many ways, and other usage can be broadly subdivided into three categories: physical, dependence and altruism.

Physical love is centred on one's needs for sexual gratification and reproduction. Feelings of intense attraction abound that motivate closer contact, which may result in physical intimacy or sexual contact. However, love of this type is often transitory in nature, evaporating once gratification has been achieved unless other loving forms take its place.

DEPENDENCY love is a form centred, perhaps unconsciously, on one's needs. It is experienced as a sense of being incomplete without the presence of a part that another person provides. This can generate intense feelings of being drawn inexplicably towards another person, driven by parts of oneself that may be hard to recognize and, on occasions, involving unaware acts of PROJECTION and TRANSFERENCE upon the object of love.

Altruistic love is centred unselfishly on another person. It is experienced when we celebrate all that another person is – their skills and their imperfections as a single entity – in one blinding, glorious moment. In this love, we seek to be with another person, to learn about them, to see them clearly without distortion and to companion them in this moment to support their life journey. This form of love differs slightly from *agape*, Christian love (Baldwin 1987), but promotes the same open giving from a theocentric motivation.

M

manifold learning a model developed by John Heron (e.g. 1989: 13) that posits four dimensions of KNOWLEDGE and learning: the experiential, the IMAGINAL, the propositional/conceptual and the practical. In structure, these four dimensions form a pyramid or up-hierarchy with the affective/experiential dimension at the base and the imaginal, the propositional and the practical levels following upward.

The first dimension is the experiential encounter, an immersion in the resonance of being in the world and in the experience, a participative attunement to others (Heron 1999: 225). The imaginal level is to do with intuitive knowing. Propositional or conceptual learning is intellectual and expressed in linguistic statements. Practical learning is to do with the acquisition and performance of skills. Each level emerges from the one below, and is a reduced precipitate of the preceding levels.

manipulation as an interpersonal behaviour, manipulation is considered positive or negative depending on the intentions of the actor. To manipulate means to direct, guide, manage, command and take control of a situation or other people and as such can be positive. Many people feel the benefit of a decisive leader who knows how to manipulate or engineer a positive outcome from a disastrous event. Steering a different course to effect a more desirable outcome can be seen as a pragmatic and creative form of manipulation.

In ASSERTIVENESS training, manipulative behaviour that seeks to control others without their consent is considered inappropriate and unwelcome. It is likely to be injurious or to affect others' rights to respect and AUTONOMY. While the intention may be unconscious and the behaviour often not predetermined or intentionally malicious, the effect on those manipulated against is often felt as abusive and creates anger and resentment.

In TRANSACTIONAL ANALYSIS, as in other psychotherapeutic theories, negative interpersonal manipulation is considered distressed behaviour and many psychological games are played from this position. For example, people with a NARCISSISTIC personality need to feel special and different. This may drive them to manipulate others, break rules believing the rules do not really apply to them, and generally seduce or coerce others to help them maintain their own sense of aggrandizement.

Another form of manipulation is to create DEPENDENCY. People who are psychological Victims, Persecutors and Rescuers (see DRAMA TRIANGLE) are all being manipulative to varying degrees and in different ways (Stewart and Joines 1987).

massage forms of massage exist throughout the world. Applications range from the use of touch for health and relaxation, which anyone can do, to specialized methods of healing (such as Shiatsu and acupressure, both based on Eastern concepts of body ENERGY), and therapeutic and developmental modes of BODYWORK, such as Gerda Boyesen's biodynamic massage. These specialized forms require the practitioner to be properly trained.

'me generation' a derogatory term that denotes an unusual amount of self-absorption, self-gratification and NARCISSISM amongst the boomer generation, those born in the USA between World War II and the mid-sixties (see Wilber 2000a).

The HUMAN POTENTIAL Movement had a part to play in creating a generation of self-development 'addicts' who used the movement to learn about being assertive, and putting 'me' first. In the context of the materially wealthy 1960s and 1970s, it appears in retrospect that young people were encouraged to believe that anything goes and that anything could be theirs, if only they knew how to ask, so acquiring an attitude of omnipotence and grandiosity.

However, this term emphasizes the negative. The 1960s and anything associated with it (including human potential) tended to be used as a scapegoat for the ills of society by right-wing politicians in the 1980s – especially ironic given the rampant encouragement of materialistic self-interestedness that characterized that era.

meditation refers to a number of different practices originating in spiritual disciplines throughout the world.

Most meditation practices are claimed to be calming and lead to an internal silence, so that new insights and understandings develop. Successful meditation can lead to physiological changes such as a lowering of blood pressure, slowing of heart rate, and alteration of brain wave patterns. Contemporary Western interest in meditation has been prompted by exploration of Eastern religions, though meditation is often practised mainly for stress management and relaxation (e.g. Bodian 1999). See also TRANSCENDENTAL MEDITATION.

Meditation usually involves concentrating and stilling the mind. Sometimes this is achieved by repeating a mantra (a word or phrase, which may be allocated by a teacher, and which in some traditions has a mystical significance).

One of the best known traditions of meditation comes from BUDDHISM (Geshe Kelsang Gyatso 1995), especially from the Zen schools. There the practice of meditation is considered to be a spiritual journey, sometimes led by a chosen teacher. It aims to increase the practitioner's powers of concentration (*samadhi*) and detachment from the effects of everyday living.

Meditating often involves taking up particular body postures, such as the lotus or half lotus. In Raja YOGA, which belongs to the Brahmin tradition, the eyes are kept open, focused on those of a senior teacher who leads the participant through his or her gaze (*drishti*). In Zen, and Buddhism generally, meditation begins by awareness of BREATHING, observing our own mental events non-judgementally, and aiming to achieve an inner stillness. Such constant and sustained attention is believed to lead to 'mindfulness', a particular kind of awareness.

mentoring Mentor, in Greek mythology, befriended and advised Telemachus, Odysseus's son, in Odysseus's absence. This concept became taken up in management circles, originally and strictly referring to a developmental, offline (i.e. not line-management) relationship created between an older, more senior member of an organization and a younger, developing manager.

Conway (in Stephenson 1998: 52) offers the following definition of mentoring in an organizational setting: 'Mentoring in organizations is a private relationship between two individuals based on a mutual desire for development towards an organizational objective. The relationship is a non-reporting one and infringes none of the organizational structures in place. It is additional to other forms of assistance, not a replacement.'

The term now applies more widely. Mentoring relationships are now common in, for example, education, between more and less experienced students. Consultants can be mentors to client managers. The distinction between mentoring and COACHING is often blurred, and is contentious, though coaching is more often focused on improving behavioural performance and need play no part in a mentoring relationship.

meta-model a fundamental model (in NLP) of the structure of language, and thus of the structure of the way people represent their experience (*meta-* is a prefix meaning 'on a higher level').

Based on transformational grammar (John Grinder, one of the founders of NLP, was originally a linguist), the meta-model was the subject of Bandler and Grinder's first NLP books (Bandler and Grinder 1975; Grinder and Bandler 1976).

Three types of transformation are seen as taking place between the 'deep structure' of one's perceived experience, and the 'surface structure' of the representation of that experience in language. These transformations are distortion, deletion and generalization. In much the same way, the map of the London underground distorts the geography of London to create an aesthetic and visually effective display; it deletes much detail of the territory in order to highlight information important to tube travellers; and it also generalizes such that stations, lines and so on are represented through uniform symbols, even though in reality they differ in many ways.

These three basic transformations give rise to a more detailed set of typical transformations, such as the 'universal quantifier' (your partner says 'You **always** do that to me'; a TV pundit says '**Everyone** believes that this is so') and the 'modal operator of necessity' ('You **have to** clear out your room'; 'We **must** do our duty').

The meta-model is a model of the structure of experience, not just of language per se, so the structure of a person's language tells us much about how they experience the world. This is not just a case of seeking to make our verbal communication more accurate. Our representations **are** our reality. Respectful probing of someone's model of the world, through using various question forms designed to address these typical limitations, can help introduce new perspectives and possibilities.

NLP works with language through other models besides this. Another, called the 'Milton model', reflects language patterns used by the hypnotherapist, Milton Erickson. 'Sleight of mouth' is Robert Dilts's coding of Richard Bandler's range of responses to questions and heckling from workshop participants. The meta-model remains the best known, and the most fundamental.

metaphor David Gordon cites the following definition (from Sheldon Kopp): 'Generally, a metaphor is defined as a way of speaking in which one thing is expressed in terms of another, whereby this bringing together throws new light on the character of what is being described' (Gordon 1978: 7).

However, metaphor is far more than a literary nicety. People organize their experience of the world according to root metaphors, and so changes or developments in these metaphors can have profound effects.

The epistemological view of Lakoff and Johnson (1980) is that 'metaphor is pervasive in everyday life, not just in language but in thought and action. Our ordinary conceptual system, in terms of which we both think and act, is fundamentally metaphorical in nature' (1980: 3). Lakoff and Johnson show how everyday activities are framed metaphorically, for example, 'argument' is often framed and conducted as 'war'.

Theories and models of personal development are based on such metaphors. For example, the metaphor of life as a transaction is obviously core to TRANSACTIONAL ANALYSIS. Metaphor is used intentionally in some therapeutic and educational processes, for example, in NLP. Metaphor is also utilized as a tool or method in personal development workshops, therapeutic processes, and organizational consulting, for example, through finding inspiration from stories, films, and myths; or as a means of communicating at an unconscious level.

mind map mind-mapping is a note-taking and note-making technique associated with Tony Buzan who popularized it with the publication of his Study Skills book, 'Use Your Head' (2000).

Drawing on the LEFT-BRAIN/RIGHT-BRAIN concept, Buzan argues that notes based on spontaneous patterns developed around a central topic or theme are much more conducive to recall than those prepared in the traditional (within Western societies) linear form. He suggests that the latter are governed by 'left-brain' thinking (predominantly logical, serial, number and language orientated) and suppress 'right-brain' thinking (more oriented towards associative, parallel, emotional, pattern, colour, rhythm, and related thought processes). Pattern notes (mind maps) utilizing key words, images and colour have, Buzan suggests, the benefit that they engage both sides of the brain.

mind-set refers to sets of assumptions and beliefs through which a person is pre-disposed to view the world, even though they may not be consciously aware of it. Usually carries the implication that the mind-set is limiting of new ideas and thinking. This is extended to organizations, such that we are used to hearing about the 'prevailing mind-set' of a company or the perceived (and perhaps questionable) need to 'change mind-sets'. An author associated with this organizational emphasis is Peter Senge, although in his book *The Fifth Discipline* (1990) he uses the term 'mental model'. See also PARADIGM.

mirroring mirroring is the imitation of another person's non-verbal behaviour, as if mirroring (reflecting back) to them their own behaviour. (Mirroring of verbal content is usually referred to as reflective LISTENING).

In NLP, mirroring (also referred to as matching, though sometimes mirroring denotes a more precise reflection) is used as a means of developing RAPPORT, on the basis that people in rapport tend to mirror each other unconsciously. It is a means of pacing a client, literally going at his or her own pace (e.g. O'Connor and Seymour 1993: 20).

Mirroring needs to be accomplished with subtlety if it is not to appear as mimicry. There are variations on mirroring such as 'crossover mirroring', in which non-verbal behaviour is reflected back in a different mode or channel (for example, mirroring the other person's voice rhythm through hand gestures).

modelling in NLP, a detailed study of the process through which a person produces a skill or experience.

This is different from more general usage of the term, where modelling refers to one person demonstrating behaviour for another. For example, a trainer might model effective listening skills when asked a question by a participant. This more general meaning is linked to the notion of a 'role model'.

The principle of modelling in NLP is that any skill is produced through a strategy, which can be identified and coded. The elements crucial to effective performance of the skill are identified, and these can be learnt by other people. Much of the focus in NLP is on the internal components of the strategy.

Dilts and Epstein (1995: 159) say: 'One of the most fundamental forms of modeling involves identifying the mental processes of people that excel at a particular task, and then comparing them with the mental processes of people who have difficulty with that same task.'

A classic example in NLP is the spelling strategy. Robert Dilts (1997), among others, claims that the inability to spell is usually not a matter of a person being unintelligent, but of using an inappropriate strategy. From repeated observation (particularly of eye accessing cues – eye movements which, according to NLP, are outward behavioural indicators of particular types of internal representation), successful spellers access an internal visual image of the word they are spelling, then experience a felt response that the spelling is correct. While this is embellished and varied according to the individual, the essence of the strategy can be learnt by those who hitherto have been ineffective at spelling.

A modelling project in NLP will codify many other aspects of experience besides the mental strategy, such as language patterns, beliefs, and more.

moral development themes of moral judgement and moral development are appearing increasingly on educational and developmental agendas, often linked to the notion of 'citizenship'.

Perhaps the best-known model of moral development, albeit one that remains controversial, is that of Lawrence Kohlberg. Kohlberg developed Piaget's ideas about childhood development, applying these to moral judgement. He proposed six stages of moral development. These are not tied strictly to age, but are experienced sequentially in time and according to Kohlberg are irreversible. Kohlberg believed that individuals are likely to exhibit signs of several stages at once, and that few people reach stage six.

The six stages (from Hampden-Turner 1981: 137) are:

- stage 1: obedience and punishment orientation; egocentric deference to a superior power.
- stage 2: naively egotistic orientation; right action is instrumentally satisfying.
- stage 3: good boy (or girl) orientation; conformity to stereotyped cultural images.
- stage 4: orientation to maintaining authority and social order.
- stage 5: social contract and interpersonal commitments orientation.
- stage 6: conscience or principle orientation with appeal to ethical universality and consistency.

These stages form three main phases: the pre-conventional (1 and 2), the conventional (3 and 4) and the post-conventional (5 and 6). According to Hampden-Turner (1981), research has shown that the level of moral judgement can be raised through discussion. The model has been criticized for being culturally biased.

motivation the study of motivation is concerned with why people behave the way they do.

In organizations, concerns about performance and control have made an understanding of motivation highly desirable – in terms both of understanding how individuals decide or become energized to pursue particular goals, and of understanding how one person (a manager) can motivate others (see, for example, Buchanan and Huczynski 1997).

Questions about human motives, and the true nature of human beings, have been asked for centuries (for example, by Aristotle) and in this sense the search for an understanding of motivation is not a modern invention.

Contemporary study of motivation, over the past five decades or so, is vast and varied (see Vroom and Deci 1992). There are many different strands. For example, some are based on the idea that motivation is fundamentally about the satisfaction of needs (for example, Maslow's HIERARCHY OF NEEDS). Some theories emphasize people as seeking satisfaction and achievement; others emphasize more the idea that people are instrumental, and thus are motivated by incentives and rewards. It can be instructive to examine the motivational assumptions behind organizational practices such as performance-related pay.

Abraham Maslow remains a key figure. Even though his work did not develop any empirical base, he did emphasize (among other things) the need for an understanding of motivation based on study of healthy people, rather than 'from psychotherapists treating patients' (Maslow 1970: 33).

Myers-Briggs Type Indicator the Myers-Briggs Type Indicator (MBTI) is a PERSONALITY inventory that classifies people into sixteen basic types.

It was developed from Jung's theory of PSYCHOLOGICAL FUNCTIONS and types by Katharine Cook Briggs, an associate of Jung's, and her daughter Isabel Myers (Briggs-Myers and Myers 1980). They believed that Jung's original typology, published in 1923, had emerged as the result of Jung's interest in psychopathology. Myers and Briggs were interested in developing the model to be applied to non-pathological situations. They believed that everyone had their own unique personality traits, which could be identified by means of an inventory. They developed this during the Second World War to help employers identify the most suitable women (who had become crucial to the work force) for

certain jobs. Since then it has been refined, and is now much used, particularly in industrial recruitment and training, despite some opposition from academic psychology.

This theory of personality types presumes that there are four critical factors, each of which consists of two opposite processes that influence how people think about and respond to events. These are perception, judging, interests in external or internal events, and attitude. Perception consists of the processes of sensing and intuiting (S, N) which are thought to be two distinct ways of attending to information. These are modified by two ways of judging, thinking and feeling (T, F). In addition, people's relative interests in either the inner or the outer world defines them as INTROVERTS or EXTROVERTS (I, E), and their attitude to life is governed by being either a perceiver or a judger (P, J).

This gives a total of sixteen different personality types. Myers and Briggs, and their followers, claim that research shows that certain combinations of these processes correlate with such things as occupations, LEARNING STYLES and choice of marriage partners.

The strength of this approach is that it assumes that each individual is unique, and that attempts to define a 'normal' human being are doomed to failure. They also stress that it is important for individuals to achieve a balance in the way in which they use these processes. Critics of this approach question the validity of the original distinctions, and the ways in which they have been defined.

mysticism a mystic is an individual on a spiritual path who holds that people have a divine connection within. Through this they grow in spiritual awareness. For a mystic, God has ceased to be an object and has become a personal experience in which they have achieved a communion with the cosmos. The mystic endeavours to live within this higher transcendental state (see, for example, Underhill 1999).

Mystical ideas are present in all orthodox religions, although the mystical teachings may be esoteric; for example, in Hebrew through the Kabbalah (see TREE OF LIFE), and in Islam through SUFISM (see also PERENNIAL WISDOM). Mysticism tends to have been marginalized in Western religions, although the teachings of the Gnostics, who have a mystical notion of the inner divine spark, are present throughout esoteric Christianity.

There is increasing interest in and influence of mystical thought in modern psycho-spiritual practices. These have emerged through the work of people such as the psychologist William James (1982), Carl Jung and Ken Wilber.

myth myths can emerge from a number of sources, such as folklore, fairy tales, legends, religious stories, great art, dreams and even the contents of psychotic episodes (see Campbell 1985; Greene and Sharman-Burke 2000).

Jung (1968c) regarded myths as the expressions of universal dispositions in mankind. He believed that they originated in the collective unconscious. He described the primal collective unconscious as full of myths and mythological motifs, which he described as ARCHETYPES. In this he strongly disagreed with Freud, whose more positivistic model of early PSYCHOSEXUAL DEVELOPMENT and the Oedipus COMPLEX was seen by Jung as essentially biological rather than mythological.

Jung stressed the impossibility of appreciating the messages in myths through conscious rationality. As with DREAMS, myths were 'a primordial language natural to . . . psychic processes' whose meaning and richness no purely rational and intellectual process could ever understand. Thus both the Christian myth, and the myth of Job, were symbolic of the process of INDIVIDUATION, which for Jung was the ultimate goal of human existence.

Myths also embody archetypal patterns within the COLLECTIVE UNCONSCIOUS, which are thought to be primordial images found in every myth. Myths also emerge from the collective, so that the myth of the Assumption of the Virgin Mary is not so much a theological truth as the collective unconscious's counter to the extreme masculinity of the traditional Christian Trinity. As with dreams and symbols, appreciation and integration of the messages of myths are considered essential to the development of the PSYCHE.

narcissism the word denotes excessive self-love and comes from the Greek myth of Narcissus, who fell in love with his own reflection. However, in a sense the opposite is the case for the narcissistic person. The child, usually between the age of 2 and 4 years old receives signals from primary caregivers that he or she is not growing up to be what others want them to be. The child's fear of annihilation or rejection forces him or her to bury the potential 'true self' and build up a compensatory false self, which appears to be what the primary caregivers want, maintained at all costs as a survival strategy. The underlying energy that maintains this false self is enormous rage.

The narcissist's need is to affirm self and obtain confirmation from others that the false self is great and exactly what is required. This inculcates an excessive and self-gratifying interest in or regard for oneself, one's own importance, abilities and so on, a strong and habitual egocentricism, and an undervaluing of others.

Narcissism is therefore a psychological DEFENCE strategy on the part of a traumatized person who can only see their own value by hyperinflating their own importance and belittling others. A need for comparison lies behind their desire to have people around, but only if in an inferior position. A person with narcissistic tendencies may be genuinely bewildered as to why other people should hold differing views, or question his or her motives.

Narcissism is characteristic of the tiny infant of 0 to 2 months who has not yet differentiated between self and the world. Many theorists refer to a 'narcissistic injury' (Johnson 1987: 39) that is endemic in most cultures. Self-help techniques such as CO-COUNSELLING, affirmation therapy and age-appropriate loving relationships heal most narcissistic injuries.

needs needs – which are essential to fulfill – are often distinguished from wants – that which we desire but do not necessarily need.

Much psychology is based on the principle that human behaviour is governed by the satisfaction of needs. This is contrasted with the integrative emphasis found in, for example, Jungian psychology and PSYCHOSYNTHESIS.

There have been many attempts to identify essential human needs, and (in management) many attempts to understand how to satisfy these in order to MOTIVATE employees; see Maslow's HIERARCHY OF NEEDS. However, none of these attempts has produced reliable or lasting knowledge. Many would argue that human needs are context-dependent.

NLP (Neuro-Linguistic Programming) Neuro-Linguistic Programming is a method for understanding the structure of subjective experience of human beings, and for utilizing that knowledge in communications. It has been defined in various other ways, for example, as 'the art of communication excellence'.

Founded in the USA by Richard Bandler (a cybernetician) and John Grinder (a linguist), NLP was based initially (Bandler and Grinder 1975) on observational studies of 'excellent communicators' (e.g. Fritz Perls, the well known GESTALT therapist). The title refers to assumed connections between internal experience ('neuro'), language ('linguistic') and patterns of behaviour ('programming'). Bandler and Grinder criticized the presupposition of some psychotherapies that personal change necessarily involves long-term therapy, possible only with insight into past experience.

NLP assumes that people are inherently creative and capable, and also, ultimately, have POSITIVE INTENTIONS for their behaviour. Communication happens through verbal and non-verbal channels, both consciously and unconsciously. People act according to the way they understand and represent the world, not according to the way the world 'is' (summed up in Alfred Korzybski's phrase, 'the map is not the territory'). Therefore change can be achieved through modifying such representations.

NLP has 'borrowed' liberally from fields such as Gestalt, linguistics and HYPNOTHERAPY and is therefore intentionally eclectic – although NLP has claimed to be not a separate, competing field of study but instead a methodology through which effective practices from other fields can be identified and coded. Arguably the underlying theory of NLP is best represented in the work of Gregory Bateson (1979). Bateson was not an NLP theorist himself, but was consulted by the founders.

Early NLP (e.g. Bandler and Grinder 1975 Grinder and Bandler 1976) emphasized a systematic coding of human experience, for example, through annotating internal or mental strategies. Grinder and DeLozier (1996) then emphasized what they called 'new code' NLP, a more holistic, BODYMIND approach. Richard Bandler now labels his practice 'Design Human Engineering'.

NLP has been criticized for emphasizing techniques more than underlying values, and for placing powerful covert tools in the hands of lay practitioners. It is now an accredited mode of psychotherapy in the UK. For an introduction to NLP see, for example, Knight (1999); O'Connor and Seymour (1993); and Robert Dilts's website (See Resources).

neurological levels an NLP model, developed by Robert Dilts, of levels of inner experience. Dilts identifies six levels (Environment, Behaviour, Capability, Belief, Identity and Spirit – though Spirit is omitted in some versions). This is a development of Gregory Bateson's model of LEVELS OF LEARNING (see Dilts and Epstein 1995: 351–54).

Dilts called his own model 'neurological levels' because he proposed originally that each level corresponds to a particular neuro-physical system: 'The environment level involves the specific external stimuli and conditions in which our behavior takes place. Behaviors without any inner map, plan or strategy to guide them, however, are like knee jerk reactions, habits or rituals. At the level of capability we are able to select, alter and adapt a class of behaviors to a wider set of external situations. At the level of beliefs and values we may encourage, inhibit or generalize a particular strategy, plan or way of thinking. Identity, of course, consolidates whole systems of beliefs and values into a sense of self. While each level becomes more abstracted from the specifics of behavior and sensory experience, it actually has more and more widespread effect on our behavior and experience' (Dilts and Epstein 1995: 353).

Dilts's model is represented as a hierarchical network. This denotes, as described in the quotation, that change at a higher neurological level (e.g. Identity) has more far-reaching consequences for the person, in that this is likely to affect an increasingly wide range of beliefs, capabilities and behaviours. However it is possible for change to a higher level to be prompted by change at a lower level too.

neurotic technically, refers to having a neurosis (in psychiatric terms, a nervous disorder). However, the categories of the psychiatric/medical model and the labelling of people in this way have been extensively challenged. In more general usage, 'neurotic' may refer to behaviour that shows unusual or excessive ANXIETY.

New Age the term 'New Age' refers generally to 'alternative' ideas and practices that characterize the transition to the era known as the 'Age of Aquarius' (when the constellation of Aquarius succeeds that of Pisces at the vernal equinox – Greene 1977: 265–66).

The term is used in many ways, however. Frost (1992) refers to a wide variety of usage, including the following:

- to denote an interest in practices and philosophies that are in fact ancient (e.g. CHAKRAS; TREE OF LIFE)
- to encompass a number of 'alternative health' practices, some of which may be ancient (for example, acupuncture; crystal healing; REIKI; auric healing; and so on)
- to refer to the beliefs and principles of a 'new age' spirituality, which is non-orthodox and non-religious but which may borrow from various religions, and which allows a person a great degree of choice in their beliefs – much criticized in particular by fundamentalist movements in the USA

- to denote the paraphernalia, consumer goods and other trends associated with the above (e.g. 'crystal shops', new age music, etc.).

'New Age' can be used as a term of abuse, when generally it denotes an unquestioning, wish-fulfilling belief in non-material and scientifically unproven solutions to personal and social problems. Whilst not going to the extreme of advocating scientism (a belief that anything not accessible to scientific study either does not exist or is worthless), it is hard to escape the conclusion that the New Age is rife with would-be gurus and ungrounded belief systems. John Rowan (1993: 11) is one author who critiques what he perceives to be a disturbing tendency towards sloppy thinking, and believes it important to understand that 'New Age' thinking does not necessarily have anything to do with SPIRITUALITY.

nominalization a characteristic of language such that processes are expressed in language in the form of objects or events (nouns). Nominalizations can be addressed using the questions associated with NLP's META-MODEL: 'Essentially, the process of nominalization occurs when the transformations of the language change what occurs in the Deep Structure representation as a process word – a verb or predicate – into an event word – a noun or argument – in the Surface Structure representation' (Bandler and Grinder 1975: 32).

'Process' is itself an example. People talk, for example, of having 'relationships', rendering a relationship linguistically undifferentiated from a spoon, a wallet or a vase that a person possesses (and which can become lost or broken). In essence, maintaining the sense of process (i.e. talking of relating rather than a relationship) represents the world in a more fluid, flexible and dynamic way. A common sense test for whether a noun is a nominalization is to ask 'could you put it in a wheelbarrow?' – my hat could, my fear of flying could not.

non-verbal communication it is reckoned that language accounts for less than 10 per cent of human communication. Non-verbal communication is therefore of great significance (e.g. Buchanan and Huczynski 1997: 50).

Non-verbal communication consists mainly of 'paralinguistics' and BODY LANGUAGE. Paralinguistics refers to nuances of meaning conveyed through the tonality and emphasis given to words. For example, an exercise used in both drama and personal development is to explore how many different meanings can be conveyed through saying 'Yes' in different ways. It soon becomes apparent that the one word *yes* can indicate joy, reluctance, obedience, defiance, enthusiasm, permission, doubt, and so on.

Non-verbal communication is the main medium for messages about RELATIONSHIP and emotional state. Words may carry content, but indicators of dominance and submission, status, liking, and so on are usually non-verbal. NLP is one mode that gives much attention and importance to non-verbal communication (see SENSORY ACUITY).

obsessive generally, being unable to let go of a subject, or having an obsessive interest in another person. Obsessiveness can involve repeated ritualistic behaviour (such as washing one's hands) resulting from hidden fears. It can also be reflected in sustained attention to a highly detailed task, for example, compiling a dictionary. See also COMPULSIVE.

occult literally, 'hidden', referring typically to esoteric ideas and practices that were available only to initiates of some mystical and spiritual traditions. The term has acquired negative connotations, partly through the efforts of formal religions to demonize opponents. Thus 'the Occult' as a label most often refers to involvement with the supernatural through practices such as Ouija boards.

Open Space Technology a large-group or conference format developed by American consultant Harrison Owen (see, for example, Owen 1995). In everyday terms, Open Space Technology is an unstructured event; however, there are principles of structuring that are often experienced as enabling and highly creative. The point is to create conditions under which exchange, interaction and creativity can happen, rather than trying to engineer these qualities through a more instrumental or controlling use of structures. It has been used with success in organ-izational development, and also in social and community projects.

Harrison Owen's website (see Resources) has several relevant papers posted (the following material is adapted from 'A Brief User's Guide To Open Space Technology'). The minimal structure of Open Space Technology includes four principles: 'Whoever comes are the right people. Whatever happens is the only thing that could have. Whenever it starts is the right time. When it is over, it is over.' Owen says: '*The leader must truly trust the group to find its own way.* Attempts on the part of the leader to impose specific outcomes or agenda will totally abort the process.'

There is also one law ('a law only in the sense that all participants must observe it or the process will not work'), known as 'The Law of Two Feet': 'Briefly stated, this law says that every individual has two feet, and must be prepared to use them. Responsibility for a successful outcome in any Open Space Event resides with exactly one person – each participant. Individuals can make a difference and must make a difference. If that is not true in a given situation, they, and they alone, must take responsibility to use their two feet, and move to a new place where they can make a difference. This departure need not be made in anger or hostility, but only after honoring the people involved and the space they occupy. By word or gesture, indicate that you have nothing further to contribute, wish them well, and go and do something useful.'

openness the quality of appearing open to others; for example, honest, transparent, available for CONTACT and able to disclose, rather than secretive, withdrawn and defended. As with DISCLOSURE, the degree of openness a person shows in any context will be influenced by the degree of safety and trust.

Also the quality of being receptive to or willing to consider new ideas, others' points of view, or new experiences (as opposed to being closed-minded).

oppression in personal development, can refer to oppression of any of a person's IDENTITY, BEING, EXPERIENCE, VALUES or preferences.

Politics and issues of oppression have often been given scant attention in personal development. A criticism of the HUMANISTIC approach is that it can operate as if, within a workshop or therapy session, oppression can be escaped or overcome by finding mutual AUTHENTICITY. Now it is more common to see this as at best naïve and, however unintentionally, perpetuating oppression by casting it as an external interference or something that a person can choose to leave at the door. See also FEMINISM.

oral stage the first stage of human PSYCHOSEXUAL DEVELOPMENT within the Freudian (psychoanalytic) school. This includes the sucking and biting phase and technically covers 0 to 18 months of age. The principle is that poor development at the sucking stage may result in a dependent personality in the adult; and fixation at the biting phase could result in an orally aggressive, sarcastic and cynical individual.

In general usage, 'oral' may refer to behaviour of, or attention given to matters relating to, eating, sucking or biting.

Organization Development (OD) an approach to organizational change which makes use of behavioural science knowledge to improve organizational functioning (see French et al. 1994). Richard Beckhard (1969) defined OD as: 'An effort which is planned, organization-wide, and managed from the top, to increase organization effectiveness and health through interventions based on behavioural science knowledge.'

OD emphasizes the need for individual employees to develop their skills in areas such as interpersonal communications, team membership, leadership and so on. It is through OD that many theories and practices of personal development have cross-fertilized with management development and organizations – see, for example, T-GROUPS.

outcome a goal or desired result. NLP assumes that people are essentially goal-orientated. Thus behaviour is regarded as teleological, in that it can be understood best in relation to its purpose or the outcome it is intended to achieve (see also T.O.T.E.).

This operates at micro, neuro-physiological levels as well as conscious and cognitive levels. It is a reflection of the systemic nature of human experience, and is not suggesting that all outcomes are consciously selected, or that people are assumed to live in a narrowly instrumental way.

There are criteria in NLP for the 'well-formedness' of an outcome. These include that the goal is stated in the positive (specifies what one wants, not the absence of what one does not want); that having achieved the outcome it can be imagined in sensorily specific terms – that is, one can state and experience what one will be seeing, hearing and feeling when the outcome is achieved – similar to the use of VISUALIZATION of successful performance in sports; that achieving the outcome is broadly within the person's control or sphere of influence; and that it is ECOLOGICAL, i.e. not harmful to others (a criterion that, interestingly, is often negated by a narrow emphasis on instrumental 'end-gaining').

outward bound training outward bound training (and related forms of outdoor development) takes participants out of the classroom and, typically, into rural, adventuring settings away from 'civilization'. There, activities such as abseiling, orienteering, and outdoor survival become the source for EXPERIENTIAL LEARNING (see, for example, Snow 1997).

Outward bound training is often used as a team development format, as issues of interpersonal relating are heightened by dependence on other people for success and even survival. It is also used for leadership training, and as Huczynski (1983) notes, it is strongly influenced by the military tradition of officer training.

Outward bound work is not only physically demanding but also, typically, isolates participants in a geographical environment. Needs for physical and psychological safety become very important. Effective FACILITATION should provide for these aspects during the experience, as well as for extensive debriefing through which participants can reflect, make sense of their experience, and interpret or conceptualize their learning.

ownership 'ownership' of a problem or issue refers to psychological and emotional, not legal, ownership. It means that a person accepts that a problem or issue is theirs, and that they rather have a level of RESPONSIBILITY for addressing it.

This cuts through the mentality of moaning 'Someone, somewhere should do something about this' or, as in Eric Berne's GAME, 'Ain't it Awful'. An image that illustrates this principle is that of the 'swamp diagram'. The more people see their problems as being someone else's responsibility, and the more people leave it to others to take action about them, the deeper they sink into the swamp of inaction.

A related usage is when a person is asked to 'own' their own PROJECTIONS: '"Owning" in the GESTALT sense means to acknowledge and take into one's awareness a particular quality or trait which already belongs to oneself' (Clarkson 1989: 107). Note, though, that the principle of ownership could also be used in a perverse way to DEFLECT others' confrontations. Say that a manager is giving a colleague feedback on how she experiences his behaviour. He feels uncomfortable and unwilling to explore the issue, and so deflects the feedback by challenging her to own her projections.

panic attack a panic attack is a strong physiological reaction to severe anxiety. It is linked to the FIGHT–FLIGHT (adrenaline) system, and all aspects of the autonomic nervous system are affected. HYPERVENTILATION, heart palpitations, sweating, and so on may occur. A panic attack is usually sudden in onset, quickly intensifying and gradually disappearing in about ten minutes. Prolonged attacks may need urgent medical treatment.

Panic attacks can be situation specific (such as agoraphobia) or generalized. They occur in many contexts, with the person reporting that the fear of dying, or losing control, having a heart attack, or going crazy (to name a few possibilities) is overwhelming. The urge to flee the perceived danger is very strong.

paradigm literally, 'an example', paradigm is also typically used to refer to a prevailing worldview. See also MINDSET.

The term seems to have become over-used. At times it refers in a highly localized way to a specific person's or organization's beliefs and assumptions, perhaps even to fleeting changes of terminology. 'New paradigms' in management seem to be hailed by the week.

Thomas Kuhn's book (1996, originally published in 1962) is the main source of contemporary usage of the term. His interest was in tracing changes in scientific thought and practice, especially changes at a fundamental level. An example is the contrast between the Newtonian view of a mechanical universe and Einsteinian relativity (which is debated in Kuhn's book).

Kuhn acknowledged that he used the term 'paradigm' in both senses noted above, thus referring both to the (philosophically deeper) 'entire constellation of beliefs, values, techniques and so on shared by the members of a given community' (Kuhn 1996: 175), and to particular examples which point the way to tackling further scientific puzzles.

paradoxical injunction paradoxes are self-reflexive statements where there is a confusion of member and class, and thus they contain an inherent contradiction (DOUBLE BINDS also have this structure). A classic example is Epimenides' paradox – Epimenides, a Cretan, stated that 'All Cretans are liars', but it is impossible to say whether that statement is either true or false.

The philosopher Ludwig Wittgenstein first speculated on the practical and behavioural implications of paradox. They may create an untenable situation, as with the spouse who tells his/her partner to 'be spontaneous', or the parent who wants his/her child to *want* to do his or her homework. This can create an impasse,

115

because it imposes a rule that the desired behaviour should be spontaneous.

In the Milan School of family systems therapy (e.g. Palazzoli et al. 1978), paradoxical interventions or tactics are apparently contrary to the goals of therapy, but are in fact designed to achieve them. 'Paradoxical injunctions' may involve symptom prescription, that is, encouraging the behaviours that are producing the 'problem'. Thus an insomniac will be forbidden to sleep, or marital couples who present a problem of 'fighting the whole time' to the therapist may be ordered to fight at particular times every day. It is claimed that this can effect second order change (see FIRST ORDER CHANGE), partly because it may destroy the original beliefs about the inevitability of the problem, and requires that it be viewed from a different perspective.

parallel process a phenomenon whereby the dynamics and patterns of one system or interaction are paralleled in the dynamics of a related system which has a member or members in common with the first system. This applies especially, for example, in therapeutic supervision, where the dynamics between the supervisor and supervisee may parallel those between the supervisee and his or her client. See also SHADOW CONSULTING.

paranoid a psychiatric term (from the Greek, meaning 'beside mind') that has passed into general usage. Clinically, paranoia is characterized by excessive suspiciousness about others and, as a result, seeking social isolation or becoming aggressive towards others.

Paranoid behaviour can be displayed by any person, for good reasons (as the popular saying goes, 'Just because you're paranoid doesn't mean they're not out to get you'). However, 'paranoid' is probably used most commonly as an insult to imply that a person is unbalanced, or that their suspicions are ungrounded.

As a descriptor of behaviour, 'paranoid' may refer to suspiciousness, which can vary from mild mistrust to fear of serious exploitation, physical or psychological harm or deception; lacking trust in others and having few confidants; tending to be argumentative in relationships; being hypervigilant and sensing danger in the most benign comments or actions; and bearing grudges for a long time and being quite unforgiving for perceived or real injuries or slights.

parent see EGO STATE.

participation the quality and/or quantity of a person's involvement in an event. In a group there might be discussion of each person's level of participation.

In some contexts the nature and level of participation can be observed and measured. This may be to give developmental feedback to individuals; or it may be a basis for drawing inferences about a person's skills and qualities in a setting such as an ASSESSMENT CENTRE.

passive-aggressive the form of behaviour that hurts without leaving much of a trace of the attacker, so that a person feels attacked or manipulated in some way but cannot pin down the cause of the hurt or how it happened (adapted from Dickson 1982: 5–6).

The passive-aggressive style is manipulative or indirect behaviour characterized by a form of attack that is mostly concealed, is denied when challenged, and is intended to press the 'guilt' button of the person being attacked.

The need of the passive-aggressive person is to be in control (in relationships, work or personal life), to get their own way while avoiding rejection and self-hurt. The passive-aggressive person fears direct confrontation, as direct aggression has resulted in serious trauma for them in childhood, yet the person is too angry to be just passive. In that sense he or she shows the same behaviours as the NARCISSISTIC personality style.

pastiming one of the six aspects of TIME-STRUCTURING in TRANSACTIONAL ANALYSIS.

A pastime is less structured or pre-programmed than a GAME, hence the individual has to invest more of him- or herself into the social transaction. An individual's personal agenda is likely to be more in the foreground and the opportunities for both positive and negative STROKES are higher. There is a greater psychological risk of rejection, but equally the possibility of more frequent and stronger strokes is present. The level of engagement is still superficial (cocktail chat), as people who pastime do just that: they talk about 'past times' without engaging with others to take action.

pathologize literally, making into a disease. This refers to the way in which one person may label another's behaviour as, for example, PARANOID. This not only attempts to define the behaviour as negative, it also introduces a quasi-diagnosis of the person.

It would be unethical for a facilitator to use their expert knowledge in this way, and in a practitioner–client relationship this would be seen as at least manipulative and probably an example of PERVERSE facilitation. Nevertheless, Grosskurth (1991) suggested that Freud and his followers pathologized other thinkers and professionals with whom they were in conflict.

Pathologizing is not confined to isolated cases of unfortunate facilitation. Many disciplines and professions concerned broadly with 'helping' – such as social work, nursing and psychiatry – are dominated by classifications of illness. Such classifications have been challenged by radical psychiatrists such as Ronnie Laing (e.g. Laing 1965), and are antithetical to the principle in HUMANISTIC PSYCHOLOGY of treating people as human beings first and foremost.

A related term is 'pathogenic', which literally means 'making ill'. There is a long-standing debate about the link between the DOUBLE BIND (which Watzlawick and others consider a pathogenic communication pattern) and schizophrenia.

patriarchy literally, rule by the father. Refers to a society in which men dominate, and a male perspective is regarded as the 'norm'. Women, and a female perspective, are thus framed as inferior and/or deviant. Patriarchy is a prime source of OPPRESSION for women (see FEMINISM). HUMANISTIC PSYCHOLOGY is dominated by white male figures; Maslow and Rogers, for example, are cited as 'fathers' of the field, but one would be hard pressed to identify a 'mother'. See John Rowan (1998: 168) on the notion of the 'patripsych'.

peak experience an experience that Maslow identified as characteristic of self-actualizing people. According to Rowan (1988: 6), Maslow describes his SELF-ACTUALIZATION theory as a two stage development, and therefore his description of peak experiences is of two kinds. The first is existential and the second mystical or spiritual. The existential peak experience could be 'completions-of-the-act, or as in gestalt-type closures and so on' (Maslow 1968). A high degree of satisfaction with the completion of creative or important tasks can give a person a peak experience, through expressing their true personal potential.

The more mystical peak experience comes with the loss of the sense of 'I', as the person experiences an expansion of consciousness and unity with nature or divine presence. This seems timeless and boundaryless, with no distinction between what is being experienced and the person who is experiencing. For Maslow, this type of peak experience seemed a high form of spiritual development and is placed at the pinnacle of his model of the HIERARCHY OF NEEDS.

With this definition, HUMANISTIC PSYCHOLOGY makes its link with TRANSPERSONAL PSYCHOLOGY, where spiritual peak experiences are accepted as one of the 'higher needs' of man (Rowan 1993). In transpersonal work, peak experiences are called 'glimpse experiences' as they are temporary perceptions of transcendence or transformation into the mystical realm.

peer learning community John Heron's (1974a) concept of a mode of collective operation, usually in an educational context, based on peerhood amongst adult learners. This is a distinct and particular form, with a strong emphasis on personal development and group dynamics, unlike the general descriptor of a 'learning community' that is routinely applied to groups of people taking educational courses. See also COM-MUNITY BUILDING.

Key principles are:
- the notion of an educated person, emphasizing SELF-DIRECTION, self-monitoring and self-correction
- participative evaluation of course objectives
- two fundamental principles of parity: equality of consideration (i.e. whatever each person brings is equally worthy of consideration); and equality of opportunity (it is equally open to anyone to contribute to or intervene in the course process at any time); this means that people's needs and contributions merit equal attention, but not necessarily that they are of equal value in relation to course objectives.

Equally important are education of the whole person (particularly education of the AFFECT, and EMOTIONAL COMPE-TENCE) and political modes of POWER sharing, particularly a progression from hierarchical to co-operative to autonomous modes of FACILITATION.

Among the implications of these principles are that the staff–student distinction is secondary to the fundamental parity between human beings; participant resources are an important source of learning; interpersonal learning is a key area; and it is necessary to have one or more primary facilitators, especially to facilitate the adoption of the peer principle.

Heron has since developed the notion of CO-OPERATIVE INQUIRY as a research approach. The functioning of the Co-operative Inquiry group (Reason 1988: 18–39) has much in common with the notion of peer learning community. We (Tosey and Gregory 1998) have revisited Heron's notion of the peer learning community in the light of application to a formal, degree course in higher education.

peer-hierarchy combination an important aspect of the DIMENSIONS OF FACILI-TATOR STYLE model (Heron 1999). The peer principle implies mutual aid and support between autonomous people who are at the same political level, that is, peers. Hierarchy means 'when somebody takes responsibility in doing things to or for other persons for the sake of future autonomy and co-operation of those persons, this is part of parenthood, education and many professions' (Heron 1999: 335).

In educational endeavours with adult learners, particularly in professional and personal development and experiential groupwork, combining peer learning with benevolent hierarchy allows participants to see each other as a rich learning resource and not become solely reliant on the facilitator. This is an essential prerequisite for a PEER LEARNING COMMUNITY.

The peer-hierarchy combination works best when the participants and facilitator(s) agree in advance which aspects of the various dimensions of facilitator styles will be peer-led, which hierarchically led and which co-operatively managed. In a new group, it is often the case that the planning, structuring and confronting are hierarchically led, while the feeling, meaning and valuing dimensions are shared. With confidence and skills building among the learning group (including the facilitator) all dimensions can eventually be managed using all three political modes as appropriate for the learning needs rather than from a sense of dependency.

perception perception has many facets. These include the faculty of perceiving; sensory perception, as in the capacity of the mind to relate sensory information to external objects; and intuitive recognition of a possible truth. The study of perception spans philosophy, general psychology, GESTALT psychology, and physiology, and also is an essential part of esoteric and TRANSPERSONAL PSYCHOLOGY – particularly through the study of CONSCIOUSNESS and INTENTIONALITY.

The faculty of perception involves taking in through sense organs stimuli from the environment (somatic and external), and with the use of INTUITION or IMAGINATION and propositional KNOWLEDGE, making sense of the incoming information. This view is acknowledged by advocates of the notion that 'the mind is an internal data-cruncher generating some surveyable facsimile or representation of the world' (Harré and Gillett 1994: 165), with psychological meaning or ideas attached to the perception.

If perception is effectively an inference-to-a comprehension-of-the-world it is said to be selective and coloured by the frame of reference, including the preferred biases of the perceiver (see also ATTENTION). These can be stereotypical perceptions – for example, if an adult male of working age walks down a hospital corridor wearing a white coat with a stethoscope hanging round his neck, he is very likely to be perceived as a medical doctor. There is a phenomenon called 'perceptual defence' where the perceptual mechanisms are selectively biased against the detection of negatively evaluative stimuli.

Perception also involves the identifying of FIGURE as distinct from ground in each percept seen in the world. This aspect of perception is a central part of Gestalt theory, along with the notion that people need to complete unfinished wholes and will use supplementary information to fill in gaps at a visual and conceptual level. Perception seems to be an intellectually constructive process that is anticipatory and dynamic. It also seems socially constructed and even culturally or socially learnt (Neisser, in Harré and Gillett 1994). Thus, perception is a dynamic relationship between the environment and how the individual makes sense of it.

In PHENOMENOLOGY, perception is regarded as the primary source of knowledge (Moustakas 1994). Intentions and sensations combine to make perceptions.

perceptual position there are three basic perceptual positions in NLP: first, second and third.

First position is an ASSOCIATED state, in which the person experiences the world through their own eyes and feeling their own body sensations and emotions.

Second position denotes experiencing the world as if from another person's perspective, imaginatively or intuitively seeing what they see and feeling what they feel. This is extremely useful in MODELLING, and is considered a natural skill for generating EMPATHY.

Third position is a detached, objective, dispassionate observer position.

A fourth perceptual position is also used. Robert Dilts (1998a) defines this as 'a perceptual position that involves being associated in the whole system or "field" relating to a particular interaction. It involves experiencing a situation with the best interest of the entire system in mind.'

perennial wisdom Willis Harman refers to Aldous Huxley's (1946) observation that religions generally have both public or exoteric, and secret or esoteric versions: 'The range of exoteric religions is fantastically diverse. However, all of the esoteric traditions are essentially the same – or, more precisely, appear to be based in some form of potentially universal spiritual experience. This common core has sometimes been referred to as the "perennial wisdom"' (Harman 1988: 83).

permission while all forms of therapy and personal development methods offer a form of permission for the individual to change, it is given very specific and overt consideration in TRANSACTIONAL ANALYSIS.

In TA it is one of the three 'P's of effective therapeutic work. These are permission, protection, and potency. All individuals voluntarily undergoing personal change need to feel a degree of protection and potency from the facilitator or counsellor who is helping them to change. Most deep changes occur at the level of counteracting serious injunctions from childhood (like 'Don't Exist', or 'Don't be Successful'). Injunctions have attached to them feared consequences of rejection or even annihilation if the individual tries to exist, or tries to be successful. Permissions can be offered from any of the counsellor's EGO STATES to the Child ego state of the client. For example (Wollams and Brown 1978: 203):

- Parent ego state of counsellor: 'You deserve to be successful'
- Adult ego state of counsellor: 'Here's how to succeed'
- Child ego state of counsellor: 'Do your thing'.

person from the Greek PERSONA, meaning 'mask', which came to stand for the role an individual played in society, and hence the individual themselves. See also SELF.

The term can refer in common-sense usage to an individual human being. It can also refer to the concept or idealized form of what a person is or might be – for example, as an aware, whole, and healthily functioning individual. There are wide variations in this type of definition – one example is John Heron's, as follows: 'The soul manifesting in alert, aware action: a being celebrating their self-determination in conscious deeds. A person emerges through their expressed intentions. 'I choose, and become a distinct person.' Through electing to do something the potential person becomes actual. Hence the person is a self-creating being. The sum total of my past acts constitutes the person I have become today. Within limits set by the fields of influence to which the everyday self is open, I am shaping my personality, making my self through my daily choices'. (Heron 1989: 127).

persona our public personality, the ARCHE-TYPALLY-based COMPLEX by which we relate to the outer world. The Latin *persona* originally meant the mask worn by an actor in order to show which character he or she was playing. From that it came to mean any ROLE or personage including life-roles and public images (Jung 1966; see also Hopcke 1995).

The term has spread out from Jungian psychology and is in general use. It is that aspect of each of us that we show to others, the face we present to the world, our public self and social role and status; hence a large part is usually played by our job or profession.

The persona is also the function by which we manage our interpersonal relations and relate to others. The roles life presents to us normally call for adaptation on our part. In order to get on at some level with people whose inner beings may well be at odds with our own, we need accepted, conventional modes of behaviour that permit the necessary interchanges of communal life to take place smoothly. From this point of view, the persona is by no means a defence against external danger, but an essential mediator between individuals that moderates their actions.

One risk is that the individual may come to believe his or her persona to be the real SELF. In these circumstances, the persona complex can cramp growth and inhibit authenticity.

personal construct theory construct theory is the study of how the individual construes their world. George Kelly, the founder of Personal Construct Theory, developed the model on the premise that all men (and women) are scientists, in the sense that we hypothesize continuously as a way of making sense of or construing our own reality (Kelly 1955).

Kelly was counteracting the scientism of his time among psychologists who were moving further away from the study of the internal experiences of people under the axiom that what could not be independently observed and measured was not scientific and therefore not worthy of psychological inquiry. Kelly's often-quoted saying, 'If you want to know what a man is thinking, ask him', led the way for the new constructivist (qualitative) research of the last thirty years.

The fundamental postulate (Bannister and Fransella 1986) is that *a person's processes are psychologically channelised by the ways in which they anticipate events.* (Processes refers to perceptions plus what one does with perceptions.) So anticipation plays an important part in understanding the present and future, as does knowledge of the past. Anticipation also implies prediction, which is the hypothesizing element of sense-making.

A personal construct system is the range of constructs a person uses most often to interpret their experiences. A limited range of constructs used in lots of situations and unchanging would be considered 'rigid' whereas a flexible, contextualized, highly differentiated use of constructs would indicate a broad and receptive perspective.

Personal construct psychologists make use of the Repertory Grid. This is a technique used to elicit from a person the relationship between sets of constructs and how such a relationship informs their behaviour.

personal development the process through which each individual gravitates towards achieving their HUMAN POTENTIAL.

Personal development, with its modern roots in the GROWTH MOVEMENT of the 1960s, is perhaps experiencing a renaissance. In businesses and organizations, personal development has often been seen as a matter of acquiring behavioural, work-related skills, without need for any form of 'inner' development. But businesses are realizing more and more that soft skills are key to performance; are clamouring for their staff to develop EMOTIONAL INTELLIGENCE; and are beginning to embrace the idea that SPIRITUALITY and the workplace might be related. Moreover, the (UK) government is actively promoting lifelong learning, emphasizing both emotional and spiritual dimensions of healthy citizenship.

There are two key dimensions of personal development, closely intertwined. One is the shedding or unlearning of DISTRESSES, habits, beliefs and so on that the person has acquired during their lifetime. The other is the unfolding of the person's full potential and integration of their facets towards what he or she may become (see, for example, INDIVIDUATION; SELF-ACTUALIZATION). In this sense personal development is concerned with the whole person (the inner and the outer, and mind, body, emotion and spirit). However, the label 'personal development' is often used in a much narrower sense, for example, to denote INTERPERSONAL SKILLS acquisition.

'Personal development' also refers to the practice of development, in whatever form (e.g. experiential workshops; counselling; self-help books).

personal history a person's BIOGRAPHY, in the sense of the story of their life, including the circumstances of their birth, cultural and familial inheritance, and the subsequent events they have experienced.

personality personality refers to those behaviour patterns which are characteristic of an individual and which tend to be consistent across situations and over time (Glassman 1995: 278). Characteristics or TRAITS are usually social or psychological constructs, rather than physiological; thus a person is said to be shy, gregarious, creative, have a depressed disposition, be boisterous, an INTROVERT or EXTROVERT, and so on.

In personal development work, personality traits may be explored to discern whether they are a true reflection of the person's perception of SELF, or whether the person believes they have acquired these characteristics by, for example, coercion or as a way of pleasing others (see DRIVERS). The aim is to explore whether the behaviour and the thinking and feelings associated with personality are maintained through habit, or fear of loss of identity, rather than owned and celebrated. For example, people who are labelled as very helpful and obliging might be invited to explore the underlying motivation for this behaviour, and whether it is causing them stress. If it seems motivated by fear they may want to find ways of changing the behaviour regardless of how socially acceptable it seems to be. Many people believe that personality traits cannot be changed; however, this is not necessarily the case.

Personality theory is the study of personality types and of how individuals acquire a recognizable cluster of traits. The age-old debate of nature versus nurture refers to different hypotheses about personality development. Some believe personality traits such as temperament are genetically determined, others that all people are born with the same propensies and that experience determines the difference.

person-centred Carl Rogers coined the phrase 'person-centred counselling' in 1951. As both a HUMANISTIC counsellor and educator, he spread the concept to education (Rogers 1961, 1983).

Rogers' principles of humanistic, person-centred education are that the processes should:
* be student-centred rather than teacher-focused
* facilitate personal growth through humanistic methods
* examine characteristics of a helping relationship
* be a shared learning experience.

Rogers' counselling model holds the same principles, with the additional humanistic values that all persons at their core are good and have the capacity to grow and to change. Rogers laid down three essential conditions under which persons are most likely to grow. These are: UNCONDITIONAL POSITIVE REGARD for the person; empathic understanding; and CONGRUENCE. These conditions are held as attitudes by person-centred counsellors when working with clients (Culley 1992).

As a philosophy, person-centredness has its roots in EXISTENTIALISM where individual accountability is valued. Sartre's notion that 'man being condemned to be free carries the weight of the whole world on his shoulders: he is responsible for the world and for himself as a way of being' (Sartre 1985: 52) echoes strongly the desire for individualism and responsibility developed in the Human Potential movement. Many personal and professional development workshops were offered in the 1970s and 1980s to help individuals know how to identify and articulate their needs and wants. Changing political emphasis from hierarchical authority to individual empowerment was facilitated by identifying needs and development from the individual's perspective, with or without facilitation, in areas such as education, counselling and social needs.

From the concept of 'person-centred' there are derivations such as learner-centred (in education) and CLIENT-CENTRED (in counselling and consulting).

perverted intervention within the communication model SIX CATEGORY INTERVENTION ANALYSIS, Heron (1990: 157) describes perverted interventions as 'quite deliberately malicious; they intend harm to the client, they seek to do clients down and leave them in some way disabled, disadvantaged and in distress'. (See also DEGENERATE INTERVENTION.)

The perverted intervention is viewed as coming from a COMPULSIVE need to transfer deep personal regressed trauma onto another as a way of alleviating the personal pain. This compulsive behaviour makes them less able to control themselves. However, there are others who intentionally plan to hurt others for the sake of hurting them and such people would be deemed amoral or even psychopathic.

Heron (1990) gives a detailed account of perverted interventions across all the six categories. An example of a perverted supportive intervention would be: 'affirming, supporting and encouraging the weak, distorted and corrupted behaviour of a person' (1990: 158).

phallic a phallic symbol is an object that resembles an erect penis. Traditionally, phallic symbols often relate to fertility and the generativity of nature. In contemporary vernacular usage, phallic can also refer to (male) behaviour that is thrusting or macho, oriented towards or glorifying the phallus.

There is also a phallic or genital stage in Freud's theory of PSYCHOSEXUAL DEVELOPMENT.

phenomenology phenomenology is a philosophical view that is interested in the way that each person experiences the world (see, for example, Spinelli 1989). It assumes that subjectivity of experience is important, and emphasizes the nature of experience before linguistic, conceptual labels are applied.

play it is in play that people are most likely to be spontaneous, uninhibited and expressive. The capacity to be playful is an important dimension of human nature. Personal development workshops frequently use playful activities, for purposes such as ENERGIZING and creative expression. *See also* GAMES.

There are various forms of play therapy, some but not all specifically for children. Virginia Axline, an associate of Carl Rogers, developed a form of CLIENT-CENTRED play therapy.

polarity response the habitual tendency of a person to respond with the opposite of an opinion or belief stated by another; or to move in the opposite direction to that in which another person is leading. The concept seems equivalent to COUNTER-DEPENDENCE; the phrase 'polarity response' is most often found in NLP, but writing on the subject is scant – Weaver (1985) is the main source cited.

politics of facilitation the politics of FACILITATION refers to the personal and role POWER of those who offer themselves as facilitators in relation to those who seek facilitation. The degree of decision-making shared by learners or participants is considered to influence them towards either self-EMPOWERMENT or OPPRESSION – a bi-polar construct that is the political dimension of facilitation.

Facilitator trainer AUTHORITY is of three types (Heron 1999: 21): 'cognitive authority, charismatic authority and political authority'. All are legitimate when used in co-operation with learners, when participants share in decisions about what is appropriate programme content, what will be assessed and how it will be assessed.

Inappropriate political authority arises when the facilitator acts from the belief that because they have cognitive authority they have the right to make all educational decisions, to direct or control the educational experience, and to assess unilaterally and demand conformity from participants.

Heron says: 'Balancing authoritative and facilitative interventions is all about the proper exercise of power; the practitioner's power over the client, the power shared by practitioner and client with each other, the autonomous power within the client. My own view is that these three forms of power need each other – always in due measure and ever changing ratios – to keep healthy' (Heron 1990: 6–7).

positive connotation positive connotation refers to regarding all 'symptoms' as somehow functional for, or beneficial to, the person or system in question.

The principle is that negative connotation, i.e. defining a behaviour as a problem, can generate resistance, particularly if the POSITIVE INTENTION or SECONDARY GAINS relating to the system are ignored. Positive connotation was a therapeutic technique of the Milan school of family systems therapy, who were influenced particularly by the work of Gregory Bateson (see PARADOXICAL INJUNCTION).

positive intention in NLP it is axiomatic that every action has, or had, a positive intent.

Having positive intentions for ourselves does not necessarily imply good behaviour to others. To assert that an action is positively intended is not to condone or excuse it, hence positive intention is not a judgement about what is useful or ethical. For example, a person may go shoplifting, with the positive intention of providing for their family's needs. Robert Dilts (1996) has addressed these and other contentious aspects.

The concept requires a distinction between an action and the intention of that action. From every action, some part of the person is assumed to derive some benefit. If the action is to be changed then an alternative way of providing the same benefit will be needed. A classic NLP technique that utilizes this principle is known as 'six step REFRAMING' (described, for example, in O'Connor & Seymour 1993: 131–34).

The notion of positive intention derived from MODELLING the work of Milton Erickson (Zeig and Munion 1999). Erickson worked from the assumption that even the most bizarre behaviour was the best option the individual had in the circumstances, and maintained a curiosity about the function of the behaviour (and possible alternatives) rather than becoming judgemental.

positive thinking *The Power of Positive Thinking* (Peale 1953) was one of the first books of the SELF-HELP genre. It expounds the view that it is more constructive to focus on the positive, or what we want, than on the negative, or what we wish to avoid.

This principle has been taken up in, for example, sports psychology (see REHEARSAL and VISUALIZATION) and many related personal development applications (see, for example, OUTCOME). Goleman (1996: 86–87) comments on the importance of hope and the real effects of one's EXPECTATIONS. On the other hand, if overdone positive thinking can become unrealistic, a form of DENIAL.

postmodernism there are different and disputed definitions of this term. In essence postmodernism represents a turning away from the idea that some absolute truth exists, and that a history is a progression towards a more complete understanding of the world.

Usher et al., considering the implications of postmodernism for adult education, say: 'The discourses and practices of modernity are characterized by an emphasis on progress and a faith in rationality and science as the means of its realization . . . Postmodernism enables a questioning of the scientific attitude and scientific method, of the universal efficacy of technical-instrumental reason, and of the stance of objectivity and value-neutrality in the making of knowledge claims' (Usher et al. 1997: 6–7).

The implications for personal development are, perhaps, an increased emphasis on questioning the nature of truth and progress purveyed by theories and practitioners.

power the concept of power is difficult to define and various usages can be found. It often has negative connotations, particularly in relation to politics or OPPRESSION, and the idea of controlling other people. In general power is taken to mean the capacity to influence other people, and/or the ability to get things done (see also EMPOWERMENT).

There are several meanings relevant to personal development. French and Raven's classic typology of sources of power is found in the field of organizational behaviour (see Buchanan and Huczynski 1997). There are five types available to people in work settings: reward (the power to grant or withhold rewards of various kinds); coercive (the power to punish); expert (specialist knowledge or expertise); legitimate (the AUTHORITY vested in one's ROLE); and referent (personal, often CHARISMATIC, qualities that lead others to accept one's influence).

'Personal power' has more SHAMANIC connotations, and has a central role in Carlos Castañeda's tales of sorcery and magical awareness (e.g. Castañeda 1974). This has influenced notions of resourcefulness and awareness found in NLP, for example.

Then there are practical and ethical issues of how practitioners and facilitators use their power. John Heron's framework of the POLITICS OF FACILITATION is helpful here. Power and other differences in the 'helping relationship' are inevitable and unavoidable, and potentially valuable as educational material – for example, an encounter

with issues of leader authority within an experiential workshop. Greater difficulties may be experienced with facilitators who proclaim themselves to be fully democratic, or who assure participants that they are sharing power. Facilitators typically have stocks of TACIT KNOWLEDGE about the content and process of working methods that participants do not possess and which it is impossible to share in order to equalize such relationships.

prejudice a strongly held BELIEF which may or may not be supported with evidence. As the word indicates, however, the belief is a pre-judgement, usually emotion-loaded, and therefore difficult to change even with presenting evidence. The prejudice may be positive or negative.

presence presence means being fully in the present with all your attention and energy; a state of being GROUNDED, intentionally aware and involved in a participative relationship with others, and CHARISMATIC through a sense of personal authority (e.g. Heron 1999: 215). It is an attribute that every person could cultivate to effect stillness, confidence and AUTHENTICITY in relationships. A high quality of presence indicates a strong degree of AUTONOMY in the helper or facilitator. Presence empowers self and others through modelling honest, in-the-present behaviour, and being attentive to the other as well as being open and aware of one's own inner STATE.

presenting problem the issue that the client, participant or student brings to the encounter to be solved. The concept is relevant in fields including psychotherapy and organizational consultancy. The presenting problem may be a symptom, a RATIONALIZATION and/or a defensive strategy masking an underlying more serious issue. The masking is usually unconscious and therefore the presenting problem needs to be taken seriously and addressed at the level offered, with an inner eye (or fourth ear – Rowan 1998: 161) to what might be behind it that also needs addressing.

Some clients may use the presenting problem intentionally as a smoke screen, fearful that exposure of the true self or true core crisis will lead to rejection. Presenting problems may be very mild, sometimes indicating that the client is minimizing the problem in the hope that he or will not be seen as a difficult case. Others may be more severe (e.g. self-harming), which is sometimes seen as challenging the potential helper to reject the client because they are too difficult or dangerous to work with (see Jacobs 1998).

presupposition in NLP, 'presupposition' refers both to a linguistic feature, and to an axiom of NLP (an epistemological presupposition).

According to NLP's model of language, 'presuppositions are what [are] necessarily true for the statements that the client makes to make sense (not to be true, but just to be meaningful) at all' (Bandler and Grinder 1975: 52). Bandler and Grinder give as an example (1975: 92) the statement 'I'm afraid that my son is turning out to be as lazy as my husband.' The presupposition here is 'My husband is lazy'. A list of forms of presupposition appears in the same book (Appendix B).

The epistemological axioms of NLP itself are derived substantially from the work of Gregory Bateson (e.g. 1979). Lists of NLP presuppositions typically include, for example:

- every limitation presented to you is a unique accomplishment by a human being
- there is no failure, only feedback
- the meaning of your communication is the response you get.

Robert Dilts (1998c) distils NLP presuppositions to two core principles: 'The map is not the territory'; and 'Life and mind are systemic processes.'

primal the pre-verbal emotional level of the personality is often referred to as the primal layer (Clarkson and Lapworth 1992: 63). Issues of bonding, ATTACHMENT and deprivation are most noticeable at this developmental stage. Working with primal issues focuses on that which is physiologically present – a person's fears, sadness, joy, rage and despair.

Arthur Janov, the founder of Primal Therapy, practised psychoanalysis in Los Angeles up until 1967. He reports that while giving therapy, 'an eerie scream welled up from the depths of the young man lying on the floor' (Janov 1973: 9). The effect of what became known as a primal scream was to change Janov's psychotherapy practice from cognitive analysis of people's neuroses to emotionally experiencing and re-experiencing major traumatic events that caused these neuroses.

Primal therapy encourages the person to work through emotional defences quickly to get to the primal scene itself, the primal pain that needs healing. For Janov, neurosis was a disease of feelings; therefore therapy started with breaking down psychological DEFENCES and working through various stages. These start with a pre-primal stage, when the person is encouraged to REGRESS to an earlier emotionally charged situation; then an accumulation of primal scenes which erupt into the high CATHARTIC primal scream stage; and finally the post-primal stage where the client regains childhood memories, integrates them into the present, and makes new interpretations about her- or himself and new positive decisions about her or his behaviour. This therapy is usually offered individually at first, followed by further regression therapy in a group. There is a London Association of Primal Psychotherapists (see Resources).

Primal Integration Therapy took applications of Janov's therapy and applied them in less controlling and more humanistic ways. Humanistic applications worked on the premise that the person did not need to be ill (neurotic) to gain healing from processing birth and infant trauma.

problem-based learning an approach to curriculum design that takes real (i.e. as experienced by the learner) problems of practice as a starting point.

Problem-based learning operates on the principle that 'learning takes place most effectively when students are actively involved and learn in the context in which knowledge is to be used' (Boud and Feletti 1997: 4). Boud and Feletti say that it originated in innovative approaches to teaching and learning in the health sciences in America.

Jarvis et al. (1998: 117) point out that problem-based learning may be seen as a variety of WORKPLACE LEARNING that is concerned with making 'learning in classrooms properly reflect the real world of work . . . Problem-based learning does not simply bring problem solving into a traditional curriculum based on disciplines. It builds a curriculum around key problems in professional practice.'

projection the fantasy of expelling a part of self (motives, attitudes and problems) unto another person and then disavowing that part, attributing it to the recipient. The projector is unaware of the projection and the recipient is often perceived as foreign, strange and frightening and therefore avoided (Ogden 1991: 35). In psychoanalytic theory, projection is a defensive mechanism in which the ego protects itself against the conflicts of the unconscious mind.

In interpersonal and group situations projections can be noted when one member gives another educational feedback (as in the 'hot seat' in GESTALT and ENCOUNTER GROUPS) only to find it triggers uncomfortable feelings in themselves. They gradually realize that the attribute or behaviour they requested the other to modify or stop is one they have denied in themselves. However, the projection may remain unconscious, so group feedback that starts with an acknowledgement of possible projections can help bring it to awareness. The disadvantage of this possibility is that experienced groupworkers may reject feedback, saying 'That's your stuff', rather than looking for the grain of truth which might be useful to them.

Ogden has written one of the most informative books on projective IDENTIFICATION as a particular psychological defence mechanism within the Object Relations School (from Melanie Klein's theory). Rowan (1998: 133) describes the two phenomena well, in that both projections and projective identification are the 'client's stuff', with projections disowned and projective identification held by the recipient. Both need to be offered back to the client at an appropriate time.

psyche from the Greek, meaning 'soul'. The concept of the psyche is central to Jung's theories about human existence. He believed that the psyche consisted of three levels: consciousness, the individual UNCONSCIOUS, and the COLLECTIVE UNCONSCIOUS. The collective unconscious contains material from ancestral experiences and phenomena, and is the true basis of the psyche.

Little of the psyche is accessible to rational consciousness. Its language is that of DREAMS, MYTHS, SYMBOLS, rituals and ARCHETYPAL fantasies. Jung believed archetypal forms were the ultimate foundation of the psyche itself, and that the psyche was the basis of all existence. He also held that its power to shape human affairs and the course of history was far greater than the human rational mind.

Jung perceived the psyche as distinct from the SOUL, and believed that it was not only a human phenomenon, but also expressed in other creatures. He warned that the over-valuing of the rational and the devaluing of the psychic material in Western culture could lead to disaster.

Jung's concept of the psyche shows his deep interest in the mysterious, the paradoxical and the unexplainable, and it is paradigmatic to his thought. This has been the basis of much criticism and rejection of his approach as being too mystifying and esoteric. It is perhaps ironic that modern psychology (which comes from the same linguistic root) has become almost exclusively concerned with the mental and behavioural dimensions of human experience.

psychic derived from PSYCHE, of or pertaining to the soul, mind and spirit.

Psychic (as an adjective) often refers to things outside the physical domain, often with connotations of the paranormal or supernatural. A 'psychic' is a person who has abilities in that domain. In some spiritual schools, such as Buddhism and Theosophy, it is held that at a certain phase of self-growth the individual becomes conscious of psychic forces. This is thought to present difficulties and its usage is often warned against.

However in personal development, as Ken Wilber suggests, 'Psychic does not necessarily mean paranormal although some texts suggest that certain paranormal events may more likely occur here. Rather it refers to psyche as a higher level of development than the rational mind per se' (Wilber 1996a: 246).

The term can also be used to denote the whole person's mind, body and spirit (e.g. 'psychic apparatus', or the usage 'psychic system' in TRANS-ACTIONAL ANALYSIS).

psychoanalysis according to Singer (1998) psychoanalysis is a reductionist approach in psychology and therapy in that it seeks the causes of a person's problems within the individual. It also breaks down the problems into parts, splitting the person up into conscious and unconscious elements and believing one can understand the whole by examination of some parts.

Psychoanalysis focuses its investigations on the unconscious as the seat of all disturbances. It works on the assumption that once the cause is brought into conscious awareness it should be possible to repair the damage by a process of integration. This can be a lengthy process, typically involving a TRANSFERENCE-laden relationship with the analyst.

Freud, the founding father of psychoanalysis was a physician and neurophysiologist who became a psychiatrist in Vienna between the first and second world wars. His own upbringing in a violent and turbulent Europe is said to have influenced his pessimistic view of human nature, including the instinctual drives for pleasure versus the death instinct. 'According to Freud, the history of man is the history of his repression' (Marcuse 1987: 11).

Freud went on to develop a personality theory that took account of this repression. The early theory focused on the antagonism between the libidinous, sexual energies and the ego (self-preservation) instinct. Later development was understood in terms of the struggle between Eros (the life instinct) and Thanatos (the death instinct). The descriptions of the ID, EGO and SUPER-EGO explain how these instincts are developed and controlled.

Psychoanalysis remains both controversial and influential. Freud's theories have been criticized in many respects and reappraised many times (e.g. Bettelheim 1985; Fromm 1982). Yet it is probably Freudian psychoanalysis that is associated most closely in the minds of the general public with psychotherapy and the inner workings of the mind. More than any other theory, Freud's ideas have become absorbed into popular culture through drama, film and literature (e.g. Peter Schaeffer's *Equus*; D.M. Thomas's *The White Hotel*, and many more), and particularly through the actual and symbolic role of the 'shrink' in America.

psychodrama an 'action method of group psychotherapy created and developed by J. L. Moreno' (Holmes and Karp 1991: 7). Moreno (1889–1974) is recognized by many as a pioneer of HUMANISTIC, existential therapeutic practice, and the originator of a wide range of ideas.

Psychodrama is a method of dramatic (re-)enactment of human encounters. 'The client does not speak separately of his life, he or she creates it through enactment, using part of the therapy room as stage area on which the specifics of that person's life are represented' (Holmes and Karp 1991: xiii).

Psychodrama is used as a therapeutic modality and as a working method in personal development workshops. Here it resembles ROLE-PLAY, but the latter is likely to be used in a more limited way, with principal emphasis on behavioural performance, in training-type settings. Psychodrama emphasizes the involvement of the whole person in human encounter.

Psychodrama is related to but distinct from dramatherapy, a recognized ARTS THERAPY. The American National Association for Dramatherapy (see Resources) says, 'Drama therapy is the systematic and intentional use of drama/theatre processes and products to achieve the therapeutic goals of symptom relief, emotional and physical integration, and personal growth.'

psychodynamic generally refers to an approach that looks at the motives, drives and needs that shape human behaviour. John Rowan (1998: 10) uses the term to denote approaches that invite people 'to explore those deep inner areas where early conflicts and early traumas are to be found'. This is a broad usage, as in this sense almost any form of psychotherapy could be described as psychodynamic.

Kurt Lewin used the term (in the form 'psychodynamics') to refer to his ideas about the energy and tensions of the psyche (see de Board 1978).

The term can also describe a partic-

ular approach to counselling and therapy that uses the conceptual apparatus of PSYCHOANALYSIS, and related models such as Melanie Klein's Object Relations, but differs in its practice (for example, by being more short-term, goal-orientated and interactive than psychoanalysis). By extension, 'psychodynamic' can indicate this set of concepts concerned with the internal dynamics of the psyche, particularly the UNCONSCIOUS, ANXIETY, DEFENCE mechanisms and TRANSFERENCE (de Board 1978).

psychological contract in addition to a formal employment contract, each person's relationship with their employer can be thought of as involving a 'psychological contract' (Rousseau 1995).

This is the set of expectations and values that a person has in mind when considering, for example, what they expect to give and receive to their job; what they perceive to be fair treatment; what they see as the organization's role in their career; and so on.

The concept can be extended to most types of relationship. The psychological contract is likely to be tacit: it is not explicitly negotiated between two parties. There will often be discrepancies and violations concerning people's sense of what is fair and equitable, and these will have real effects on commitment, loyalty and goodwill.

psychological functions the four basic modes whereby consciousness apprehends reality, i.e. sensation, FEELING, thinking and INTUITION. Significantly (Jung respected ASTROLOGY), the functions correlate closely with the four traditional astrological elements of water, air, earth and fire (see also TAROT). The words for the functions were given their specific psychological sense by Jung, following work by Schopenhauer, in his classic *Psychological Types* (Jung 1971).

The thinking function tells us what something is: it is rational, analytical, logical, precise, systematic and procedural; it draws logical inferences, and judges objectively in terms of true or false. The feeling function does not refer to emotion, but rather to a sensibility that discriminates and appreciates an object by the empathic feelings it evokes. The sensation function tells us simply that something is there: uncomplicatedly experiential, it relates to immediate concrete sensory perception, seeing the facts without judging them. Intuition, unconcerned with sensory data, goes beyond the immediately apprehended. Imaginative and psychically alert to insights, it can dream up novel solutions, grasp the meaning of things inwardly, and perceive connections and underlying patterns without mental steps or sufficient information.

Everyone has all four functions; however, each person typically has one that is (for them) much more efficient and easier to use, which Jung called the superior function. The function that is furthest from this natural lead function is the least accessible for the individual and liable to be infantile and troublesome, even powerfully disruptive; Jung termed it inferior. In brief, an individual's psychological type is determined by which of the two attitudinal orientations (INTROVERT or EXTROVERT) and which of the four functions he or she habitually employs. External pressures may modify the innate sequence, and so also – episodically – may developmental stages (Von Franz 1971). Jung's typology is much employed in modern psychological tests such as the MYERS-BRIGGS TYPE INDICATOR. Jung restricted himself to the eight basic types (extroverted thinking, etc.), which in most cases, is probably an adequate delineation.

psychological type see PSYCHOLOGICAL FUNCTIONS.

psychologism a psychologistic explanation of experience or events privileges a psychological perspective over other (e.g. sociological, ideological, political) frames of reference. The term is defined by Graeme Salaman in relation to the study of work organizations as follows: 'When the structure of organization is regarded as the result of neutral principles and pressures (not ideologies and interests), events within the organization, and individuals' positions and experiences, must be seen as the result of members' attitudes, abilities and competence. The structure of the organization is given; therefore what must be changed, if change is desired or necessary, is members' behaviours. This excessive emphasis on the individual as responsible for organizational performance, I call *psychologism*'. (Salaman 1979: 202).

The significance here is of how problems come to be defined as issues of 'personal development', and whether this is justified. Psychologism can make problems appear necessarily to be the responsibility of the individual person, or amenable to change by the individual. Examples are rife in the literature of self-improvement, and areas such as the management of change – where, for example, unsuccessful change may be attributed to individuals' failure to 'love' change sufficiently, regardless of economic and other structural dimensions of the issue. In therapy, a therapist may 'psychologize' a client or their issue when they ignore power relations and insist on (say) dreamwork.

psychology 'Psychology', said William James, one of the first scholars of psychology in 1890, 'is the science of mental life', where mental life was considered to denote the human mind or spirit. Psychology is an offshoot of philosophy, and the study of the PSYCHE (including the nature of consciousness, mental life and the causes of behaviour) became a discipline in its own right from the beginning of the 1900s.

Psychology was initially an introspective study, of which PSYCHOANALYSIS is a good example. It became more an empirical and experimental science and simultaneously a behavioural science from the 1920s to the 1950s, starting with Pavlov and his dogs, through to Skinner's (1938) BEHAVIOURISM. Memory, PERCEPTION, and all types of sensory and behavioural experiences, individual and group, which could be observed, manipulated and measured were subject to laboratory investigation. At its peak in the 1950s, most experimental psychologists considered that any study of the mind that was unamenable to scientific manipulation was irrelevant.

A reaction against psychoanalysis and behaviourism helped create what became the 'third force' in psychology, HUMANISTIC PSYCHOLOGY (Maslow 1970). This aimed to place the whole person back at the centre of psychology.

Psychology remains a strong academic and professional discipline, using primarily behavioural and cognitive theories, and working in domains from the clinical to the occupational. A recent development has seen a fourth 'force', TRANSPERSONAL PSYCHOLOGY, become a division of the mainstream profession in the British Psychological Society.

psychometrics psychometric tests aim to measure individual psychological TRAITS. They are used frequently in recruitment, careers counselling, ASSESSMENT CENTRES, and training. A caution is if they rely on expert interpretation or are used to make psychological judgements more than to provide information to the person for their own development. A very wide range of tests and profiles is available, some recognized and validated as psychological instruments. Many profiles do not seek or claim academic or professional validity, but exist to provide helpful feedback and insight.

psychosexual development Freud (e.g. Freud 1923) defined child development from retrospective stories from his adult clients. His theory is based on sexual instincts and how he perceived children to navigate what he considered the dangerous journey of unconsciously driven sexual development. The stages are related to erogenous zones, which provide the child with sexual gratification at different ages.

The stages are, first, the ORAL STAGE (sucking and biting phase, 0–18 months); the ANAL STAGE (18 months to 3 years); the PHALLIC (genital) stage, with its Oedipal COMPLEX and (supposed) fear of penile castration in boys and penile envy in girls (age 3–5 years); the latency period (age 6–12 years) – not explained in Freudian theory apart from stating that with resolution of previous stages, the child can concentrate on other developments, such as psychosocial and cognitive development; and finally the stage of adult genital sexuality (age 12+ years).

For Freudians, if the previous developmental stages have been traversed in a healthy manner, the sexual instincts lie dormant under the developed control of the SUPEREGO.

Erik Erikson built on this model of development with his notion of the LIFE CYCLE.

psychosomatic literally, BODYMIND, from the Greek *psyche* and *soma*. Refers in general usage to symptoms that are considered mental rather than physical in origin, and sometimes used to discount the significance or reality of the symptom. In this respect, some see orthodox medicine as holding the contradictory view that the body can be treated in isolation from the mind and the emotions (thus denying the bodymind principle), while accepting that the mind can produce physical symptoms.

psycho-spiritual education a label used in some places to refer to programmes of study intended to develop PSYCHIC abilities and spiritual awareness (e.g. Soskin 1996). Psycho-spiritual education is seen as a process of connecting to, or drawing out, the inner being or HIGHER SELF, which is seen to be largely cloaked by the outer PERSONA, or Lower Self. Acknowledgement of the Higher Self is thought to enable dissolution of imbalance in emotional, physical or mental layers. This begins a process of spiritual unfoldment, towards SELF-AWARENESS and growth.

Such studies typically have their roots in a combination of Eastern and Western mystical traditions, modern psychology, and psychic and spiritual development. The approach has some similarities with TRANSPERSONAL PSYCHOLOGY. However, transpersonal psychology takes into account the spiritual aspect of individuals and operates primarily in psychotherapeutic and counselling modes (see, for example, Rowan 1993). Psycho-spiritual studies aim to encompass spiritual, psychic and healing practices.

Psychosynthesis Roberto Assagioli founded Psychosynthesis in the early 1900s to provide a more inclusive model and a more intuitive methodology than PSYCHOANALYSIS offered. It became popular in the 1970s and is known for its creative use of the IMAGINATION, as well as its emphasis on SPIRITUALITY and WILL (see Assagioli 1965, 1975a, 1975b; Hardy 1989).

Psychosynthesis suggests that when human beings are able to cultivate a 'Dis-identified I' (free themselves from the contents of their consciousness through developing awareness) they realize that their lives are both aspirational and purposive, and become more available to the influence of the Superconscious (see ASSAGIOLI'S EGG). They are then more able to integrate the elements of their personalities and substitute more appropriate behaviours.

Assagioli developed methodologies pioneered by Freud, Jung and Desoille, as well as meditative techniques from his interest in the spiritual life. The Egg Diagram attempts to offer a complete picture of consciousness, and its understanding of the Journey of the Soul points towards an EXISTENTIAL and spiritual conception of the dynamics of human life.

In recent years Psychosynthesis has remained popular, and in needing to articulate a professional and practical psychotherapy it has integrated aspects of other approaches. It remains unique in its powerful psychology of context and will.

psychotherapy originally known as the 'talking cure', psychotherapy emerged from Sigmund Freud's practice as an alternative to physical treatments of mental illness. Psychotherapy is one form of personal development and help for the human condition, which in the UK claims professional status.

It can be helpful to distinguish psychotherapy (as a generic term for various modes of practice) both from PSYCHOANALYSIS, which is the particular practice founded by Freud, and from psychiatry. The latter is a medical specialism in the UK, whereas in the USA a psychiatrist is in effect equivalent to a psychoanalyst in the UK (see Rowan 1998: 17).

Psychotherapy (see Feltman and Horton 2000) is considered as an appropriate method of help for many kinds of problems. It is a non-clinical, growth-oriented activity, 'an intentional and committed process of personal development' (Rowan 1993: 98). Thus being in psychotherapy can be a developmental choice, and certainly does not mean that a client necessarily has any particular clinical or mental problems.

There are many different schools of psychotherapy, including those who follow mainly Freud, Jung, or some of their disciples. Among these are the PSYCHOSYNTHESIS school of Roberto Assagioli, GESTALT Therapy, TRANSACTIONAL ANALYSIS, RATIONAL-EMOTIVE

THERAPY and NEURO-LINGUISTIC PROGRAMMING. What all of these have in common is that they seek to enable people who are distressed to understand the sources of their pain, and/or help them to find their own internal resources so that healing or growth takes place. Most schools of psychotherapy believe that every person has the necessary coping skills, but may need some kind of helpful relationship to enable these to come to the fore.

There have been some useful and challenging critiques to psychotherapy in recent years, such as Masson (1992), and James Hillman and Michael Ventura's (1992) wonderfully titled *We've Had a Hundred Years of Psychotherapy and the World's Getting Worse*.

quantum developments in quantum physics during the 20th century led to commentary (e.g. Capra 1992; Penrose 1994) on the apparently increasing convergence of current notions about the material world and consciousness. This metaphor of the 'quantum' nature of consciousness and humanity has been popularized by authors such as Chopra (1990).

The possibility that the universe is organized on holographic principles has stimulated many writers on personal development (e.g. Houston 1982). It indicates possibilities for understanding phenomena of consciousness that a science predicated on a linear, mechanistic view of the universe seems unable to provide.

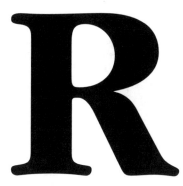

racket system from TRANSACTIONAL ANALYSIS, more recently called the script system.

Erskine and Zalcman (1979) who developed the model, say: 'The racket system is defined as a self reinforcing, distorted system of feelings, thoughts and actions maintained by script bound individuals, and has three inter-related and interdependent components: the Script Beliefs and Feelings, the Rackety Displays and the Reinforcing Memories' (Erskine and Zalcman 1979: 51).

Rackets are self-reinforcing psychological processes. The existential LIFE POSITION will determine whether the person will act out a racket of Victim, Persecutor or Rescuer (see also DRAMA TRIANGLE). The script system is not the same as the SCRIPT (which is a child's decision about how he or she will be in the world). The script is the decision, the script system explains how the script is maintained and what the maintenance process is. The link between rackets and the script is that the racket/script system acts as fuel to keep the script alive.

The system is a spiralling negative feedback loop where a current event (for example, being made redundant, even with a golden handshake) could catapult the person into a depressive state, coming from a life position of 'I'm not OK', to feeling rejected (inter-nal state), isolating her- or himself from friends who are still working (observable behaviour) and fantasizing about being rescued, which does not happen.

The person then uses this event (current memory of redundancy) to link back to all the other times (old emotional memories) that she or he has been left out of things (such as not having lots of boy/girlfriends, and not being picked first for school games, to not being her/his parents' favourite child). Fantasies of being emotionally rescued lodge in the memory as if real. The script system feeds the script decision of 'I'm not loveable', with the main injunctions from parents being 'Don't be close' and 'Don't trust (others).'

rapport a harmonious and trusting relationship between people. Rapport is a basis for much personal development practice, particularly following Carl Rogers' emphasis on EMPATHY. It is taught specifically in NLP. For example, O'Connor and Seymour (1993: 234) describe rapport as 'the process of establishing and maintaining a relationship of mutual trust and understanding between two or more people, the ability to generate responses from another person.'

The early work of Bandler and Grinder (1979) identified ways in which skilled communicators generated rapport. The process relies on matching, for example, body posture (see MIRRORING), voice patterns, breathing, and/or the REPRESENTATIONAL SYSTEM of the person with whom one is interacting. This is considered to happen naturally between people who are good friends. NLP encourages people to be aware of this dimension of interaction, hopefully without using it mechanistically to engineer responses. Rapport is considered an initial foundation for a productive interaction.

rational-emotive behaviour therapy a form of therapy developed by American clinical psychologist Albert Ellis (see Yankura and Dryden 1994) in the 1950s. Unlike most HUMANISTIC approaches, rational-emotive behaviour therapy (REBT) is primarily a cognitive approach. Originally it was probably humanistic more in its intentions for the client – that they should be assisted to achieve their goals and realize their potential – than in Ellis's reportedly highly directive style.

Ellis's central principle was that people experience the world according to their BELIEFS, and that thought, emotion and behaviour are closely related. The implication is that many problems are the result of beliefs, rules and expectations that people have constructed themselves, including, for example, SELF-FULFILLING PROPHECIES. In other words, people are literally the authors of their own disappointments (see Rowan 1998: 107).

The rational-emotive approach continues to be used widely in counselling (Dryden 1999). The approach generally seeks to identify, confront and revise irrational and self-defeating thoughts, and does not concern itself with the source of such thoughts in actual past events.

rationalizing finding a reason for something, explaining away a statement or behaviour by putting forward reasons for its occurrence, perhaps in order to excuse inappropriate behaviour, defuse conflict, or DEFLECT attention

from its possible significance.

More generally, the culture of the HUMAN POTENTIAL movement is sceptical of people who tend to intellectualize problems, who may be considered too much 'in their heads'.

reality the question 'What is reality?' is of course a perennial philosophical issue. In relation to personal development, it is often taken that whatever the person defines or experiences as real **is** real to them. This does not imply an extreme subjectivist or solipsistic view. Reason (1994), for example, summarizes a view of a participatory universe, which is neither wholly objective nor wholly subjective.

Different theories and traditions within personal development are likely to embody particular views on the nature of reality, which may define the developmental agenda of that mode. For example, a typical BUDDHIST view is that the world we experience is entirely illusory, with contemplation offering the route to ENLIGHTENMENT.

According to NLP each person operates according to their 'map of the world', and as Alfred Korzybski stated, 'The map is not the territory.' NLP's approach is to encourage people to increase the choices available in their map of the world, rather than to attempt to change 'outer reality', which is likely to be self-defeating.

As John Heron remarks, recent years have seen an increasing emphasis on the notion of creating one's own reality. He says: 'New-age populists speak a great deal of creating your own reality. In doing so they sometimes exploit the ambiguity of the phrase in irresponsible ways and do not pause to clarify what it does and does not mean. It clearly does not mean creating any old world that suits your fancy. It is not a formula for omnipotent solipsism except in the minds of the deranged. There is no such thing as my own reality in any absolute and exclusive sense of ownership and possession. For reality is essentially public and shared; it depends on a consensual view of its status and credentials. I can have a distinct and idiosyncratic perspective on this shared reality, but this purely personal view is interdependent with the public account' (1992: 249).

rebelling rebellious behaviour can have positive and negative aspects. Adolescence is a time when many people learn to rebel against authority, and this can be seen as effectively a normal developmental stage. Rebellion can also cut through unhealthy levels of CONFORMITY, and challenge OPPRESSION. In this case, rebellion can be a powerful political tool to bring about radical change in law or oppose tyrannical regimes.

Where it is a more COMPULSIVE or automatic behaviour, rebelliousness is related to a PASSIVE-AGGRESSIVE stance (Tilney 1998). Resistance to performing may be demonstrated through stubbornness, forgetfulness, deliberate inefficiency and procrastination. Rebellious behaviour may involve swinging from being very judgemental to seeking parental nourishment.

In TRANSACTIONAL ANALYSIS, the concept of the Rebellious Child is an important manifestation of the Child EGO STATE. It is as though the child has learned that he or she can receive more STROKES (recognition and attention) by doing the opposite to what the parent wants him or her to do. Adults who regress to Child behaviour often show the same non-constructive characteristics, such as rule-breaking at work and driving well over the speed limit, hoping not to get caught 'by the system' at one level yet also being highly critical of a system that does not seem to police effectively.

rebirthing rebirthing uses a form of BREATHING technique (circular breathing) to increase sensory (kinaesthetic) awareness and allow for deep body relaxation. The method was developed by Leonard Orr in the early 1970s and became very popular in the USA and Europe (Leonard and Laut 1983).

It involves re-experiencing your own birth, based on the theory that the trauma of being born can remain within the body at different layers, and needs to be released. The particular breathing techniques are often accompanied by deep CATHARSIS indicating the release of body-bound traumas. The hoped-for outcome is the healing of long-standing physical or emotional difficulties.

While rebirthing is said to be a SELF-HELP technique, the beginner is actively encouraged to undergo training in the technique and facilitation of their psychological processes with a trained Rebirther for up to twenty sessions. Psychological support in the initial stages of rebirthing is advocated as it is considered a powerful personal development process. Rebirthing can be done 'dry' or in water, much like a birthing pool or bath, in which case it is done under supervision (see also Begg 1999; Dowling 2000). There is a British Rebirthing Society (see Resources).

reflection reflection in the context of adult learning means looking back on (or, metaphorically, holding up a mirror to) experience in order to consider its meaning and potential learning. In Kolb's EXPERIENTIAL LEARNING CYCLE it is the stage that enables learning to emerge from experience.

Boud et al. (1985) have studied reflection in detail, and emphasize that reflection is 'not a single-faceted concept . . . but a generic term which acts as a shorthand description for a number of important ideas and activities' (1985: 8). They have put forward a three-stage model of:
1. returning to experience
2. attending to feelings
3. re-evaluating experience.
See also REFLECTIVE PRACTITIONER.

reflective practitioner Donald Schön's concept of the self-developing professional practitioner, who uses reflection-in-action to monitor and modify their practice. This is achieved through application of principles of 'action science', which Schön developed with Chris Argyris.

Schön comments on reflection-in-action as follows: 'Both ordinary people and professional practitioners often think about what they are doing, sometimes even while doing it. Stimulated by surprise, they turn thought back on action and on the knowing which is implicit in action . . . There is some puzzling, or troubling, or interesting phenomenon with which the individual is trying to deal. As he tries to make sense of it, he also reflects on the understandings which have been implicit in his action, understandings which he surfaces, criticizes, restructures, and embodies in further action. It is this entire process of reflection-in-action which is central to the "art" by which practitioners sometimes deal well with situations of uncertainty, instability, uniqueness, and value conflict' (Schön 1983: 50).

Schön's is a widely-known model of professional learning. It is not without its critics. Usher et al. (1997) contend that Schön's examples lack REFLEXIVITY and tend to emphasize a technicist approach to professional learning – in other words, one concerned with pragmatic effectiveness more than critical reflection. Bill Torbert's ACTION INQUIRY is a variant that has some significant differences.

reflexivity specifically, application of a concept or practice to itself, or to oneself (as reader/author/proponent). More broadly, the practice of examining ideas and practices for the nature of the assumptions and beliefs embedded within them, recognizing that theories and practices themselves construct reality. In education, 'to work reflexively is to enquire as to who is enabled to speak by the educational milieu and who is silenced by it' (Reynolds 1997b: 323).

Reflexivity is in one sense a feature of SELF-AWARENESS. Thus reflexivity concerns the capacity to be aware of our own motivations, assumptions, thoughts and feelings simultaneously with acting in the world. Usually reflexivity is seen as more searching than REFLECTION.

In another, related sense, reflexivity refers to the way in which language is not a neutral description of the world, but constitutes a way of perceiving and knowing. There is no knowing or understanding that is separate from the world itself; in this sense perception and language are self-referential.

See also CRITICAL REFLECTION.

reframing the process of reframing involves an event or action being assigned to a different category or setting, thereby effecting a change in meaning. The new category or setting is the frame, which needs to fit the 'facts' of the same problematic concrete situation, yet alter its meaning, and therefore the response of the individual to it. According to Watzlawick et al. (1974) meaning is the product of the ways in which events have been thought about.

Bandler and Grinder (1982) developed the use and techniques of reframing in NLP. Like Watzlawick, they believe that all therapeutic change involves reframing, in which the client undergoes a profound shift in his or her perception of originally problematic events in their lives. Such shifts involve a re-ordering of information, bringing about a change in perception. Bandler and Grinder hold that the way in which the therapist or counsellor uses language can profoundly influence how such changes are made. A problematic situation may be reframed as a challenge, or other meanings sought, which are congruent with the client's worldview.

The idea that in using language we automatically assign events to categories means that counsellors who are careful listeners, and understand the relationships between language and the making of meaning, are able to make powerful reframes for their clients. Reframing is part of the basic approach in BRIEF THERAPY.

regression in personal development, regression means re-entering a previous phase of life, usually childhood. However, even a three-year-old child will show signs of regressing to a younger pre-verbal age if very excited or traumatized. Most psychological GAMES (in Transactional Analysis terms) are played out from an unconscious regressed state.

Regression per se has a positive or negative value depending on whether it is consciously intended and whether the experience is welcomed or seen to be effective. In many forms of personal development work, clients are invited to go back to a previous event which has emotional impact and which has left the client feeling 'unfinished'. The intention is to help the client get in touch with the feelings associated with the event and work with those feelings for psychological healing.

Regression therapy developed out of Janov's work on PRIMAL therapy, with basically the same therapeutic intention, although the methodology differs. Laing (1983), while an advocate of regression work, was insistent that for regression to be therapeutic it had to include recession. By this he meant that going back should also involve going deeper into the unconscious experience. So the regression is not just chronological (as in stage hypnotherapy) but deep into the psyche for the purpose of understanding and healing.

The most important part of all regression therapy is the integration and acceptance of the past into who we are in the present.

rehearsal actual or mentally imagined rehearsal of a performance of some kind. For example, people typically rehearse (go through in their minds) what they are going to say in a difficult encounter.

This process can be done intentionally and systematically, as described by Robert Dilts: 'Mental rehearsal relates to our ability to practise a process or activity in our minds. In NLP, mental rehearsal is used to strengthen or improve behavioral performance, cognitive thinking patterns and internal states. When applied to behavioral performance, mental rehearsal involves creating internal representations, in the form of images, sounds and feelings, of some behavior or performance we desire to enact or improve (as an actor might silently rehearse lines for a play)' (Dilts 1998b).

Mental rehearsal (a slight misnomer, as the rehearsal is by no means purely cognitive) is used extensively in sports psychology. It is reckoned by some that mental rehearsal can be as effective as actual practice (see VISUALIZATION). Rehearsal in the sense of practice at behaviours and interactions is used in ROLE-PLAY.

Reiki Reiki is the name given to a system of energy channelling and healing that originates from the work of Dr Mikao Usui (1864–1926), a Japanese teacher who is believed to have studied the healing methods described in the Buddhist Lotus Sutras and Christian teaching. There are many similarities between Reiki and a Tibetan Buddhist healing technique involving an empowerment being transmitted from teacher to student.

The term Reiki comes from the two kanji (pictograms) used to represent it: *Rei*, translated as 'universal, transcendental spirit, a boundless essence'; and *Ki*, translated as 'life force energy'. The energy is consistent with the *chi* energy of Chinese medicine, and *prana*, found in Hindu teaching and YOGA. This energy is present in all living things.

Reiki teaching suggests that the ability to increase the availability of Ki to self and others is inherent, although often latent, in all people. The process of re-awakening and increasing the ability to channel energy is undertaken through a series of ATTUNEMENTS that balance and heighten the vibratory frequencies of the CHAKRAS. Guidance is also given as to how the energy can be channelled and interpreted. See McKenzie (1998) and Quest (1999).

rejection the breaking or denial of emotional ties, rejection – whether by a lover, by peers, or others – is typically a very distressing human experience that may impact significantly on SELF-ESTEEM. Fear of rejection is common in many contexts, though there is little written specifically on the subject. Some self-help books deal with rejection in personal relationships; and in business, sales personnel are often trained in how to deal with rejection. It is possible for a person to reject a part of his or her own self.

Kohut (1984: 192) states that the child has three basic needs that must be fulfilled if the self is to develop fully. These are the need to be mirrored, the need to idealize and the need to be like others. The first of these just does not happen if the child experiences rejection, and this then adversely effects the other needs too.

relationship generally refers to a patterned and usually well established, non-transient interaction between a person and another person, or between a person and some other feature of the world (e.g. 'my relationship with money'). See also I–THOU.

In personal development generally, relationships – with partners, family, friends, work colleagues and so on – are often the focus (see, for example, GENDER). This is particularly so in forms of COUPLE THERAPY and family therapy, where the practitioner typically works with the live process of relating. The relationship between therapist or counsellor and client is also the subject of much writing in the field (see, for example, Rowan 1998).

Many modes of therapy and theories of human development consider that patterns of relationship learnt in early childhood are crucial to psychological and emotional health in later life.

The word 'relationship' is a NOMINALIZATION, which means it can appear to be a 'thing' rather than a dynamic process. Gregory Bateson emphasized the error of seeing the world as consisting of separate 'relata' (people, objects, etc.), and the neces-sity of perceiving dynamic relationships or circuits.

In this systemic way of thinking, there are two fundamental patterns of relating, symmetry and complementarity. Bateson said: 'I applied the term *symmetric* to all those forms of interaction that could be described in terms of competition, mutual emulation and so on (i.e., those in which A's action of a given kind would stimulate B to action of the same kind, which, in turn, would stimulate A to further similar actions . . .). In contrast, I applied the term *complementary* to interactional sequences in which the actions of A and B were different but mutually fitted each other (e.g. dominance-submission, exhibition-spectatorship, dependence-nurturance)' (Bateson 1979: 208).

relaxation a state in which the person is free of unnecessary emotional and physical tension. Many techniques are designed to assist relaxation – see, for example, MEDITATION and AUTOGENICS. Also many BODYMIND methods will produce or enhance states of relaxation. Many SELF-HELP sources exist, such as the enduringly popular (but one hopes ironically titled) *Relaxation and Stress Reduction Workbook* (Davis et al. 2000).

representational system refers in NLP to how we code information internally into one or more of the five sensory systems. Visual, Auditory, Kinaesthetic (touch) are the three main representational systems, plus Olfactory (smell) and Gustatory (Taste). So not only do our five senses perceive the world, but also representations of those senses are used internally to store information.

Representational systems are reflected in language. In NLP, a phrase like 'I see what you mean' is taken as a literal report of the person's internal experience. In other words, this person is probably making sense through an internal visual image (though not necessarily consciously or intentionally).

Each of us tends to prefer one of the senses, and this preferred sense is called the lead system. A person with a visual preference, in these terms, may use phrases such as 'get into focus', 'wanting clarity', 'looking ahead to a bright future'. By contrast a person with a kinaesthetic preference will use terms such as 'feeling heavy', 'wanting to get a grip on things', and 'being comfortable' with the way things are going. Bandler and Grinder's early work (e.g. Grinder and Bandler 1976) identified a spontaneous ability in excellent communicators to respond with the language of the same representational system of their clients, so contributing to RAPPORT.

The preferred representational system is also reflected in external behaviour such as voice tone, posture, breathing and gestures, an illustration of NLP's assumption that mind and body, thought and behaviour, operate as a whole, connected system.

repression repression is an unconscious psychological DEFENCE mechanism. It involves repressing aspects of memory, desires and emotions considered to be too dangerous for survival. Freud emphasized the dilemma of repression by stating that human life was full of intense, persistent conflict and that there was a need to repress many of our most basic instincts to function as social beings, hence the existence of the SUPEREGO. However, he also stated that excessive repression created most of the problems his patients experienced. The main focus of PSYCHOANALYSIS is to bring out the repressed material of the unconscious mind for analysis and healing.

rescuing sometimes referred to as 'Red Crossing', rescuing means to do something for somebody else who you believe cannot do it for him or herself. Therefore rescuing refers to a psychological role position of Rescuer (see DRAMA TRIANGLE) rather than a real-life, legitimate role with a real-life need for help.

All forms of psychological rescuing constitute a DISCOUNT of the other person's ability to manage their own affairs, be these feelings, behaviour, finance or life in general. Part of the discounting is a grandiosity, that is, that the Rescuer can do better than the Victim. By implication, rescuing involves an invitation into a symbiotic relation: Rescuers need Victims and Victims need Rescuers or Persecutors, and many long-term relationships are established and maintained as long as this PSYCHOLOGICAL CONTRACT is maintained.

resentment Fritz Perls saw GUILT as projected resentment, and thus suggested that an individual's feeling of guilt would disappear if they could identify what they resented (Kovel 1978: 170).

resistance the opposition of one part of a system to change in the system.

Resistance can happen at an intrapsychic level (one part of the self opposes therapeutic change) or at a social level (e.g. a group of staff resist organizational change).

Management consultant Peter Block says: 'Resistance is a predictable, natural, emotional reaction against the process of being helped and against the process of having to face up to difficult organizational problems' (1981: 113).

The term 'resistance' has negative connotations, and it is often the case that resistance is defined from the perspective of the agent that desires change to happen. Various consulting and personal change approaches would counsel strongly against attempts to 'overcome' resistance, and instead would suggest inquiring into the needs and intentions of the 'resistant' part.

In NLP, for example, it is assumed that a part that objects has a POSITIVE INTENTION, and may well have important information about the wisdom of the change for the whole organism (see ECOLOGY), or about some action (e.g. honouring or acknowledging the past) that will help the change to be accepted.

responsibility in GESTALT, Perls reframed responsibility as response-ability, so it was not about duty or obligation (see SHOULDS) but about the ability to respond, to choose, and to act. Responsibility is therefore a key EXISTENTIAL capacity of the healthy individual.

'When we lose touch with the existential truth of our own responsibility, we become alienated from our existence; we seek to blame or praise others for what we do and credit or discredit ourselves for what others do . . . Perls did not mean by this that the individual is personally responsible for all situations in which he finds himself . . . However, he is still actively responsible for how he lives out his life in this environment. For example, Frankl has described . . . how his fellow prisoners in concentration camps remained active in the meaning they gave to their lives, even though they were usually unable to change the bitter circumstances in which they existed' (Clarkson and Mackewn 1993: 61).

The more extreme version referred to by Clarkson and Mackewn, i.e. suggesting that each individual has total responsibility for their fate and circumstances, is espoused in some forms of LARGE GROUP AWARENESS TRAINING such as EST.

re-stimulation this usually refers to emotional re-stimulation or memory re-stimulation, which results in the person re-experiencing the emotion of a particular event.

Re-stimulation may be joyous as well as distressed, as when a mother of teenage children sees or hears another young child's laughter, and re-experiences the joy of her own children laughing at that age. However, most writers address the re-stimulation of old traumas that may become inappropriately displaced into distorted behaviour. Therapeutic care requires being sufficiently aware around events that may re-stimulate trauma, and finding a safe place and the means to discharge the DISTRESS, re-integrate the experience, and gain insights into how archaic distress is still held in the mind-body. CO-COUNSELLING and other forms of cathartic work are intended to reduce re-stimulation of distress (see Heron 1992: 214).

retroflection a process of turning energy in on oneself rather than expressing it outwardly. Retroflected anger is common, when a person becomes angry with themselves rather than directing it towards the person or event that stimulated the anger, usually out of fear of reprisal. Another form of retroflection arises when we do to ourselves what we would like from others. So instead of asking for nurturing from others we might nurture ourselves, through smoking or drinking. Retroflection is a blocking tactic identified in GESTALT theory, a type of BOUNDARY disturbance that avoids here-and-now CONTACT with others (Sills et al. 1995).

rite of passage a rite of passage is a ceremony or other ritual marking a significant transition from one status to another (e.g. birth, adulthood, death).

The term 'rites de passages' was coined by French anthropologist Arnold van Gennep in 1909 (see Holm and Bowker 1994). He argued that the structure of rites from various sources is characterized by three phases of separation, transition, and reincorporation. This closely resembles the three stages of TRANSITION and of the HEROIC QUEST.

Examples of rites of passage are found in all known societies. They include weddings, graduation ceremonies, funerals and so on. In contemporary Western society, such rites of passage have become less marked or less significant, especially for those who do not belong to religious or spiritual communities. In adult life, the career is often the most prominent context in which we experience changes of status. Personal development may also provide many people with the sense of purpose and meaning that often appears to missing from modern society – as evidenced, for example, by the burgeoning interest in SPIRITUALITY and spiritual traditions.

rituals rituals generally are patterned events or interactions with identifiable social or cultural significance. They may be very formalized (as in religious services) or informal. In organizational behaviour, a ritual is defined as 'a repetitive sequence of activities which expresses and reinforces the key ideas, values, beliefs and norms of the company' (Buchanan and Huczynski 1997: 523). Rituals of various kinds can be used in groupwork (see Heron 1999), for example, to open up the transpersonal dimension.

In TRANSACTIONAL ANALYSIS theory, rituals represent one type of TIME STRUCTURING. Rituals are familiar social interactions (transactions) where the psychological risk, although higher than in WITHDRAWAL, is still very low. The interactions are 'safe' accepted social norms, such as mutual greetings, the 'proper way' to behave at business meetings and so on. STROKES are mutual and low risk in terms of 'getting it wrong' or fear of rejection.

role role is a complex, core concept of social psychology and organizational behaviour, among other disciplines (see, for example, Buchanan and Huczynski 1997). It is important in many approaches to personal development. See also GROUP ROLES.

The concept of role is, as the term suggests, a dramatic metaphor, denoting the part or social function that a person occupies. The concept of role is core to PSYCHODRAMA. We all play many roles in life. Some we think of as part of our IDENTITY, such as being a father or mother. Our job is an occupational role. Other roles are marked as temporary, such as being a participant in a training course.

While we shape the way we play our roles, we are also influenced by the EXPECTATIONS and norms that roles attract, as well as the constellation of complementary roles (for example, trainer and participant) with which the role interacts (known as the 'role set'). Often these expectations and norms operate as assumptions that we are unaware of until they are transgressed. For example, the actions of Robin Williams's character in the film *Dead Poets' Society* may be seen as problematic for the school more because they violated norms and expectations about the roles of teachers and pupils, and so threatened the social order, than because of their inherent intent. A classic analysis of the enacted nature of social life is Erving Goffman's *Presentation of Self in Everyday Life* (1959).

Sometimes in personal development it appears that roles and some notion of the 'authentic self' are set in opposition, as if roles are barriers to or distractions from AUTHENTICITY. This is a problematic view. Undoubtedly roles can be used as masks (see PERSONA), and everyone has experienced the sense of artificiality and constraint this can bring. But it is contentious to argue that roles are either undesirable or could be avoided. An alternative view is that we each perform variable roles according to the context in which we find ourselves. Whilst we may retain a sense of a 'core SELF', social roles enable different facets of our identity to be expressed.

role model originally, a person who is an example (or in the opinion of others, should be an example) for others in similar roles in society. By extension this has come to refer to any iconic public figure whom others might aspire to be. Thus footballers such as David Beckham, and pop stars such as the Spice Girls, are often called 'role models', sometimes as if to admonish them because of the likelihood that children will imitate their behaviour.

role-play a training and education format in which participants take specified roles to rehearse or act out an interaction. Used to practice particular skills (e.g. assertiveness); to explore interactions from inside the shoes of other actors, and so to increase empathetic understanding of others' experience; and to explore options for handling a given scenario. Thus it may lead to attitudinal and/or behavioural change, as well as promote SELF-AWARENESS. A current practical guide is Bolton et al. (1997).

Role-play has the advantage that participants can experience the behavioural and emotional dimensions of the issue. While the situations are simulated, the whole person can be engaged. This is used as a therapeutic process in PSYCHODRAMA, from which role-play derives.

In practice people often feel uncomfortable with role-play's performative aspects and apparent artificiality. It is a powerful tool for experiential learning that needs careful preparation and sensitive facilitation.

scapegoat a person who is made to carry the blame, or (metaphorically) the sins of others. The term 'scapegoat' derives from Old Testament sources. On the Day of Atonement (Yom Kippur) a goat symbolically bearing the sins of the children of Israel was sent out into the wilderness.

The scapegoating of an individual is, in psychological parlance, the result of others' PROJECTION of their own faults, hostilities or anxieties. Thus scapegoating is a form of psychological DEFENCE.

There is a Scapegoat Society (see Resources) 'for those concerned with the dynamics of attributing blame to others – the core of scapegoating and demonizing. The Scapegoat Society is both for people who have experienced being a scapegoat, and for people working professionally to resolve scapegoat problems'.

schizoid refers to patterns of behaviour, the main characteristics of which are a lack of desire for INTIMACY, indifference to opportunities to develop close relationships, a restricted range of emotional expression with other people, and a reduced degree of satisfaction from being part of a family or social group. Those with schizoid tendencies are emotionally flat and have difficulty expressing strong feelings of any type, anger or joy.

People who display schizoid behaviour are usually introverted, preferring their own company and are often called 'loners'. In Jung's typology of PSYCHOLOGICAL FUNCTIONS, they are thinkers and theorists with under-developed awareness of sensory and feeling functions. The latest technological industries can offer such people ideal working conditions at computer terminals as typically they do not like interacting with people.

script in TRANSACTIONAL ANALYSIS theory, founder Eric Berne made the audacious assertion that 'Each person decides in early childhood how he will live and how he will die, and that plan, which he carries in his head wherever he goes, is called his script. By age six his important decisions are already made . . . It may not be what he wants, but it is what he wants to be' (Berne 1972: 36).

The decision is seen as a survival decision, made under stress and early childhood trauma. According to Berne the script has seven components:

The script payoff: a message (curse) in the form of an outcome that the parent gives to the child, about how he is to end his life – can be winning, losing or banal and is linked to the LIFE POSITION.

Injunctions: an 'unfair, negative command' that will keep the child from lifting the curse, and the most powerful element of the script apparatus.

Script provocation: to encourage behaviour which fuels the payoff.

These are called script controls. The following three components are counter-acting forces, equally damaging to the person:

A prescription or counter injunction: a directive on how to pass time while waiting for the script action, determining the person's style of life (Berne 1972: 119). The prescription comes into play between the ages of 6 and teenage years and is known as DRIVER behaviour.

Adult program: the 'how to' carry out the script. Parents and other significant figures can ROLE MODEL how to act out the script in real life.

Scripty impulses, or the demon: the Rebellious Child fighting against the script, but like a self-saboteur. Berne likens it to the ID in psychoanalysis and thus it could be described as a form of death instinct.

The final component is sometimes called the spellbreaker:

The antiscript or internal release is not part of the script itself but is a release from the script, which may or may not lead to autonomous aspirations. This, lodged in the emerging Adult EGO STATE of the child, carries the sense of hope or rescue. Sometimes it is time-limited – e.g. 'When I have left home I will start meeting my own needs' – but if the age of leaving home was not stipulated this could be delayed indefinitely and so maintain rather than end the script.

All script behaviours involve DISCOUNTING. The child is considered capable of having an autonomy (healthy) decision if parenting and other life events have been satisfactory up to that point. While it is difficult to say that some individuals are 'script free' throughout childhood, this is implied and is the goal in TA psychotherapy.

secondary gain 'A psychoanalytic term referring to the indirect, interpersonal advantages which the neurotic derives from his condition, e.g. compassion, increased attention, freedom from responsibilities, and the like' (Watzlawick et al. 1967: 287).

Secondary gain is considered to take place at an unconscious level and may come in the form of sympathy, attention, support, being excused from responsibility, and so on. On the surface it may seem rational for the conditions which lead to these gains to be changed. The person themselves may well espouse the desire to change. But in practice if we fail to take account of, and cater for, the needs that are met in the form of secondary gains we may find that change is resisted.

self there are many variations on the meaning of the self. It is a concept central to many theories of personality and personal development in ancient and modern times. For example, the Chandogya Upanishad (Huxley 1946: 10) regards the HIGHER SELF and the lower self as quite distinct. John Rowan (1998: 76) addresses the notion of the 'real self', which he equates with Ken Wilber's CENTAUR level of human development.

In Jungian psychology (and spelt with a capital) the Self is an ARCHETYPE, 'the God within, and the individual in seeking Self-realization and unity becomes the means through which God seeks his goal' (Jung 1983: 20). The Self is the whole person, conscious and unconscious, that develops through INDIVIDUATION.

In relation to the Freudian concept of EGO, the self is experienced as having a distinct separate identity from the id, ego and superego in that it embraces them all and can be witness to their functions. While the psyche is a self-regulating system between the conscious and unconscious, which are seen as two parts of one system, the self embraces the whole PSYCHE, conscious and unconscious. The ego is only a part expression of selfhood in manifestation.

Rogers, Maslow and other humanistic psychologists viewed the 'self-concept' or one's self-image (in other word's the person's view of and attitude towards themselves) as crucial to their health and development. See also SELF-ACTUALIZATION and SELF-ESTEEM.

self and peer assessment self-assessment is a reflexive process engaged in by individuals (self and peers) for the purpose of obtaining an accurate appraisal of knowledge, skills and attributes in particular areas of work and personal development. At Surrey it emerged as a method of professional development (e.g. Kilty 1979) and has since been used in formal higher education (Gregory and Tosey 2000).

Heron (1974a) stated that an educated person is one who is SELF-DIRECT-ING, self-monitoring and self-correcting. Self-assessment supports this principle and aims to facilitate the person to learn from experience, to learn how to learn, to be self-organizing, and to identify their capacity to learn and transfer skills across contexts.

The content and procedures of the self-assessment, and the standards and criteria against which the person assesses their knowledge and behaviour, are usually agreed with peers in advance. The involvement of peers in the self-assessment process is as a reflective mirror, a counterpoint against unwitting self-deception, to reduce 'blind spots' and to validate accurate self-assessment (see JOHARI WINDOW). The peers' assessment often serves to emphasize the 'overstated, understated or omitted strengths and weaknesses in the self assessment and in the peers' assessment of the person' (Heron 1999: 109).

Under the principle of self-direction the self-assessor is encouraged to be proactive. The power and ownership of the learning stay with the learner.

self-actualization Maslow (1970) studied successful leaders in the 1940s, seeking to understand the essence of job satisfaction and life satisfaction. The result of this study was the HIERARCHY OF NEEDS, of which self-actualization is the pinnacle, the highest point of the human potential and achievement.

For Maslow, the self-actualizing person is one who has worked through many layers of human conditioning, emotional and other psychological trauma, has learned to be in touch with their creativity and full potential, and has a sense of purpose which is higher than material gains (Rowan 1993).

Maslow thought that people who had PEAK EXPERIENCES, particularly of the mystical type, were demonstrating self-actualizing development. Those who worked with these experiences and actively opened themselves up to being fully human would eventually experience a state of BEING that is mystical and transcendent, or Divine.

self-awareness awareness of one's own nature and behaviour; seeing ourselves as others see us. The issue of the extent to which people can be self-aware is a philosophical one. Disciplines such as social psychology, EXISTENTIALISM and others also have their own views and debates on the subject.

In personal development there is no ultimate definition of what self-awareness is. It encapsulates what is expressed by, for example, the exhortation inscribed above the Delphic oracle ('Know thyself'); and by Robert Burns's poem, 'To a Louse':

O wad some Power the giftie gie us
To see oursels as ithers see us!
It wad frae mony a blunder free us,
An' foolish notion:
What airs in dress an' gait wad lea'e us,
An' ev'n devotion!

John Rowan says: 'Most courses which teach about dealing with other people now include some emphasis on understanding yourself, and use humanistic thinking and humanistic methods – often unacknowledged. They have to, because any attempt to understand or work with others on any kind of emotional level has to involve some self-understanding, some self-awareness' (from Association for Humanistic Psychology website, see Resources).

Methods as diverse as ASTROLOGY, the ENNEAGRAM, the MYERS-BRIGGS TYPE inventory, and 360° FEEDBACK are intended to promote self-awareness. In addition it is almost always an aim in personal development workshops to enhance participants' self-awareness through drawing attention to their behaviour and their impact on others. See also JOHARI WINDOW.

self-directed learning the humanistic principle that learners, rather than teachers or trainers, take charge of their own learning; a preference or capacity for learning in a self-directed manner. Also the process by which learners do some or all of the following: diagnose their needs; define learning goals; identify resources and methods; and assess their progress (see LEARNING CONTRACT; SELF AND PEER ASSESSMENT).

Key authors contributing to the concept of self-directed learning are Stephen Brookfield, Cyril Houle, Malcolm Knowles and Allen Tough (see Jarvis et al. 1998: 77–87). Rylatt and Lohan (1995) identify the six principal claims made about the benefits of self-directed learning as follows:

- it improves motivation to learn
- it improves a person's adaptability to change
- it provides improved flexibility in learning
- it is aligned to what we understand to be the way adults learn
- results of learning are easier to identify
- in the right circumstances it is the most cost-effective process.

Practices adopting the principle of self-directed learning are found in formal education, management training and WORKPLACE LEARNING. It is largely presupposed in methods such as the AUTONOMY LAB and OPEN SPACE TECHNOLOGY.

self-esteem self-esteem is the value we place on ourselves. Argyle (1969: 356) divided the self-concept into two components, self-image and self-esteem. Self-image is the particular way we each perceive ourselves.

Self-esteem is based on the positive, negative, or neutral evaluation a person gives to attributes of self (Coopersmith 1967: 4–5). A high self-esteem is a personal judgement of high self-worth, based on an acceptance of self as being generally 'all right'.

Self-esteem is influenced by environmental (social) circumstances and can fluctuate according to context. Making comparisons of self with other people helps to form attitudes of self, as does the decision we make about our mission in life (that is, what we believe we are in this world to do). Comparisons may have first been initiated by parents or teachers and form a foundation of self-identity which the child INTROJECTS out of awareness. So phrases like 'I've never been able to draw, dance, sing, be as good as the next person', indicate an uncritical acceptance of self based on others' judgements when the person (child) was too young for independent thinking. See also LIFE POSITIONS – our self-esteem can be viewed as related to our 'existential position'. The only position that shows a healthy self-esteem is of course the 'I'm OK – you're OK' position.

One of the main concerns with self-esteem is the human capacity for negative judgement about self (McKay and Fanning 2000). Judging and rejecting self causes emotional pain, which we then seek to avoid by taking fewer social, educational or career risks. We limit our ability to, for example, have open relationships with others, express our SEXUALITY, be the centre of attention, hear and accept criticism, and ask for help or solve problems. We erect psychological defences to keep others out for fear of REJECTION, but we have already rejected ourselves.

self-fulfilling prophecy a concept originally from the sociologist Robert Merton. There are various studies that illustrate the way that EXPECTATIONS or labels influence behaviour or performance. Such expectations and labels can operate as 'self-fulfilling prophecies' in that they determine how people are treated and assessed, sometimes regardless of actual behaviour or other information. For example, there has been research (Rosenthal 1968) into the effect of teacher expectations on pupil performance. The overall message of this research is that there can be a link, though the explanation for this effect is disputed.

The notion of the self-fulfilling prophecy is related to the 'Pygmalion Effect' and the 'halo effect', although there are nuances of difference between them. The halo effect is the principle that a person's outstanding qualities in some respect lead us to perceive them overall in a favourable light, potentially ignoring their faults or negative qualities. According to Buchanan and Huczynski (1997: 57) the term was first used by educational psychologist Edward Thorndike in 1920. The halo effect, therefore, can be thought of as creating a self-fulfilling prophecy.

The Pygmalion effect is different again. The title of George Bernard Shaw's play derives from Greek mythology, where Pygmalion was a sculptor who fell in love with one of his own statues – which subsequently came alive. Shaw's play is the story of a teacher who trains a working class woman in order to pass her off as a refined 'lady'. Whilst overtly successful, the woman eventually rebels and reverts to her original identity. The story therefore has tones of the poten-

tial for people to transform, but with undertones of the dangers of teachers and men manipulating people for their own ends, and/or of the way men use power in relation to women. What this shares with the notions of the self-fulfilling prophecy and the halo effect is the emphasis on the potential influence of other people's perceptions or expectations on an individual's identity and self-worth.

self-help 'self-help' is a philosophy or principle with several nuances of meaning. At root it is the principle that individuals can control, or should be in control of, their own well-being and growth (see also AUTONOMY). Many feel this to be important for psychological health. The self-help principle of Samuel Smiles (originally 1882, see Smiles 1996) enjoyed prominence in the 1980s and 1990s, with a normative emphasis that each person should stand on their own two feet. Self-help in this sense was seen as more enabling and effective than external help, which could inhibit the person's capacity for autonomy.

In Western cultures, knowledge about help and support for the human condition is often, and perhaps increasingly, the province of psychological professions. The self-help genre, though of variable quality and reliability, contradicts this tendency and makes core ideas and practices available to many people who for financial or social reasons cannot access, or are sceptical of, professional help. In this respect, self-help literature is political. The emphasis of some self-help literature on the individual pursuit of happiness, and its formulaic approach to 'success', can be disquieting – fuelling self-obsession more than self-awareness – although such promises are not exclusive to the self-help genre.

A self-help group is an active form of self-help. Such groups are usually formed by people with a common interest or predicament, to give mutual support, provide information and enable action. Self-help groups may be local and informal (e.g. a community men's group), but they include issue-based associations (e.g. for victims of abuse) and widespread operations such as Alcoholics Anonymous (see TWELFTH-STEP PROGRAMME).

self-hypnosis also 'auto-hypnosis'. The practice of hypnotizing oneself, by following a procedure to enter a state of deep relaxation. Used in AUTOGENICS and NLP, for example; see also HYP-NOTHERAPY.

sensitivity training a generic term given to intensive, experience-related work in small groups (see also ENCOUNTER GROUP; T-GROUP refers specifically to the techniques developed in Bethel and by the National Training Laboratory).

Sensitivity Training started in 1946 at the New Britain Teachers' College, Connecticut (see, for example, Back 1972). It was then designed to explore the use of small groups as a vehicle for personal and social change. The group leaders were Kenneth Benne, Leyland Bradford, and Ronald Lippitt, working under the overall direction of Kurt Lewin.

The goal of Sensitivity Training is change through self-expression, rather than self-expression for its own sake. The experience tends to be emotionally intensive and occurs at the intersection between the purely personal and the interpersonal. Through interaction with others, open expression of emotion, unexpected feedback and the guided exploration of feelings, the participant feels that he or she transcends limitations and can access powers, experiences and abilities previously closed to them. The group acts as an accelerator, and members temporarily or permanently take on great importance for each other (see Weschler and Reisler 1959).

sensory acuity in NLP, 'the process of learning to make finer and more useful distinctions about the sense information we get from the world' (O'Connor and Seymour 1993: 235).

The paradigm for sensory acuity in NLP is Milton Erickson, the hypnotherapist (e.g. Zeig and Munion 1999). As a child, Erickson was ill and confined to bed for long periods. Reportedly, he began to notice that he could discern, for example, who had just entered the house according to the sound of the door being opened. In his professional life, Erickson was known for being able to discern subtle changes in a client's breathing pattern and muscle tone.

A particular model of behaviour usually not noticed consciously is that of eye-accessing cues. This links observable eye movements with the REPRESENTATIONAL SYSTEM that a person is likely to be using internally. The standard form of the model (for a right-handed person, as seen by an observer) is as follows:

- up left: constructed pictures (visual)
- up right: remembered pictures (visual)
- level left: constructed sounds (auditory)
- level right: remembered sounds (auditory)
- down left: feelings (kinaesthetic)
- down right: internal discussion (internal dialogue/auditory)
- straight ahead: visualization (visual).

The model has been challenged, mainly by experimental psychologists who have failed to substantiate the model's claims (perhaps, it is suggested, due to the nature of the experiments themselves). But the main point in NLP is to encourage attention to details that are potentially useful, but normally below conscious awareness; and to proceed on the principle that, until demonstrated to the contrary, there is a systematic relationship between each person's external behaviour and their internal thought processes.

seven rays from the work of Alice Bailey (1880–1949), the seven rays is a map of existence – 'the seven basic streams of energy pervading our solar system, our planet and all that lives and moves within its orbit' (from The Lucis Trust website, see Resources).

Bailey's work is in the theosophical tradition, which essentially takes a rational and empirical route to spiritual knowledge and development. Alice Bailey's writings on the rays were channelled from a discarnate Tibetan sage and formed a five-volume work on Esoteric Psychology known as *A Treatise on the Seven Rays* (Bailey 1970).

The rays have links with both colour (seven colours of the rainbow) and the CHAKRAS (seven centres of human energy in the body). With each ray are associated various essential qualities. These are:
- the first ray of will and power
- the second ray of love and wisdom
- the third ray of active intelligence and adaptability
- the fourth ray of harmony through conflict, of beauty and of art
- the fifth ray of concrete knowledge and science
- the sixth ray of idealism and devotion
- the seventh ray of ceremonial order and ritual.

The rays can be used as a form of personality profile.

sexuality sexual preference or orientation (as distinct from GENDER); or the quality of a person's sexual expressiveness. See also TANTRA.

Sexuality is core to a person's IDENTITY. While many social taboos about sex remain, recent years have seen greater acceptance and understanding of, for example, female sexuality and gay and lesbian sexuality. The diversity of sexual expression and the significance of sexuality in society are increasingly apparent. Fear and prejudice still abound, nevertheless, and represent a significant source of inhibition or OPPRESSION for many people.

Sexual needs are basic human needs and sex is also a fundamental form of human expression. Sex was central to Freud's theories of human behaviour (see LIBIDO) and to Reich's ideas about ENERGY. Various forms of sex therapy are available.

shadow a term generally used to refer to a part of the individual PSYCHE that contains aspects of the personality that are unacceptable to the EGO at its present stage of development.

The shadow elements are unwanted and sometimes frightening because they challenge our perceived sense of who we are and how we present this to the world – our PERSONA – and are therefore consigned to the unconscious. Despite this the shadow tends to leak into consciousness in several ways, mainly by being split off and projected onto others, or by appearing in dreams.

If these parts are consciously explored and integrated into the ego the personality becomes richer and closer to a truer manifestation of the self, and the energy that was being used to repress the shadow is released. Both these occurrences allow for a more holistic and effective functioning of the individual.

The concept is particularly associated with Jung and analytical psychology, although there is evidence that he was building on an idea originally formulated by Nietzsche. Jung's theoretical basis stems from his assumption of opposites (syzygy): in the case of the psyche, two opposing forces are the shadow in the unconscious balancing the conscious ego. The aim is not to eradicate the shadow (this is regarded as impossible) but to bring it into consciousness for integration – a process known as confronting and coming to terms with the shadow, a key element of INDIVIDUATION in Jungian analysis.

Jung and post-Jungian writers disagree as to the positive and/or negative qualities of the shadow, the extent to which it originates from the individual and/or COLLECTIVE UNCONSCIOUS, and its relationship with other psychic archetypes and complexes, such as the ANIMA and ANIMUS.

Classically, shadow is a term that has been in the province of individual therapy, although Jung himself referred to countries as having a shadow. The last decade has seen two main developments. A concept of shadow (arguably over-simplified at times) has been applied to both group (Gemmill and Costello 1990) and organizational development (Egan 1994, Bridges 1992, Bowles 1991). Secondly, particularly in the USA, shadow integration has moved into the area of self-help (Zweig and Wolff 1997): an idea that some traditional Jungians might view as irresponsible.

shadow consulting shadow consulting is a form of practitioner supervision that utilizes the principle of PARALLEL PROCESS. This emphasizes that the dynamics and patterns of the consultant–shadow consultant interaction are likely to parallel dynamics between the consultant and the client organization.

The term was invented by Marjan Schröder (1974; see Casey 1993: 76): 'The term shadow consultant denotes a consultant who, at the request of a colleague and by means of a series of mutual discussions in which he uses a socio-scientific approach, helps evaluate and, if necessary, change the diagnosis, tactics, or role adopted in a certain assignment' (Schröder 1974: 580).

A number of practitioners in the field of organizational consultancy, including David Casey, have developed shadow consulting as a peer supervision format.

shamanism a shaman (the word is of Siberian origin) is a 'walker between the worlds', a member of a tribe or society who performs a spiritual function but who typically is excluded from the social life of the community (Matthews and Matthews 1985). See also URBAN SHAMANISM.

Shamanic or shamanically-derived models and practices are common in personal development training. Examples include the notion of the VISION QUEST, used in management training; the medicine wheel, the American first people's spiritual map (Sun Bear et al. 1991); and medicine cards (Sams and Carson 1988).

shoulds Fritz Perls (see GESTALT) identified 'shoulds' as messages or obligations that are often INTROJECTED from childhood, schooling and elsewhere. Examples are the ideas that one should always be polite; should respect one's elders and betters; should always be punctual; and so on. Through identifying whatever 'shoulds' we have taken in, we can realize that we have choice about whether to follow such imperatives.

single- and double-loop learning a concept of learning developed by Chris Argyris, a key author in the field of organizational learning, based on the work of Gregory Bateson (LEVELS OF LEARNING).

Morgan defines single-loop learning as 'an ability to detect and correct error in relation to a given set of operating norms', and double-loop learning as 'being able to take a "double look" at the situation by questioning the relevance of operating norms' (Morgan 1997: 87).

In other words, single-loop learning is concerned mainly with the achievement of goals, but the assumptions and values behind the theory-in-use are not questioned.

Argyris's work, both individually (for example, Argyris 1994) and jointly with Donald Schön, has influenced significantly the thinking of subsequent writers such as Peter Senge (1990).

Six Category Intervention Analysis a model of communication developed by John Heron while he worked within the Human Potential Research Group in the 1970s and 1980s (Heron 1990). The model can be used to analyse, guide, and develop skills in, facilitative interventions. Its premise is that all communication, particularly verbal communication, can be classified under six categories:

- **prescriptive**: directing another's behaviour, and sometimes their thinking and feeling. The degree of prescription varies from strong commands to facilitation of self-direction
- **informative**: the intention is to impart knowledge and interpretation to the other to enable them to work from an informed, more resourceful position
- **confronting**: this intervention seeks to raise the other's awareness to what may be unconscious or denied patterns of rigid behaviour and thinking. Permission to confront another is significant here; within a facilitative relationship the right to confront is agreed within the work CONTRACT
- **cathartic**: the aim of a CATHARTIC intervention is to facilitate the release or discharge of emotions in the other person. A major part of personal development work is educating the client or participant to find ways of releasing blocked energy so that it can be used more constructively and creatively
- **catalytic**: seeks to draw out, to facilitate the client or participant to tell their story, and to elicit self-discovery and constructive problem-solving based on their own inner wisdom. Empathic communication is a core skill of this intervention
- **supportive**: the helper seeks ways of affirming the value of the other person. Being supportive is an underlying attitude of all the interventions in a helping relationship. Actively demonstrating support involves skills such as appropriate self-DISCLOSURE, touch, and expressing the worth of the other even if the behaviour is not supported.

The first three categories are authoritative (the practitioner directs, informs or confronts the client), the second three are facilitative (the practitioner follows, supports and assists the client in the expression of feelings). All categories have equal value when used appropriately (see also DEGENERATE INTERVENTION and PERVERTED INTERVENTION).

socialization 'The process through which an individual's pattern of behaviour, and their values, attitudes and motives, are shaped to conform with those seen as desirable in a particular organization, society or sub-culture' (Buchanan and Huczynski 1997: 122). Socialization is in effect a learning process, through which we INTROJECT beliefs, attitudes and norms of behaviour. Personal development is often concerned with unravelling the effects of socialization.

soul for most spiritual and religious movements the soul is the name given to the capacity within the human person to be in union with Spirit or Divine Light, sometimes called the Holy Spirit. It is this capacity that enables humans to bridge between the human and divine world; or in Wilber's map (see Rowan 1993) the soul inhabits the subtle self.

Many see the human soul as the lowest of the spirits, a monad, that is the ultimate unit of living beings, substantially united with the human body, the highest of physical things, so that man appears, as it were, as 'the horizon and the dividing line of spiritual and physical nature' (Buber 1965: 129, quoting Thomas Aquinas).

For Plato, what soul is like and the nature of its existence could be described only in symbols or myth. Plato said: 'All soul is immortal, for what is always in motion is immortal . . . Now, since it has been proven that what moves itself is immortal, a man need feel no hesitation in identifying it with the essences and definition of soul. If then it is established that what moves itself is identical with soul, it inevitably follows that soul is uncreated and immortal' (Plato 1973).

In non-industrial societies the soul is considered a 'thin insubstantial human image, in its nature a sort of vapour, film, or shadow. Mostly palpable and invisible, yet also manifesting physical powers. This is similar to Plato's Myth of Er where he uses a similar concept to encompass your entire identity' (Hillman 1996: 9).

In SUFISM, the Spirit working in man is the soul (Witteveen 1997). Inayat Khan (a Sufi mystic, 1882–1927) compared the soul to a ray of the divine sun and believed that the divine spirit expresses itself in all beings and in all aspects of the manifestation. Therefore all material and mental atoms are part of the heavenly radiance, that is, they have divine light and this light is its soul.

spatial sorting in NLP, the use of different physical locations to map and differentiate between STATES, PERCEPTUAL POSITIONS, or different components of an experience. For example, a person who is considering their present feelings and circumstances, recalling a past incident, and thinking about their future goals, may be guided to stand or sit in a distinct location for each of past, present and future.

The principle in NLP, particularly as developed by Robert Dilts (1998b), who also refers to this as 'psychogeography', is that this helps to reduce cross-contamination from one state to another, and also ANCHORS each state to its chosen physical location.

Spatial sorting appears to have been influenced by Fritz Perls's 'empty chair' technique in GESTALT.

spirit spirit is considered the vital inanimate essence of a person or animal or plant. It is discarnate energy. Heron defines spirit as 'a moving vitalizing principle that is anterior to our normal distinction between the animate and inanimate' (1998c: 8). Ken Wilber says of the nature of spirit: 'Spirit transcends all, (matter, life, mind, and soul) so it includes all' (Wilber 1996a: 18).

John Rowan (1993: 120–21) brings together four positions on personal and spiritual development, offering a model of the nature of the work at the different levels and suggesting how best to work with them. The fourth position or highest level is that of Spirit, part of the Causal Self, the SELF that is not ego-defined, which surrenders in divine union and seeks salvation in Unity-emptiness.

spiritual intelligence 'spiritual intelligence' (or SQ) is a recently-coined phrase that seems intended to extend Goleman's concept of EMOTIONAL INTELLIGENCE (EQ). Like EQ, its lineage is from Howard Gardner's concept of multiple INTELLIGENCES.

Several books with 'spiritual intelligence' in their title have now been published, perhaps the best known being Zohar and Marshall (2000). Another example is Levin (2000). According to Zohar and Marshall (2000: 3–4), spiritual intelligence is: 'the intelligence with which we address and solve problems of meaning, the intelligence with which we can place our actions and our lives in a wider, richer, meaning-giving context, the intelligence with which we can assess that one course of action or one life-path is more meaningful than another. SQ is the necessary foundation for the effective functioning of both IQ and EQ.'

Zohar and Marshall have assembled evidence from a number of disciplines, including psychology, neurology, anthropology and cognitive science. This is helpful; however, the claim that SQ is a new discovery appears built on the argument that 'in Western psychology the self, or personality, has no centre' (2000: 152). The suggestion that Western psychology has yet to address notions such as the core SELF or the realm of the TRANSPERSONAL is contentious when one considers the work of, for example, Roberto Assagioli, Carl Jung, John Heron and Ken Wilber.

spirituality as a process, journeying to

develop conscious awareness of unity with the HIGHER SELF. The term 'spirituality' may also refer to a realm of experience or consciousness; or to the religious or spiritual beliefs to which a person subscribes.

Heron defines the realm of the spiritual as 'a comprehensive, all-pervasive, dipolar consciousness-life that appears to include human consciousness-life, to be beyond it and to be within it . . . (that is) spirit as transcendent and present consciousness and spirit as present and immanent life' (1998c: 8).

The spiritual journey is concerned with developing a sacred, divine or inner, non-material or mystical way of living. Some experience a spiritual path within the framework of a religion; others do not impose religious interpretation on their spiritual experiences (see PEAK EXPERIENCE).

Most spiritually oriented people will speak of moving towards the Light, making the connection between the spark of divine light within self (see SOUL) with the cosmic or Divine Light or transcendent divinity (Heron 1998c). Many authors seem to use SOUL and SPIRIT as synonymous, yet most would see the soul as the alchemist's container where spirit, earth and divine meet.

splitting a concept central to Melanie Klein's theories of object-relations (see, for example, de Board 1978: 25), also addressed by Donald Winnicott (1991).

Essentially, splitting involves the INTROJECTION of good qualities and the PROJECTION of bad qualities; and consequently the development of a compliant, external self that is split from 'true' inner desires. Klein's ideas about splitting concern the psychic world of the young infant. It is not so much a defensive strategy as a failure to complete integration of internalized relationships between the parent and child. However, it is a dynamic that can be experienced at any age or in any context, for example, in an 'us and them' situation in the workplace.

spontaneity a quality of the developed person, emphasized in, for example, CO-COUNSELLING. Spontaneity in the form of fun and laughter contributes significantly to well-being, and can often be neglected in people's stressful lives.

stages of development many models depict personal growth and DEVELOPMENT as a series of stages that are experienced as sequential through time. Classic examples are Piaget's work (based on child development), and Erikson's LIFE CYCLE.

A model increasingly used in the sphere of management and leadership is Bill Torbert's 'stages of managerial development' (e.g. Fisher et al. 2001). This derives from, and develops, Loevinger's theory of ego development (Loevinger and Wessler 1978).

This model has, variously, six, seven or eight stages of development, labelled:

- Opportunist
- Technician
- Diplomat
- Achiever
- Strategist
- Ironist
- Magician

The idea is that at each stage, a particular set of principles or 'governing frame' guides one's worldview and actions. The opportunist, for example, literally takes an opportunistic view, seeing the world as there to be exploited but also assuming that others act in this way.

An individual may reach a particular stage of development and stay there. In organizations, according to data gathered by Fisher and Torbert over many years, most managers measure at one of the first three stages. Progression through these stages can result from intentional personal development.

Torbert considers the transition from Achiever to Strategist to be highly significant, particularly in the management context to which this model is usually applied. See also ACTION INQUIRY.

state an internal state is the nature and quality of a person's phenomenological and physiological experience of the world at a point in time.

An internal state can include the conscious and the unconscious, and mind as well as body (e.g. dreams, emotions, internal dialogue, feelings such as agitation, and psychic, mystical or spiritual sensations). There is a strong case for seeing internal states as multiple and context bound.

Different models have their own maps of, or approaches to, internal states. In NLP, state refers to a particular configuration of neurology and physiology. Any given state can be MODELLED in NLP as having a distinctive combination of, for example, posture, breathing, language patterns and internal representations. NLP is particularly interested in states that are 'resourceful' – in other words, in which the person feels CENTRED and has access to their capabilities. NLP also refers to 'state control', which refers initially to a person's ability to maintain a resourceful state – poise and confidence – but more widely means the ability to maintain or change any state at will.

story-telling 'Human meaning-making rests in stories. Life making calls for accounts, for story, for sharing. To be human is "to be entangled in stories"' (von Eckhartsberg, cited in Reason 1988: 82).

Story-telling is a traditional form of communication with many possible functions – entertainment, myth-making, oral history, and more. The notion of the 'teaching story' is particularly associated with the SUFIS. Idries Shah has introduced this form to the West, and has published several volumes of stories about the Mullah Nasrudin, the Sufi 'wise fool'.

Story-telling is used in education and in therapy (for example, Gersie and King 1990). More recently, story-telling has been introduced into organizations as a way of acknowledging, capturing and working expressively with people's experience of work.

stress physiologically, the heart and the body are considered stressed when worked consistently under or over the optimal level. Stress is diagnosed when the adrenergic system goes into overdrive as a response to the sense of danger and demand for adrenaline within the mind and body system. This trigger of danger can be purely physiological.

However, there is a strong psychological component, in so far as if the person thinks the event or situation is of danger to them or if work is too much or too demanding, they will physiologically and psychologically respond in the same way, the total effect being the same whatever the origin.

Boredom, under-excitation and powerlessness can create just as serious physiological stress as over-excitation and over-work.

There is a great deal of literature on workplace stress and stress management. See, for example, Buchanan and Huczynski (1997: 153–56); James and Arroba (1999).

strokes a stroke is a unit of recognition, such as (at its simplest) saying 'Good morning.' Understanding how people give and receive positive and negative strokes, and change unhealthy patterns of stroking, are powerful aspects of work in TRANSACTIONAL ANALYSIS.

Berne (1961) observed that people need this form of recognition, as evidence of their existence and value, to survive and thrive. Hence the treatment of 'sending someone to Coventry', that is, deliberately ignoring them for any length of time, is psychologically damaging and can now be legitimate grounds for a complaints procedure in the workplace.

Strokes may be conditionally positive or conditionally negative, depending on the culture of the group, and the competence of the individual in the activity (Stewart and Joines 1987: 91).

sub-modalities in NLP, qualities of, or fine distinctions made within, internal representations (see Bandler and MacDonald 1988; O'Connor and Seymour 1993: 41). For example, an internal image has qualities of size, location, whether moving or still, colour or black and white, contract, saturation, focus, and so on. These qualities and distinctions are treated as significant and utilized in many NLP methods, typically concentrating on those sub-modalities that vary and so make a difference in any instance.

sub-personality although we may wish to be consistent, in fact we express ourselves through many different selves, behaviour styles or identities, according to the context of the situation and what we believe is expected of us. These parts of ourselves, which make up a kind of inner family, are known as sub-personalities (see, for example, Rowan 1990; Stone and Winkleman 1985).

The body therapist Wilhelm Reich suggested that our behavioural styles were predictable according to the Character Type we developed in childhood. Roberto Assagioli (1975b), the founder of PSYCHOSYNTHESIS, thought that our sub-personalities were the expressions of our souls, according to the universal principle of the manifestation of the One into the Many.

Some theorists have focused on the relationship between conflicting sub-personalities, and others on the power of the disowned parts of our personality. While not pathologizing the presence of sub-personalities, Assagioli and others recommended inner work of recognizing and consciously naming the different parts (for example, the Critic, the Martyr, the Perfectionist). Active imagination dialogues may be encouraged with the overall aim of facilitating creative interaction within the psyche.

Sufism Sufism (e.g. Witteveen 1997) is usually understood to be the mystical or esoteric tradition of Islam, although it has not necessarily been owned officially as such. Sufi figures well known in the West include the 14th-century poet, Rumi, and the contemporary thinker and educator, Idries Shah, author/compiler of the Mullah Nasrudin teaching stories.

Doris Lessing (1997), in a summary of Idries Shah's work and influence, says: 'It took 800 years to get Sufi thought accepted by orthodox Islam, and since then Moslems have claimed it as their own ... The Sufi reality predated Islam, has always been introduced, secretly or openly, into every culture. "We work in all places and at all times." (The word "Sufism" is not liked by Sufis: they see it as a typical Western abstraction, away from the living reality of the Sufi Way, which is embodied in people.)'

See also PERENNIAL WISDOM.

suggestopedia a process that enables the learning of, for example, language through unconscious processing, using, for example, music in classroom sessions. A form of ACCELERATED LEARNING, based on the notion that it is the whole BODYMIND, not just the conscious mind, which learns.

The practice originated as follows: 'Suggestopedia is the creation of a doctor and psychiatrist, Georgi Lozanov from the University of Sofia, Bulgaria. The method was developed in the 1960s after 20 years of therapeutic practice and research into hyperamnesia, and began from an experiment to induce enhanced memorization in schools' (Hooper-Hensen 1992: 197).

Hooper-Hensen also notes that the term 'suggestopedia' is misleading, and has unwanted connotations in the English language. Lozanov now uses the term 'desuggestive learning', and eschews the use of any form of hypnosis.

The Society for Effective Affective Learning (SEAL – see Resources) was founded in 1983 to promote Lozanov's work, and since has broadened to include all learning methods with similar aims and principles.

superego in Freudian theory (see PSYCHO-ANALYSIS) the superego is that part of the psyche that introjects societal mores and values and represses the instinctive drives (the pleasure principle) in favour of such mores to survive in a socio-cultural environment. The superego seems to be the originator of unconscious REPRESSION and other psychological defensive strategies.

supervision usually, accredited practitioners of any form of personal development are required to have professional supervision. Whether or not supervision is required formally, it is considered an essential good practice in therapeutic work, and desirable in other contexts.

John Rowan (1998: 192) defines the function of supervision as 'to enable the therapist or counsellor to become aware of blind spots and prejudices and mistakes and inadequacies, and to work on them in such a way that professional development takes place'.

In humanistic work, supervision would honour principles such as SELF-DIRECTEDNESS of the client and so is likely to aim for a balance of support and challenge, having due regard to professional and ethical guidelines. It may use processes such as SELF AND PEER ASSESSMENT.

support can refer to an act of support (a 'supportive intervention' in terms of the SIX CATEGORY INTERVENTION ANALYSIS model), such as a comforting word and presence; and to the 'support system' that everyone can be said to have, which may or may not include specific 'support groups' (see SELF-HELP).

Mulligan (1988: 134) says 'support can range from simple greeting or welcoming, through praise and appreciation to giant acts of benevolence and constructive patronage. You can be supported as a person through having your values, ways of being and who you are affirmed, or by an advocate who stands up for your rights and needs.'

A person's support system is his or her network of friends and family, work colleagues, the home, the activities, places and things he or she enjoys, and perhaps professional helpers. Some people have difficulty asking for or accepting support, and consider this a sign of weakness. But such independence is unrealistic – we exist in an INTERDEPENDENT world, as expressed in John Donne's phrase, 'No man is an island'.

symbols the Jungian tradition holds that the unconscious communicates with the conscious through symbols. In this sense, symbols are essentially expressions of unconscious information, which has not yet been recognized or consciously formulated. They have been described as a vital link between the known and the unknown. They are distinct from signs, whose meaning is usually immediately and unambiguously recognized. They are found in DREAMS, MYTHS, folklore, fantasy, ritual, and art. It is thought that even medical symptoms may have a symbolic function.

In Jung's view, symbols may carry information about future events, as well as past or present situations. They belong to both the personal and the COLLECTIVE UNCONSCIOUS. Central to this approach is the use of dream exploration and amplification in Jungian analysis, in order to make unconscious information accessible to the consciousness of individuals.

Jung (1968d; see also Storr 1983) interpreted the Mandala symbol as an indication of an individual's wholeness and maturity. For the Jungian therapist, a client's symbols can provide useful diagnostic insights. For the client, or symbol maker, symbols can be images carrying rich subjective meaning, and contain existential themes. They can also produce an emotional response whose meaning may never be entirely clear to individuals, but which continues to unfold. There may be many meanings to a symbol. In the Jungian tradition, one of the tasks of the therapeutic relationship is to provide a context for exploration of the power and messages believed to be inherent in symbols and their role in the process of INDIVIDUATION.

synchronicity a meaningful relation between events that are synchronous but not causally connected. The word was coined by Jung (1969). He was not the first to conceive of such acausal connections. Input also came from Einstein, whose conversations about relativity inspired Jung in his intellectual journey into non-locality.

A typical synchronistic event would be an internal realization of something which personally is highly significant to the individual at the same time as he or she sees an accidental occurrence which appears to emphasize that very same inner state. Another common form is that of a vision or dream indicating something – internal or external – that is then confirmed in external reality. Within the psychotherapeutic field, synchronicities are aids to psychological and spiritual growth, often connected to significant personal transformations.

Just about all parapsychological, and related, phenomena, from horary astrology to TAROT CARDS, presuppose or operate according to the principle of synchronicity. Some believe that synchronicities are happening all the time, and that if we would only open ourselves to their presence, we would see that everything is touched with mystery and replete with meaning (see Grasse 1996).

The view of reality which underlies the concept of synchronicity, in whatever form, is a challenge to the modern scientific worldview of the majority of individuals living in the West. The idea that all things are interconnected, that the nature of our reality is symbolic, and that nothing is without meaning or happens by chance, has, however, been the accepted conventional viewpoint of most periods of world history.

synectics synectics is a creative problem-solving methodology developed by W.J.J. Gordon (1961). It makes use of metaphor and analogy to break free from constraining assumptions or mind-sets – essentially, by making the strange familiar, or by making the familiar strange. Gordon believed that the emotional and irrational components of creative behaviour are more important than the intellectual, but need to be understood and used as tools in order to increase creative output. Synectics is used in business, education, and other settings (for example, Nolan 1989).

systems thinking a way of thinking about the world that utilizes principles of systems theory. This view underlies NLP, BRIEF THERAPY and forms of family therapy.

Campbell et al. (1991: 17) cite Bateson's definition of a system as 'any unit structured on feedback'. Senge et al. say: 'A system is a perceived whole whose elements "hang together" because they continually affect each other over time and operate toward a common purpose. The word descends from the Greek verb *sunistánai*, which originally meant "to cause to stand together". As this origin suggests, the structure of the system includes the quality of perception with which you, the observer, cause it to stand together' (Senge et al. 1994: 90).

There are many different versions of systems theory. In essence this view is characterized by seeing human systems and action as predicated on FEEDBACK and recursion. It will also tend to see the patterns at the systemic level as determining the behaviour of individuals in the system, rather than the other way round (the latter is more usual in a person-centred, individualistic view of the world). Thus in systemic family therapy, symptoms displayed by one family member are regarded as an output of the whole family's functioning, not as signs of that individual being ill.

A form of systems thinking was popularized in the 1990s by Peter Senge's book, *The Fifth Discipline*. Senge put forward a number of 'laws of the fifth discipline' (Senge 1990: 57–67) which express the distinctive, arational (i.e. not rational in a logical, linear sense, but not irrational either) flavour of this worldview. Similar principles were expressed in environmental pioneer Barry Commoner's 'four laws of ecology':

- Everything is connected to everything else.
- Everything must go somewhere.
- Nature knows best.
- There's no such thing as a free lunch.

Senge advocated systems thinking as one of the core disciplines of learning organizations, including substantial reference to personal development, or 'personal mastery', which includes a notion of spiritual development. However, the personal development aspect is not strongly developed, and the general flavour of systems thinking at Senge's academic institution, the Massachusetts Institute of Technology (MIT) is technical.

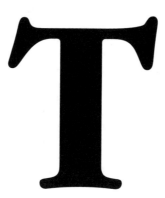

tacit knowledge   Michael Polanyi (1891–1976), a Hungarian medical scientist and later philosopher, argued that formal, explicit KNOWLEDGE relies on personal, tacit knowing (see Polanyi 1966).

Polanyi believed that all knowledge is personal and experiential, and that much personal knowledge is out of awareness, or remains unarticulated, or is of a different order to the type of knowledge that can be articulated in theory. The concept is widely used though some challenge the validity of the distinction made between tacit and explicit knowledge.

In recent years the concept has been applied in an organizational context, relating to both WORKPLACE LEARNING and knowledge management (see, for example, Nonaka and Takeuchi 1995), partly in an attempt to explain why it is so hard to codify knowledge and competence.

tai chi chuan   a form of graceful, rhythmic, meditative exercise originating in China. An example of a BODYMIND approach, in principle Tai Chi Chuan is a physical expression of TAOIST philosophy. Its aim is to stimulate and nurture chi, our life energy. It affects the nervous system, massages internal organs and tones the physical body. In addition it assists relaxation and can help to reduce anxiety. Its movements originate in the martial arts, and it is also related to forms of Chinese medicine through the principle that illness arises from blockages to the flow of chi.

tantra   in Sanskrit *tantra* means a way of expansion, and it refers to esoteric practices found in Hinduism and Buddhism. In relation to personal development, tantra refers principally to practical and sensual methods for opening and expanding consciousness, and producing transcendent experience, particularly through sex. Also referred to as sacred sex.

Taoism   Taoism is a religion and philosophy (or way of being) originating in China. The originator of Taoism is believed to be Lao Tzu, who wrote one of the most famous Taoist texts, the *Tao Te Ching* (see Lao Tzu 1969). Lao Tzu aimed initially to develop a philosophical and psychological approach that would help to reduce social conflict, to some extent as an alternative to Confucianism. Taoism later became a formal religion, and remains one of the three major religions of China.

Tao is an indefinable concept usually translated as 'The Way', which implies living in harmony with the universe and surrendering to its flow. A related principle is that of 'wu wei', which refers to being effective through minimal action.

Taoist thought has been very influential on much of the growth movement (see e.g. I CHING; TAI CHI; YIN AND

YANG), thanks in particular to the interest of Alan Watts (Watts 2000). John Heider's *Tao of Leadership* (Heider 1986) is a lovely example of Taoist philosophy related to contemporary facilitation.

Taoism is directly or indirectly significant in complementary medicine and many NEW AGE practices. Its principles might also be seen as the earliest example of SYSTEMS THINKING.

tarot cards a deck of cards used for divination, and to represent the archetypal journey of personal development.

Tarot card decks are found in many Indo-European cultures. Some believe they came from ancient Egypt. Alternative views include that of Stewart (1988) who traces the symbology to the Merlin texts (written out by Geoffrey of Monmouth in the 12th century) and related Celtic sources. Modern decks make links to various esoteric or psychological traditions, for example, Jungian psychology, and Arthurian legend.

Tarot decks have four suits, usually wands, cups, coins and swords (many 'themed' decks are available that vary the actual suits) – indeed these are the suits of standard playing cards today in countries such as Italy. These symbolize respectively the four 'elements' of fire, water, earth and air. The suit cards constitute the 'minor arcana'.

Tarot decks also have 22 cards known as the 'major arcana'. These represent the symbolic journey of the soul from birth on this planet (card 0, 'The Fool'), to return (card 21, 'The Universe'). Some authors (Stewart is one) link the major arcana directly to the twenty paths in the TREE OF LIFE. There is a view that the Tarot functioned as a thematic 'storybook' within the Kabbalah's oral, story-telling tradition. In other words, instead of the knowledge system being written down it was conveyed orally, facilitated by the imagery and structure of the Tarot.

The Tarot can be used in personal development both as this symbolic representation of development, and as an aid to reflection and meditation. See Pollack (1997) for a general introduction to the origins and applications of the Tarot.

T-group 'T-group' stands for 'training group'. The T-group method is a variety of SENSITIVITY TRAINING, personal and/or team development, in which participants are supported in exploring their interpersonal relationships. The role of 'leader', or FACILITATOR, is generally one that may intervene in group process or interpersonal conflict, but otherwise does not structure or lead the group. Often a T-group will have no task other than to study its own process. The absence of an overt task, in principle, focuses attention on GROUP DYNAMICS and interpersonal interaction.

T-groups are the American version of similar work in the UK by the Tavistock Institute (see Resources), the latter involving a more explicitly PSYCHODYNAMIC view of groups. Roger Harrison (1995) comments on the cultural differences between British and American approaches. T-groups were a core method of ORGANIZATION DEVELOPMENT in the 1960s – for example, they were used extensively in ICI.

According to Aronson (1994: 183), 'The first T-Group was an accident that happened when participants in a workshop conducted by Kurt Lewin asked to sit in on the observers' debriefing sessions. The result was a lively and exciting debate, and the practice continued.'

Typically, time is represented on a line (James and Woodsmall 1988), thus the farther back in time I experienced something, the further my representation of that memory will be stored along my timeline towards the past. Not everyone's timeline is continuous, however.

Timeline is often used to create SPA-

TIAL SORTING in NLP exercises. For example, a participant might walk along a line representing their time-line, moving back towards the past to re-encounter an experience, perhaps making an appropriate change, then walking towards the present and future again to experience the benefits of having made that change. This practice relies on NLP's assumption that our representations of the past affect our experience, rather than what 'actually' happened.

time management the skill of managing time, usually implying efficient use of time as a resource, and good self-organization, in order to achieve personal and/or professional goals (for example, success in a managerial job; balancing home and work life; and so on). For example, John Adair's (1998) principles of time management are to develop a personal sense of time; identify long term goals; make medium term plans; plan the day; make the best use of your best time; organize office work; manage meetings; delegate effectively; make use of committed time; and manage your health. He suggests applying these principles to all parts of one's life.

The flavour of many approaches to time management is instrumental and achievement-orientated, with emphasis on controlling time and one's life – concerned, in short, with doing and not with BEING. Covey (1992: 150) describes the concept of a fourth-generation time management approach, saying that 'rather than focusing on *things* and *time*, fourth-generation expectations focus on preserving and enhancing *relationships* and *results*'. Covey has posed the question, 'How many people on their deathbed wish they'd spent more time at the office?'

timeline in NLP, in common with many other modes and theories, it is accepted that experience of time is subjective. In particular, each person has his or her own internal REPRESENTATION of time. This means, for example, that I might literally represent the past as being 'behind me' and the future stretching out in front. But many different kinds of representation are possible.

time-structuring a term used in TRANSACTIONAL ANALYSIS to describe different forms of interpersonal activity (Stewart and Joines 1987: 335).

Berne (1968) concluded that there was a basic need for human beings to structure their time and he called this 'structure hunger'. This hunger motivated people to engage in interpersonal transactions. People have different degrees of hunger and a person's strategies of structuring time gives a good indication of their psychological development and their need for STROKES, positive or negative. Eric Berne (1961) described six ways that human beings spend time: WITHDRAWAL; RITUAL; PASTIMES; activities; GAMES; and INTIMACY.

Activities focus on HERE AND NOW communication, directed towards solving a problem or achieving some goal. For example, my typing this definition is an activity. The level of recognition in the form of STROKES can be much higher than in most other time-structuring modes, but still less than in intimacy, depending on the amount of involvement and directed energy the individual puts into the activity.

T.O.T.E. stands for Test–Operate–Test–Exit. Developed by Miller et al. (1960), the T.O.T.E. is used in NLP as a fundamental model of human functioning. It underlines the 'Programming' element of NLP. It is essentially a cognitive model.

'The T.O.T.E. concept maintains that all mental and behavioral programs revolve around having a *fixed goal* and *a variable means to achieve that goal*. This model indicates that, as we think, we set goals in our mind (consciously or unconsciously) and develop a *test* for when that goal has been achieved. If that goal is not achieved we *operate* to change something or do something to get closer to our goal. When our *test* criteria have been satisfied we then *exit* on to the next step' (Dilts and Epstein 1995: 144).

touch touch is a universally important human experience, as well as one around which many taboos exist.

Touch is significant because of its PRIMAL and intimate nature. Using touch is common in humanistic approaches and personal development workshops, in complete contrast to the Freudian approach, where the analyst remains detached physically and visually. As Rowan (1998: 92; 118) points out, this is based on a different view of TRANSFERENCE in humanistic practice.

In a workshop, an ice-breaker may encourage people to make some form of physical contact. ENERGIZERS often involve mutual massage. Expression of feelings is encouraged, for example, through hugs, and touch can assist CATHARSIS. Deeper work will often involve physical contact, or exploring issues through physical means.

BODYWORK methods, of course, use touch intentionally and integrally. In other modes, where touch is not explicitly a working medium, practitioners may need to take care with their use of touch so that it is not experienced as invasive, sexual, or otherwise an inappropriate use of the facilitator's POWER.

tough love the notion that love is not weak sentimentality; and that being loving does not rule out loving confrontation, setting and holding BOUNDARIES, or being ASSERTIVE. In varied usage, sometimes clearly maintaining respect for the 'recipient' of the tough love but at others simply a euphemism for harsh, imposed measures. The origin of the phrase is unclear.

training a generic term usually indicating a format or process in which a trainer aims to equip participants with particular, specified knowledge and skills. The difference between training and education, and whether such a distinction is useful, is a matter of debate. Typically, training is more geared towards the acquisition of a known range of skills or knowledge for a specific, applied purpose, whilst (formal) education is more cerebral and diffuse. Education (which means, literally, 'drawing out', so developing the person by encouraging their talents, potential and inherent qualities) usually refers to formalized institutions, systems and processes of teaching and LEARNING. This position is blurred by increasing emphasis on vocational education, a significant trend within LIFELONG LEARNING.

trait a term used mainly in psychology, a trait is considered an enduring personality quality or characteristic, whether learned or innate, found to varying degrees in more than two thirds of the population of any culture. Examples of traits are height, IQ, sociability, determination, INTROVERSION, EXTROVERSION and so on.

Understanding our own personality profile continues to be popular, evidenced by the quantity of PSYCHOMETRIC tests and personality inventories on offer in SELF-HELP publications, counselling, occupational psychology, and management and leadership training.

Transactional Analysis Transactional Analysis (TA) is a theory of personality as well as a powerful, systematic psychotherapy for personal growth and change. 'Transactions' refer to communication exchanges between people. Transactional Analysts are trained to recognize which EGO STATES people are transacting from and to follow the transactional sequences so they can intervene and improve the quality and effectiveness of communication (cited on the ITAA website – see Resources).

The theory of Transactional Analysis was developed by Eric Berne in the 1950s to offer health care practitioners (psychiatrists, social workers, psychotherapists, doctors and nurses) a more accessible model to understand human nature, and a more effective therapeutic method than the elitist PSY-CHOANALYSIS of that time.

TA is divided into five main sections: Structural Analysis (personality development); Functional Analysis (interpersonal communication theory); SCRIPT analysis; GAME theory; and RACK-ET analysis (Stewart and Joines 1987).

There are now three main professional applications of TA: clinical (psychotherapy and counselling), educational and organizational. It has an international membership, finding application in all cultures across the world.

Transcendental Meditation a technique of deep relaxation derived from the Ayurvedic tradition by Maharishi Mahesh Yogi (see Resources). It is a distinctive meditative practice that has been adapted for use outside monastic settings. Adopting TM practice does not imply, or require, support for the social, political and religious institutions that have been founded by TM practitioners. There is controversy about the status of studies which are claimed to prove the effectiveness of Transcendental Meditation, although there seems little reason to doubt that there are benefits as from other forms of MEDITATION.

transference the term literally means a distortion of a present object representation on the basis of experience in a previous object relationship (in Freudian terminology 'object' refers to a person or other material thing outside the intrapsychic world of the individual). 'One's feelings about a present object are altered in accordance with feelings originating in a previous relationship (Freud, cited in Ogden 1991: 81).

The transference can be either positive or negative. If the past experience was negative, such as abusive AUTHOR-ITY or poor parenting, then a counsellor or employer or others in authority in the present could be viewed through the distorted perceptions of the individual and be responded to in ways that seem displaced. The process is intrapsychic, that is, not dependent on the other person.

Counter-transference is equally an intrapsychic phenomenon. Here the practitioner transfers their own feelings or experiences from past relationships onto the client. The practitioner's unconscious needs and conflicts act as an interfering influence on their interpretation of the client and on the therapeutic relationship (Ogden 1991: 81).

Transference and counter-transference are a dynamic force in psychoanalytic theory, and in other psychotherapies since, and are the basis for the requirement of the therapist or counsellor to experience their own therapy. This is, for example, so that practitioners do not use clients to meet unconscious distressed or inappropriate needs.

This phenomenon of transference and the issue of how to use it therapeutically is not dissimilar to the management of projective identification (see PROJECTION). In both cases, the therapist separates out his or her own feelings and thinking from those experienced as coming from the client. The projected feelings are analysed by the therapist to understand the internal world of the client. Where necessary such understandings are reflected back to the client to facilitate the client's own understanding of their internal world.

transformation literally, change of form. Transformation may imply a dramatic or deep-seated form of CHANGE. But usage is rendering the term redundant; almost every workshop or SELF-HELP book is accompanied by hyperbolic claims that it has been, or will be, transformational. Presumably, any non-transformational personal development is no longer considered exciting or profound enough to contemplate.

This is an unfortunate tendency that contributes to the sensationalizing of personal development and plays into the hands of those who promise or demand quick fixes.

Transformation can refer to a change from one STAGE OF DEVELOPMENT to another in a specified model of personal growth. For example, John Rowan (1993) talks of 'breakthrough experiences', significant transitions that link to Ken Wilber's CENTAUR stage of development. A related idea is Willard Frick's concept of the 'symbolic growth experience' (Frick 1987).

transformation game the Transformation Game was developed at Findhorn, the spiritual community based in Scotland. It is a board game format designed to promote SELF-AWARENESS both through the content and through the interactions with other players. Other games with a similar intent have been developed. Findhorn continues to offer experiences of the Game itself, as well as facilitator training (see Resources).

transformative learning based on the work of Habermas, who posited three main types of learning (technical, practical and emancipatory). American educator Jack Mezirow pursued the third type and so developed his concept of transformative learning.

This, as Mezirow conceived it, implies a significant re-shaping of a person's meaning schema – their understanding of, and beliefs about, the world. According to Jarvis (1995: 97), Mezirow 'suggests that learning is the process of making meaning from experiences as a result of the learner's previous knowledge, so that learning is a new interpretation of experience'. As Jarvis notes, Mezirow's concept of learning has a primarily cognitive emphasis.

Mezirow associates his concept of 'perspective transformation' with major life changes, saying that such transformation 'can occur either through an accretion of transformed meaning schemes resulting from a series of dilemmas or in response to an externally imposed epochal dilemma such as death, illness, separation or divorce, children leaving home, being passed over for promotion or gaining a promotion, failing an important examination, or retirement' (Mezirow 1991: 168).

transition 'The psychological process people go through to come to terms with the situation' [of CHANGE] (Bridges 1995: 3).

Several models of life change and loss portray a process of transition from a starting state of shock, through a number of stages towards an end state of resolution or reintegration. One original source, often reproduced in texts on the management of change as well as on life transitions, is the work of Elizabeth Kübler-Ross (1970), who studied the experience of bereavement (see GRIEF). Another source (Adams et al. 1976) looked at changes in SELF-ESTEEM experienced during transition. Their stages were labelled as follows:

• immobilization
• minimization
• depression
• acceptance of reality, letting go
• testing
• search for meaning
• internalization.

Such models highlight the emotional shifts likely to be encountered in times of change. While these have been helpful for understanding the process of psychological and emotional adjustment involved in change, there is sometimes a tendency to use them in an instrumental and stereotypical way, with the purpose of hastening progress towards the final phase. As Kübler-Ross's work indicates, this runs the risk of keeping people cycling through the depressive stage.

Some more recent work on transitions is by William Bridges, an

American psychologist and management consultant. Bridges (1995, 1996) emphasizes the difference between change and transition, arguing that many change-management processes fail to attend to transitions. He highlights three main phases of transition:

1. letting go (of an old identity, an old reality, an old strategy)
2. crossing the wilderness between the old way and the new (the 'neutral zone')
3. making a new beginning and functioning effectively in a new way.

See also RITE OF PASSAGE.

transitional object in Winnicott's version of PSYCHOANALYTIC theory of infant development, the transitional object is a magical internalized object, controlled by the infant to help the separation process of the child as an independent person. Winnicott puts it, simply, that the transitional object 'may be the bit of cloth that once belonged to the cot-cover, or was a blanket or mother's hair ribbon. It is a first symbol, and it stands for confidence in the union of baby and mother based on the experience of mother's identification with the child' (Winnicott 1986: 50).

In healthy development the baby endows the object with what he or she perceives to be the powers of the omnipotent parent, while gradually internalizing these qualities. The important principle is that the child needs to believe that this is of his or her own creation. When the transitional phase is hampered by inconsistent parenting or other trauma the child believes he or she created this too. He or she will internalize the vulnerability of the parent, which then becomes the child's own vulnerability. As a result, self-identification is said to be fragmented.

Winnicott's ideas have been applied to the workplace in relation to change – see Morgan (1997: 236).

transmutation refers to the intentional transformation of distress into a more constructive state: an alternative to CATHARSIS. Heron (1990: 79) says: 'This means that the distinctively agitated, hurting energy of the distress is changed and refined into the calming, peaceful energy of a positive emotional state. And this is done by a silent, behaviourally imperceptible rearrangement of the structures of consciousness. Whereas catharsis can clearly be elicited and facilitated, so that we have cathartic interventions, this is not so with transmutation. It is an imperceptible, internal self-help method.'

transpersonal beyond the normal boundaries and limitations of individual personhood. From *trans*, the Latin preposition for 'across, beyond or through', and 'personal'.

The origins of the term 'transpersonal' are explored by Vich (1988: 109–110). There have been numerous attempts at definition. Grof's is probably the most successful: a transpersonal experience, he says, is 'when consciousness has expanded beyond the usual ego boundaries and has transcended the limitations of time and space' (Grof 1988: 38).

'Transpersonal' is, in essence, a morally neutral reference to a particular domain which avoids the value judgements at the heart of the concept 'spiritual' (see SPIRITUALITY). The term is generally used in contexts dealing with the psychology of religious and spiritual experience and the theoretical base underpinning our understanding of this. It is most usually met in the phrase TRANSPERSONAL PSYCHOLOGY.

The term can also refer to the planes that these experiences are thought to relate to, or to fields of study that deal with the world in a holistic fashion or which are relevant to transpersonal studies (e.g. anthropology or mythology). As giving direct experience of these planes, MYSTICISM and non-ordinary states of CONSCIOUSNESS are core concerns. John Rowan (1993) has written an excellent guide to transpersonal counselling and psychotherapy.

Transpersonal Psychology that branch of knowledge concerned with experiences that are connected with the TRANSPERSONAL domain.

As a separate, scientific, academic discipline Transpersonal Psychology is relatively new. Effectively it developed from HUMANISTIC PSYCHOLOGY. The phrase 'transpersonal psychology' originated in the mid-sixties. According to Vich (1988), Stanislav Grof used it in a lecture in September 1967. Maslow and Grof favoured it in place of 'trans-humanistic' or 'transhuman', apparently, to indicate the expansion of (humanistic) psychology to include a spiritual dimension. Finally, when the Journal of Transpersonal Psychology was founded (1968), the editors (who included Maslow and Sutich) settled upon it for the new periodical as fitting for their conception of a new and proper area of psychological enquiry (Vich 1988: 107).

Though it also investigates observable personal responses to its core material – such as individual spirituality, religious experience, rituals, and so on, particularly if they are outside orthodox religious traditions – the distinctive feature of this discipline is that its ambit includes experiences that ostensibly come from planes beyond the ordinary four-dimensional space-time world. To the usual description of the human PSYCHE it adds a domain that is beyond the ego, the personal unconscious or even the single individual. In transpersonal experiences the sense of identity expands into regions normally considered 'other'.

The Transpersonal Psychology perspective tends to be inclusive rather than exclusive, incorporating insights from more limited viewpoints (psycho-analytical or Humanistic psychology, for example). In addition to its multi-disciplinary embrace, it sees all cultures and historical ages as within its scope, and has consequently helped to revive the ancient wisdom traditions such as Christian mysticism, Kabbalah (see TREE OF LIFE), Gnosticism, TAOISM, and Zen BUDDHISM. All of these indicate the possibility of spiritual development beyond the normal level of the ego and the intellect. East and West, past and present, objective data and subjective experience, physical and spiritual, all offer potentially relevant material.

The success of this discipline in rehabilitating knowledge from outside the modern scientific tradition is increasingly recognized. Wilber's work, in particular, though undoubtedly disputable, has gone a long way towards an overall integration of previously opposed currents into an all-inclusive model (Wilber 1980, 1996; see also Rowan 1993).

trauma from the Greek, meaning 'a wound'. An extremely distressing event that may be the source of psychological problems for a person. Also refers to the experiencing of such an event. Someone who is traumatized may be in shock, catatonic or having a PANIC ATTACK. See also COPING BEHAVIOUR.

tree of life in the Kabbalah (a generic term for the secret oral teachings of Jewish mysticism – alternative spellings include Qabala – see e.g. Epstein 1978), the journey of personal and TRANSPERSONAL development is represented as a tree. The tree has ten centres or spheres of consciousness, called sephiroth. These are connected by a total of 22 paths, which some claim are directly related to the 22 major arcana of the TAROT. The tree of life is used as a map of development in various contemporary sources (for example, Matthews and Matthews 1986; Myss 1997).

trust exercise an experiential exercise, often physical in nature, that requires, and thereby aims to build, a level of trust between participants. A well-known trust exercise is the blind walk. In pairs, one partner is blindfolded and the other is the guide who must assist the blindfolded person to explore their world safely.

As another example, one person stands in the centre of the circle of participants. Those in the circle stand close enough to each other to leave no gaps, and just over an arm's length from the person in the centre. The person in the centre stands tall and straight, with feet together and, maintaining this posture, allows themselves to fall towards any part of the circle. Those in the circle cushion this person with their hands and arms, gently pushing them back towards the centre, from where they topple again. With the facilitator monitoring physical safety, both the person in the centre and the participants can then extend their movement, depending on the level of safety and trust they develop. Thus the person in the centre might close their eyes, those in the circle might propel the person more firmly.

Another way to build interpersonal trust is to use exercises that involve self-DISCLOSURE.

twelfth-step programme the 12th-Step Programme provides a way for the recovering 'addicted' person to live life. It is of particular interest as a method of development and SELF-HELP that helps to address addiction. The Steps enable people to modify characteristic issues that contribute to addiction, such as issues of control (see, for example, Bateson 1973), either-or thinking, confusion about feelings, and relationship difficulties. The ultimate goal is learning to take RESPONSIBILITY rather than externalizing problems, and learning to accept, forgive and love oneself.

The 12th-Step Programme was developed by Bill W and Dr Bob, founders of Alcoholics Anonymous in 1935. The steps provide a set of 'suggested' principles/guides to developing honest and fulfilling relationships with self and others in order to remove the desire to return to an addiction. They are intended to enable members to connect or reconnect with their SPIRITU-ALITY.

Here is the text of the Twelve Steps, which first appeared in *Alcoholics Anonymous,* the A.A. book of experience:

1. we admitted we were powerless over alcohol – that our lives had become unmanageable
2. came to believe that a power greater than ourselves could restore us to sanity
3. made a decision to turn our will and our lives over to the care of God, as we understood him
4. made a searching and fearless moral inventory of ourselves
5. admitted to God, to ourselves and to another human being the exact nature of our wrongs
6. were entirely ready to have God remove all these defects of character
7. humbly asked him to remove our shortcomings
8. made a list of all persons we had harmed, and became willing to make amends to them all
9. made direct amends to such people wherever possible, except when to do so would injure them or others
10. continued to take personal inventory and when we were wrong promptly admitted it
11. sought through prayer and meditation to improve our conscious contact with God, as we understood him, praying only for knowledge of his will for us and the power to carry that out
12. having had a spiritual awakening as the result of these steps, we tried to carry this message to alcoholics, and to practice these principles in all our affairs.

As a method of personal development, the programme is thought to work through seeing reality 'as it is' as opposed to the addicted person's distortion of it; learning to believe in the possibility of positive change; learning to ask for help from other people; believing in a positive higher power; and moderating the obsession with oneself by giving service within the group.

There are many active 12th-Step Groups, such as Alcoholics Anonymous (see Resources), Debtors Anonymous, Workaholics Anonymous, and many more. The term '12-step programme' is also used more generally, often to refer to formulaic processes of self-help and personal development.

U

unconditional positive regard Carl Rogers, one of the founders of HU-MANISTIC PSYCHOLOGY, gave the definition of an enabling relationship as one of positive regard, EMPATHY, and respect (Rogers 1967: 39–40). Unconditional positive regard implies a positive regard for the being of the person, notwithstanding any concerns one might have about the person's behaviour.

According to Rogers (1967: 41–47), helper attitudes that facilitate growth 'will be acceptance-democratic with an ability to develop a person-to-person relationship; ability to understand the person's meanings and feelings (or an attitude of a desire to understand) (**empathy**); a sensitivity to the person's attitudes; a warm interest without any emotional over-involvement, (**positive regard**). Trustworthiness is important if the relationship is to be helpful . . . which is about being CONGRUENT or transparent, that the helped person can see who you are as well as what you do, i.e., **genuineness or congruence**'.

This definition, in various guises, is the foundation stone for humanistic psychotherapy, counselling and facilitation.

unconscious the unconscious is contrasted with the CONSCIOUS. Understanding of the nature of the unconscious varies greatly with the perspective taken. See also CONSCIOUSNESS.

From Freud we inherit the idea of the unconscious as a repository of what is unwanted or repressed (see also DREAMS). Jung took a more optimistic view, with the unconscious as a rich source of imagery and SYMBOLS. Jung also introduced the idea of the COL-LECTIVE UNCONSCIOUS.

Various people – Gregory Bateson, and Fritz Perls, for example – have advocated the 'wisdom of the unconscious', entailing the idea that our conscious, rational minds are really rather short-sighted and limited and should not be trusted with guiding our entire existence. Such people also saw the unconscious mind as operating according to different, non-literal and non-linear, principles. The unconscious mind, in this sense, is engaged intentionally in personal development in modes such as NLP.

unfinished business whatever has been left unsaid or uncompleted. In GESTALT therapy, 'unfinished business' is whatever prevents the completion of a gestalt of experience, and thus continues to demand attention and prevent 'closure'.

Unfinished business often refers to what one person needs to say to another. For example, voicing resentment can allow the person to let go of that resentment. The term is also used to refer to longer-term unfinished business, such as that left from childhood experience. The incomplete gestalt continues to draw on psychological energy and to interfere with human functioning.

urban shamanism urban SHAMANISM is an attitude to life whereby the inter-connectedness of all things brings meaning and purpose into everyday activities. Urban shamans acknowledge the earth as a living and communicative being, see all obstacles on their paths as worthy foes to help them sharpen their intent, and use ritual and ceremony to stay in sacred contact with natural law.

The intellectual champion of shamanism was the Jungian anthropologist Joseph Campbell, supported by Joan Halifax, and later Clarisa Pinkola Estes (1992). However, the leading writer in the sphere of applicable shamanism has been the mysterious Carlos Castañeda (1970, 1973, 1974). From the late 1960s he introduced the world to the still-existing pre-Columbian wisdom of native America and such concepts as the 'warrior's unshakeable intent', the 'Beneficial Tyrant', and the arts of Seeing and Dreaming.

Castañeda's vision was developed, systematized and made available to the public through the work of Harley 'SwiftDeer' Reagan (1980). Other complementary approaches have been made by the West African Malidoma Patrice Somé (1994), Martin Prechtel, and the dance therapist Gabrielle Roth. There is a further stream which focuses on the European Celtic tradition and its application to modern life.

Urban shamanism can be said to have two main paths: first the psycho-spiritual arena of developing personal mastery over the emotional self and outer challenges; and secondly the ceremonial side where the accoutrements of shamanism (drumming, burning herbs, dance, and ritual) are more prominent.

validation valuing or honouring of a person. Used in CO-COUNSELLING, where to validate is to affirm a person's being.

values ideas that a person believes to be worthwhile or feels to be right.

Values are closely related to ATTITUDES and to BELIEFS. Whether or how they are distinguished may depend on the theory or model being used. Usually, values are more feeling-based whereas beliefs are more cognitive in nature. Values are thought of as underlying and may be deeply-held, whereas attitudes are more transitory and social.

Values clarification exercises, usually designed to make values explicit and to support a participant's capacity to choose his or her values freely, are sometimes used in workshops.

vision Vision can refer to:
- the sense of sight
- the visual REPRESENTATIONAL SYSTEM
- a MYSTICAL revelation
- an inspirational image (see VISUALIZATION).

'Vision logic' is a term Ken Wilber (1980) uses to denote the 'logic' of INTUITION, SYMBOLS and IMAGERY.

vision quest the term 'vision quest' is from American first nations' traditions (see, for example, Foster and Little 1989). A vision quest or its equivalent is found in many cultures, and is a form of initiation ritual (see RITE OF PASSAGE) or search for self-discovery.

Typically, a person goes out alone into some natural setting or wilderness and waits for, invites or seeks an inspiring vision that helps them to connect with their core SELF and their purpose.

Like many methods from spiritual disciplines, the concept of a vision quest is offered as a contemporary personal development training. It is being made palatable for management training; and is even being used as a brand name.

visualization visualization is a mental process using 'the mind's eye' as a way of accessing IMAGERY and internal information. It deals with inner events through visual rather than verbal thought and may be done consciously (as in remembering or imagining) or unconsciously (as in dreaming).

The conscious process can be seen as a way of tapping into the unconscious through images in order to bring about a desired outcome, whether that is a memory, a wish or a visual idea or plan. This is something which can be done by oneself or with a 'guide' (i.e. someone trained in the use of images), alone or in a group.

The earliest evidence of the applied use of conscious visualization would seem to be cave paintings and the people, animals and scenes depicted there from memory or imagination. These paintings are believed by some to have been ways both of recording what had been seen, and of anticipating what was hoped for (i.e. successful hunts) (Jung 1964).

The history of visualization includes its use in early religions and philosophies as a tool for personal growth and transformation, while SHAMANIC healers visualized going on a journey into a person's world in order to restore them to health (Samuels and Samuels 1975). These continue to be among the ways in which it is used today, whether through therapeutic interventions and techniques or as part of organizational and professional development training.

The assumptions behind such techniques as 'creative visualization' (Gawain 1995) and 'imagework' (Glouberman 1989) are that it is possible to bring about what people want to create in their lives.

voice work a mode of personal development based on developing the voice. Essentially a whole-body and whole-person activity, as voice production depends on BREATHING, posture and movement, is directly linked to emotional EXPRESSION, and has a spiritual dimension too.

Voice work as a mode of personal development for the general public can operate at many levels. Some practitioners have a background in music or singing, and draw on traditions from around the world, including Tibet, Mongolia and more. Others have had a primary interest in the psychological and emotional significance of voice, and experience an enhanced ability to sing as a delightful added benefit.

'Voice Movement Therapy' is a particular mode of expressive arts therapy. See also CHANTING.

W

warrior an ARCHETYPE of the human capacity for focused aggression (e.g. as displayed by the trained martial artist), which can be constructive in appropriate circumstances. This archetype is present in spiritual traditions throughout the world (for example, Trungpa 1988).

The Way of the Peaceful Warrior is the title of a classic human potential 'autobiographical' novel by Dan Millman (2000), the story of his personal growth and athletic success guided by a shamanic mentor, the gas-station attendant Socrates. The idea of the peaceful warrior is also represented by historical figures such as Mahatma Gandhi.

See also URBAN SHAMANISM.

well-being see HEALTH.

wholeness the quality of being whole, or experiencing oneself as whole. See also HOLISTIC.

Many modes of personal development emphasize the desirability of wholeness, or claim to work with 'the whole person'. Clarkson (1989: 17) notes, for example, that GESTALT will usually acknowledge 'intrapsychic, behavioural, physiological, affective, cognitive and spiritual aspects of the client's life'.

Will although all psychologies are interested in human motivation the study of Will has had few adherents. Among these are Rank, Adler, Assagioli, Frankl,

and May. While Adler and Rank focused on the power and struggle concerned with the employment of the Will, Roberto Assagioli's PSYCHOSYNTHESIS went furthest to delineate its nature and aspects, highlighting the challenge and liberation of the act of choice.

Assagioli (1975a) considered the Will to be the counterpart to the Self's function of awareness. Importantly, he distinguished between the Victorian 'Strong Will', and other aspects such as Skilful and Universal Will. He believed that understanding the nature of Will was crucial to mankind: 'It is imperative to narrow the gap between man's external and inner power.' Besides evolving a psychology of Will, on a personal level he recommended a two-pronged approach: simplifying the external life, and developing inner powers.

EXISTENTIAL psychologists, like Rollo May (1953), were more interested in the concepts of maturity, responsibility, and freedom which the deliberate and conscious employment of Will implies. They noticed the human being's reluctance to engage in life at such a level of commitment.

withdrawal when used within the TRANSACTIONAL ANALYSIS model of TIME-STRUCTURING, refers to a need for private time or a psychological withdrawal as a defensive strategy. Either way, the only STROKES a person can receive in withdrawal are self-strokes, and there is minimal psychological risk of receiving 'rejection' strokes from others. It is in psychological withdrawing while still being physically present that the concept of 'withholding self' makes conceptual sense.

workplace learning workplace learning refers, literally, to learning that a person acquires, or which is available, in the course of work. The term is of contemporary significance because of, for example, emphasis from the UK government as well as employers on the potential of, and the necessity for, workplace learning for economic reasons. Related terms in usage are work-based learning and work-related learning.

According to Raelin (2000), work-based learning differs from classroom learning in that:

- it requires REFLECTION on work practices – as distinct from acquiring skills or content knowledge
- learning arises from action and problem-solving within a working environment (see ACTION LEARNING)
- knowledge creation is a collective activity
- it requires the meta-skill of LEARNING TO LEARN.

This view represents those writers and practitioners who (as with the notion of INFORMAL AND INCIDENTAL LEARNING) emphasize learning that does not use traditional classroom methods. Perhaps ironically, therefore, some workplace learning initiatives (such as 'professional universities') make extensive use of classroom methods, and one can detect a significant trend towards the formalization of workplace learning in related government policies.

workshop usually an interactive, experiential event, less formal than a training course; or a session within a training course or educational programme.

yin and yang the TAOIST tradition held that yin and yang were two kinds of cosmic energies which imbued all creation. They are often perceived as opposites by Westerners, but traditionally were believed to be complementary, each containing some of the other.

Chinese philosophy and medicine allocates every part of the created world its yin and yang qualities. It identifies an ENERGY, chi, which binds them together, and flows within and around them. Everything is classified in terms of its yin and yang qualities. Yang is generally thought of as male, creative, light, heat, hard, dry; spirit and action. Yin is considered to represent the female principle, receptive, dark, cold, soft, wet; creative and passive.

Yin and yang are part of TAOIST cosmology. They are believed to have emerged from an original heavenly circle before the beginning of time. They then became separated into creation, which is considered to be yang, and matter, which is yin. The well-known yin-yang symbol of Taoism symbolizes the cosmos, human beings, compass points and the seasons. They are considered as inseparable, and unable to exist without each other.

yoga a practice of meditation and exercise, sometimes quasi-religious, more often health-related. Yoga literally means 'a yoke', alluding to the disciplined nature of the practice. It represents a form of BODYMIND development.

There are multitudinous forms of yoga, some associated directly with traditions from India or Tibet, others associated with particular teachers. Certain yogic exercises may be used to raise KUNDALINI.

One classic type is hatha yoga, which emphasizes the breath as a means of controlling and enhancing the life-force (prana). It also uses many bodily postures, known as 'asanas'.

Zen see BUDDHISM.

Resources

Inclusion of terms referring to practices or bodies should not be taken as approval or recommendation of those practices or bodies. The authors do not accept responsibility for, and do not endorse the content of, any service or website listed here.

Associations

The American National Association for Dramatherapy
5505 Connecticut Ave., N.W. #280
Washington, DC 20015
USA
Tel: 202 966–7409
Fax: 202 966–2283
Website: www.nadt.org
Email: nadt@danielgrp.com

The Association for Humanistic Psychology (AHP)
1516 Oak St
#320A
Alameda
CA 94501–2947
USA
Website: ahpweb.org/index.html
Email: ahpoffice@aol.com

AHP in Britain (AHPB)
BM Box 3582
London WC1N 3XX
UK
Tel: 0345 078506
Website: ahpb.org.uk (many useful links at ahpweb.org/involve/websites.html)

Association for Humanistic Psychology Practitioners (AHPP)
AHPP Administrator
Box BCM AHPP
London WC1N 3XX
UK

The Association for Management Education and Development (AMED)
62 Paul Street
London EC2A 4NA
UK
Tel: 0207 613 4121
Fax: 0207 613 4737
Website: www.amed.management.org.uk
Email: julian@management.org.uk

The Association for Neuro-Linguistic Programming (ANLP)
Caroline Coughlan
ANLP Administration Office
PO Box 10, Porthmadog LL48 6ZB
UK
Tel: 0870 870 4970
Fax: 0870 444 0790
Website: www.anlp.org
Email (public enquiries):
admin@anlp.org

The Association for Transpersonal Psychology
PO Box 29030
San Francisco
CA 94129–0030
USA
Tel: 415 561–3382
Fax: 415 561–3383
Website: www.atpweb.org
Email: atpweb@mindspring.com

The British Association for Counselling and Psychotherapy (BAC)
1 Regent Place
Rugby
Warwickshire
CV21 2PJ
UK
Website: www.counselling.co.uk

The British Autogenic Society
(The Administrator)
Royal London Homeopathic Hospital
Great Ormond Street
London WC1N 3HR
UK
Tel/Fax: 0207 713 6336
Website: www.autogenic-therapy.org.uk

The British Rebirthing Society
South Manor Road
Catcott
Bridgwater
Somerset TA7 9HT
UK
Tel: 01278 722536

The Chartered Institute of Personnel and Development
CIPD House
Camp Road
London SW19 4UX
UK
Tel: 0208 971 9000
Fax: 0208 263 3333
Website: www.ipd.co.uk/start.asp

European Association for Integrative Psychotherapy (EAIP)
PO Box 2512
Ealing
London W5 2QB
UK

The European Association for Transactional Analysis (EATA)
EATA, c/o Martine Huon
Les Toits de l'Aune Bat. E
3, rue Hugo Ely
F–13090 Aix-en-Provence
France
Website: www.eatanews.org/index.html
Email: info@eatanews.org

The International Enneagram Association
1060 N. 4th Street
San Jose, CA 95112
USA
Tel: 408 971–5905
Website: www.intl-enneagram-assn.org/enneagrm.html
Email: IEAStaff@intl-enneagram-assn.org

The International Foundation for Action Learning (IFAL)
c/o Department of Management Learning
The Management School
Lancaster University
Lancaster LA1 4YX
UK
Tel: 01524 812254
Website (world-wide):
www.tlainc.com/ifal.htm
Website (UK):
www.btinternet.com/~saraswati.soc/home.htm

The International Institute for Bioenergetics
144 E. 36th Street
New York, NY 10016
USA
Tel: 212 532–7742
Fax: 212 532–5331
Website: www.bioenergetic-therapy.com
Email: iibanet@aol.com

The International Transactional Analysis Association (ITAA)
436 14th Street, Suite 1301
Oakland, CA 94612–2710
USA
Tel: 510 625–7720
Fax: 510 625–7725
Website: www.itaa-net.org
Email: itaa@itaa-net.org

The Society of Alexander Teachers (UK)
129 Camden Mews
London NW1 9AH
UK
Tel: 0207 284 3338
Fax: 0207 482 5435
Website: stat.org.uk
Email: info@stat.org.uk

The Society for Effective Affective Learning (SEAL)
The Society for Effective Affective Learning (SEAL) was founded in 1983 to promote Lozanov's work (see SUGGESTO-PEDIA) and has since broadened to include all learning methods with similar aims and principles.
PO Box 2246
Bath BA1 2YR
UK
Tel/Fax: 01225 444024
Website: www.seal.org.uk
Email: admin@seal.soceal.demon.co.uk

The UK Council for Psychotherapy (UKCP)
167–69 Great Portland Street
London W1N 5FB
UK
Tel: 0207 436 3002
Fax: 0207 436 3013
Website: www.psychotherapy.org.uk
Email: ukcp@psychotherapy.org.uk

Centres, networks, support groups

Alcoholics Anonymous
General Service Office of AA (UK)
PO Box 1
Stonebow House
Stonebow
York YO1 2NJ
UK
Tel: 01904 644026
Fax: 01904 629091
Website (Int.): www.alcoholics-anonymous.org/english/F–2_d1.htm
Website (UK): www.alcoholics-anonymous.org.uk

Alternatives
Alternatives is a non-profit making organisation that has been running a successful lecture series since 1989 in:
St James's Church
197 Piccadilly
London W1
UK
Tel: 0207 287 6711
Website: www.alternatives.org.uk
Email: alternatives@ukonline.co.uk

Centre for Action Research in Professional Practice
University of Bath
Bath
BA2 7AY
UK
Tel: 01225 826826
Fax: 01225 826473
Website:
www.bath.ac.uk/carpp/index.htm

Centre for Gender Psychology
The Centre for Gender Psychology
128a Northview Road
London N8 7LP
UK
Tel: 0208 341 4885
Website: www.genderpsychology.com
Email: info@genderpsychology.com

Circle Dance
Grapevine magazine is the network's quarterly journal. At the time of writing its editorship is held by Frances Fawkes (tel: 01647 277227).

Co-Counselling International (UK)
Website:
www.dpets.demon.co.uk/cciuk/index

Community Building in Britain [CBiB]
Peter Cooper
52 Sole Farm Avenue
Bookham
Leatherhead KT23 3DE
UK
Tel: 07974 961301
Email: PeterCBiB@aol.com

Connections
c/o David Jaques
7 Stanley Road
Oxford OX4 1QY
UK
Tel: 01865 724141
Fax: 01865 203255
Website: www.treda.co.uk/connections
Email: davidjaques@i-way.co.uk

Cortijo Romero

(UK contact address)
c/o Little Grove
Grove Lane
Chesham HP5 3QQ
UK
Tel: 01494 782720
Fax: 01494 776066
Website: www.cortijo-romero.co.uk

Douai Abbey

Douai Abbey
Upper Woolhampton
Reading
Berkshire RG7 5TQ
UK
Tel: 0118 971 5300
Fax: 0118 971 5203
Website: members.aol.com/douaiweb
Email: douaiabby@aol.com

The Educational Kinesiology Foundation

Ventura
CA 1–800–356–2109
USA
Website: www.braingym.org
Email: edukfd@earthlink.net

Enlightenment Intensives

Website:
www.enlightenment-intensives.org.uk

Esalen

'Esalen was founded in 1962 as an educational center devoted to the exploration of unrealized human capacities. It soon became known for its blend of East/West philosophies, its experiential/didactic workshops, the steady influx of philosophers, psychologists, artists, and religious thinkers, and its breathtaking grounds blessed with natural hot springs. Once home to a Native American tribe known as the Esselen, Esalen is situated on 27 acres of spectacular Big Sur coastline with the Santa Lucia Mountains rising sharply behind.'

Esalen Institute
Highway 1
Big Sur, CA 93920–9616
USA
Website: www.esalen.org/index.shtml

Findhorn

'The Findhorn Foundation is at the heart of one of the best-known intentional communities in the world. It is a major international centre of adult education and personal and spiritual transformation, offering people many ways to visit, live and work here. We are located in northern Scotland.'
The Findhorn Foundation
The Park
Findhorn
Forres IV36 3TZ
Moray
Scotland
Tel: 01309 690311
Fax: 01309 691301
Website: www.findhorn.org/index.html
Email: reception@findhorn.org

The Gestalt Centre

62 Paul Street
London
EC2A 4NA
UK
Tel: 0207 613 4480
Fax: 0207 613 4737
Website: ds.dial.pipex.com/gestaltc
Email: gestaltcentre@dial.pipex.com

Human Potential Research Group

School of Educational Studies
University of Surrey
Guildford
Surrey GU2 7XH
UK
Tel: 01483 300800
Website:
www.surrey.ac.uk/Education/hprg/
hprgindx.htm

The Independent Practitioners' Network

A UK national organisation of psycho-practitioners who seek to hold accountability to their clients in ways that are congruent with their values and skills.
Website: ipnosis.postle.net

The Institute of Noetic Sciences

'For 25 years, the Institute of Noetic Sciences has been at the forefront of research and education in consciousness and human potential. From the beginning we have pursued this inquiry through rigorous science.' Website includes an archive of many useful articles on consciousness and related subjects.

101 San Antonio Road
Petaluma, CA 94952
USA
Tel: 707 775–3500
Fax: 707 781–7420
Website: www.noetic.org

International Centre for Co-operative Inquiry (John Heron)
Website:
zeus.sirt.pisa.it/icci/welcome.html#ICCI
The International Cyberspace for Co-operative Inquiry:
Website:
www.voyager.co.nz/~jheron/page4.html
See also The South Pacific Centre for Human Inquiry.

The London Association of Primal Psychotherapists
Tel/fax: 0207 482 0858
Website: pumpkinpie.com/lapp/index
Email: info@lapp.org

The Lucis Trust
Suite 54
3 Whitehall Court
London SW1A 2EF
UK
Tel: 0207 839 4512
Fax: 0207 839 5575
Website: www.lucistrust.org/lucispub

The Manchester Gestalt Centre
7 Norman Road
Manchester M14 5LF
UK
Tel/Fax: 0161 257 2202
Website:
www.mgestaltc.force9.co.uk/index.htm
Email: mgc@mgc.org.uk

Metanoia
North Common Road
Ealing
London W5 2QB
UK
Tel: 0208 579 2505
Fax: 0208 566 4349
Website: www.metanoia.ac.uk
Email: mail@metanoia.ac.uk

The Minster Centre
17 Mapesbury Road
London NW2
UK
Tel: 0208 450 3311
Website (under construction):
www.os94.dial.pipex.com

NLP Education Network
Jeff Lewis
24 Oaklands Lane
Smallford
St Albans
Herts AL4 0HR
UK
Tel: 01727 856200
Fax: 01727 842181
Website: www.new-oceans.co.uk/ednet/index.htm
Email: Jeff_Lewis@new-oceans.co.uk

Non Mainstream Psychotherapy and Counselling Resources on the Internet
A resource maintained by psychotherapist Nick Totton.
Website: www.psyctc.org/mirrors/non-main/nonmain.htm

Oasis
Oasis Human Relations
Hall Mews
Clifford Road
Boston Spa
Wetherby LS23 6DT
UK
Website: www.oasis-centre.demon.co.uk/home.htm
Email: info@oasishumanrelations.co.uk

The Open Centre
The Open Centre
3rd Floor, 188 Old Street
London EC1V 9FR
UK
Tel/Fax: 0207 251 1504
Website: www.opencentre.com
Email: info@opencentre.com

The Psychosynthesis and Education Trust
92/94 Tooley Street
London SE1 2TH
UK
Tel: 0207 403 2100
Fax: 0207 403 5562
Website: www.psychosynthesis.edu
Email: psychosynthesis.eductrust@btinternet.com

Relate (UK)
Herbert Gray College
Little Church Street
Rugby
Warwickshire CV21 3AP
UK
Website: www.relate.org.uk/main.htm

Re-vision (Centre for Integrative Psychosynthesis)
97 Brondesbury Road
London NW6 6RY
UK
Tel: 0208 357 8881
Fax: 0208 357 9661
Website: www.re-vision.org.uk
Email: info@re-vision.org.uk

The Scapegoat Society
The Scapegoat Society
Forest Row
East Sussex RH18 5JF
UK
Website: www.scapegoat.demon.co.uk

Schumacher College
'Founded in 1991, Schumacher College is an international centre for ecological studies. The foundations of a more sustainable world view are explored through a combination of intellectual inquiry, work and reflection.' (Dartington Hall website)
The Old Postern
Dartington Hall
Totnes TQ9 6EA
UK
Tel: 01803 865934
Fax: 01803 866899
Website: www.gn.apc.org/schumachercollege
Email: schumcoll@gn.apc.org

The Skyros Centre
c/o 92 Prince of Wales Road
London NW5 3NE
UK
Tel: 0207 267 4424
Tel: 0207 284 3065
Tel: 0207 284 3063
Website: www.skyros.com
Email: www.skyros.com

The South Pacific Centre for Human Inquiry
11 Bald Hill Road
R.D.1 Kaukapakapa
Auckland 1250
New Zealand
Website: www.human-inquiry.com
Email: jheron@human-inquiry.com

Spectrum
'As far as we know, Spectrum is the largest combined training centre and practice committed specifically to the development of humanistic psychology in the world and one of the most established.'

7 Endymion Road
London N4 1EE
UK
Tel: 0208 341 2277
Fax: 0208 340 0426
Website: www.spectrumtherapy.co.uk/home.htm

The Tavistock Institute for Human Relations
'The Tavistock Institute is an independent social science research, advisory and training organisation.'

The Tavistock Institute
30 Tabernacle Street
London EC2A 4UE
UK
Tel: 0207 417 0407
Fax: 0207 417 0566
Website: www.tavinstitute.org
Email: central.admin@tavinstitute.org

Transcendental Meditation
Website: www.transcendental-meditation.org.uk

The Viktor Frankl Institute
'The Viktor Frankl Institute is a non-profit scientific society for Logotherapy and Existential Analysis.' Website includes access to an extensive bibliography.

Langwiesgasse 6
A–1140 Vienna
Austria
Tel/Fax: 1914 2683
Website: logotherapy.univie.ac.at
Email: logos@ap.univie.ac.at

The Wrekin Trust
20 The Chase
Reigate
Surrey RH2 7DH
Tel/Fax: 01737 779386

Personal development: reference and self-help sources on the Web

Buddhist Studies WWW Virtual Library
Website: www.ciolek.com/WWWVL-Buddhism.html

Byzant
'Aims to help you explore, enjoy and examine a range of subjects encompassing mysticism, symbolism, philosophy, psychology, poetry, spirituality and beyond.'
Website: www.byzant.com

The Catholic Encyclopedia
'It differs from the general encyclopedia in omitting facts and information which have no relation to the Church. On the other hand, it is not exclusively a church encyclopedia, nor is it limited to the ecclesiastical sciences and the doings of churchmen. It records all that Catholics have done, not only on behalf of charity and morals, but also for the intellectual and artistic development of mankind.'
Website: newadvent.org/cathen

Classics in the History of Psychology
An Electronic Resource developed by Christopher D. Green, York University, Toronto, Canada (ISSN 1492–3173). Includes online access to classic articles.
Website:
psychclassics.yorku.ca/index.htm

A Dictionary of Philosophy of Mind
By Chris Eliasmith, Department of Philosophy, Washington University in St. Louis.
Website:
artsci.wustl.edu/~philos/MindDict/index.html

A Dictionary of Postmodern Terms
On the site of Postmodern Therapies' News.
Website: www.california.com/~rathbone/lexicon.htm

Robert Dilts (NLP)
Robert Dilts's homepage includes many articles on NLP. There is also a link to his newly published NLP encyclopedia (www.nlpuniversitypress.com).
Website: www.scruz.net/~rdilts

Enneagram Monthly
Website: www.ideodynamic.com/enneagram-monthly/EM_quoi.htm

The Expanded Dictionary of Metaphysical Healthcare
By Jack Raso, MS, RD (Subtitled 'Alternative Medicine, Paranormal Healing, and Related Methods'.)
Website: www.hcrc.org/diction/dict.html

The Global Ideas Bank
'A Global Ideas Bank for socially innovative non-technological ideas and projects.'
Website: www.globalideasbank.org

G.O.R.I.L.L.A. (Denis Postle)
'G.O.R.I.L.L.A. was founded in response to developments in the "caring for the human condition" trade in the UK . . . I wanted to have a place where dissenting voices could be heard and where a positive program of research and development into viable alternatives could find support.'
Website: www.lpiper.demon.co.uk

Guide to the Transpersonal Internet

'This guide covers the small but rich portion of the Internet with transpersonal content. It was first published as an article in the ATP Newsletter in Fall 1997 (last updated 1/01).'
Website: www.virtualcs.com/tpi.html

John Heron

See under 'Centres': International Centre for Co-operative Inquiry; The South Pacific Centre for Human Inquiry.

The History of Psychology Website

'The site provides a gateway for teachers and students to over 1000 World Wide Web resources related to the history of psychology.'
Website: elvers.stjoe.udayton.edu/history/welcome.htm

Inner Self Magazine

Website: www.innerself.com/index.htm

InterConnections

'Our aim is to provide you with up-to-date information on all aspects of holistic living.'
Website: www.interconnections.co.uk

Oikos: Towards an Ecology of Mind

'This page makes the bridging connections from Ecology [as having to do with nature, the environment etc.] to Psychology [as the attempts to understand our human experiencing].'
Includes links for Gregory Bateson.
Website: www.oikos.org/psicen.htm

Harrison Owen (Open Space Technology)

Website: www.mindspring.com/~owenhh

Red Feather Dictionary of Critical Social Science

Abbreviated version of the 3rd edition of the Red Feather Dictionary, available in hard copy from Westview Press.
Website: www.tryoung.com/Dictionary/shortdict.html

John Rowan

See under 'Associations': Association for Humanistic Psychology.

Peter Russell

Website: www.peterrussell.com/index2.html

Skeptic's Dictionary

'Over 400 skeptical definitions and essays on occult, paranormal, supernatural and pseudoscientific ideas and practices with references to the best skeptical literature.'
Website: skepdic.com

SpiritWeb

'Comprehensive website promoting spiritual consciousness since 1994.'
Website: www.spiritweb.org

Stanford Encyclopedia of Philosophy

Principal Editor: Edward N. Zalta.
Publisher: The Metaphysics Research Lab at the Center for the Study of Language and Information, Stanford University, Stanford, CA.
Website: plato.stanford.edu/contents.html

Rudolph Steiner Archive

Website: www.elib.com/Steiner

Suite 101

An 'online publishing community'.
Website: www.suite101.com

Bill Torbert

Website: www2.bc.edu/~torbert

The University of Alberta's Cognitive Science Dictionary

Website: web.psych.ualberta.ca/~mike/Pearl_Street/Dictionary/dictionary.html

Web Dictionary of Cybernetics and Systems

Website: pespmc1.vub.ac.be/ASC/INDEXASC.html

Ken Wilber Online

Website: wilber.shambhala.com

Other general resources/reference sources

Amazon
Website (Int.): www.amazon.com
Website (UK): www.amazon.co.uk

Encyclopaedia Britannica
Website: www.britannica.com

Encyclopedia.com
More than 14 000 articles from *The Concise Columbia Electronic Encyclopedia*, 3rd edition.
Website:
www.encyclopedia.com/home.html

Harcourt Academic Press Dictionary of Science and Technology
Website:
www.harcourt.com/dictionary/browse/soc.html

Internet History Sourcebooks Project
An extensive source on ancient, medieval and modern history, includes text extracts such as one from Samuel Smiles on 'self-help'.
Website: www.fordham.edu/halsall

References

Adair J (1998) The John Adair Handbook of Management and Leadership. London: Thorogood.

Adams J, Hayes J, Hopson B (1976) Transition: Understanding and Managing Personal Change. London: Martin Robertson.

Argyle M (1969) Social Interaction. London: Tavistock Publications.

Argyris C (1994) On Organizational Learning. Oxford: Blackwell Business.

Aronson E (1994) Communication in sensitivity-training groups. In French WL, Bell CH, Zawacki RA (Eds) Organization Development and Transformation. (4th edn) Burr Ridge, IL: Irwin.

Assagioli R (1965) Psychosynthesis: A Manual of Principles and Techniques. New York: Viking.

Assagioli R (1975a) The Act of Will. New York: Penguin.

Assagioli R (1975b) Psychosynthesis: A Collection of Basic Writings. Wellingborough: Turnstone Books.

Assagioli R (1992) The Act of Will. New York: Penguin Arkana.

Assagioli R (1994) The Act Of Will: Self-realisation Through Psychosynthesis. London: Aquarian Edition.

Back KW (1972) Beyond Words: The Story of Sensitivity Training and the Encounter Movement. New York: Russell Sage Foundation.

Back K, Back K (1999) Assertiveness At Work: A Practical Guide to Handling Awkward Situations. London: McGraw-Hill.

Bailey AA (1970) Esoteric Psychology: A Treatise on the Seven Rays, Vol. 1. Lucis Publishing (www.lucistrust.org/lucispub).

Baldwin W (1987) Agape: A Devotion on 1 Corinthians 13. Oldham: Christian Print and Publishing Co Ltd.

Bandler R, Grinder J (1975) The Structure of Magic: A Book about Language and Therapy. Palo Alto, CA: Science and Behaviour Books.

Bandler R, Grinder J (1979) Frogs Into Princes. Moab, UT: Real People Press.

Bandler R, Grinder J (1982) Reframing: Neuro-Linguistic Programming and the Transformation of Meaning. Moab, UT: Real People Press.

Bandler R, MacDonald W (1988) An Insider's Guide to Sub-Modalities. Cupertino, CA: Meta Publications.

Bannister D, Fransella F (1986) Inquiring Man: The Psychology of Personal Constructs. (3rd edn) London: Croom Helm.

Bateson G (1973) Steps to an Ecology of Mind. London: Paladin, Granada. (New edn available 2000.)

Bateson G (1979) Mind and Nature. Glasgow: Fontana/Collins.

Bateson G, Bateson MC (1988) Angels Fear. London: Rider Books.

Battram A (1998) Navigating Complexity. London: The Industrial Society.

Beckhard R (1969) Organization Development: Strategies and Models. Reading, MA: Addison-Wesley.

Begg D (1999) Rebirthing. London: Thorsons.

Belbin MR (1996) Team Roles at Work. Oxford: Butterworth-Heinemann.

Berne E (1961) Transactional Analysis in Psychotherapy. New York: Grove Press.

Berne E (1968) Games People Play. Harmondsworth: Penguin.

Berne E (1972) What Do You Say After You Say Hello? New York: Grove Press.

Bertalanffy L (1975) Perspectives on General Systems Theory. New York: George Braziller.

Bettelheim B (1985) Freud and Man's Soul. London: Flamingo, Fontana Paperbacks.

Bion W (1961) Experiences in Groups. London: Tavistock Publications.

Blake RR, Mouton JS (1964) The Managerial Grid. Houston: Gulf Publishing Company.

Block P (1981) Flawless Consulting. California: University Associates. (2nd edition 1999; San Francisco: Jossey Bass.)

Bly R (1990) Iron John: A Book About Men. New York: Addison-Wesley.

Boadella D (Ed.) (1991) In the Wake of Reich. (2nd edn) Boston, MA: Coverture Ltd.

Bodian S (1999) Meditation for Dummies. New York: Hungry Minds Inc.

Bohm D (1980) Wholeness and the Implicate Order. London: Routledge and Kegan Paul.

Bolton GM, Bolton G, Heathcote D (1997) So You Want to Use Role-Play? Stoke-on-Trent: Trentham Books.

Boud D (Ed.) (1988) Developing Student Autonomy in Learning. (2nd edn) London: Kogan Page.

Boud D, Cohen R, Walker D (Eds) (1993) Using Experience for Learning. Buckingham: Society for Research into Higher Education and Open University Press.

Boud D, Feletti G (Eds) (1997) The Challenge of Problem Based Learning. (2nd edn) London: Kogan Page.

Boud D, Keogh R, Walker D (Eds) (1985) Reflection: Turning Experience into Learning. London: Kogan Page.

Bowlby J (1969) Attachment and Loss. London: Hogarth and the Institute of Psychoanalysis.

Bowlby J (1979) The Making and Breaking of Affectional Bonds. London: Routledge.

Bowles ML (1991) The organization shadow. Organization Studies 11(3): 395–412.

Bozarth JD (1986) The basic encounter group: an alternative view. Journal for Specialists in Group Work 11(4): 228–32. Available online at personcentered.com/group1.htm; accessed 15 Dec. 2000.

Brennan B (1988) Hands of Light. New York: Bantam Books.

Bridges W (1992) The Character of Organisations: Using Jungian Types in Organisations. Palo Alto, CA: Consulting Psychologists Press.

Bridges W (1995) Managing Transitions. London: Nicholas Brealey.

Bridges W (1996) Transitions: Making Sense of Life's Changes. London: Nicholas Brealey.

Briggs-Myers I, Myers PB (1980) Gifts Differing. Palo Alto, CA: Davies-Black Publishing.

Brookfield S (1987) Developing Critical Thinkers. Milton Keynes: OU Press.

Buber M (1947) Tales of the Hasidim. In Vardey L (Ed.) God in All Worlds: An Anthology of Contemporary Spiritual Writing. London: Chatto and Windus.

Buber M (1958) I and Thou. New York: Charles Scribner's Sons.

Buber M (1965) Between Man and Man. New York: Collier Books, Macmillan Publishing Company.

Buchanan DA, Huczynski AA (1997) Organizational Behaviour. (3rd edn) London: Prentice Hall.

Buzan T (2000) Use Your Head. London: BBC Publications.

Cairnes M (1998) Approaching the Corporate Heart. Australia: Simon and Schuster.

Campbell D, Draper R, Huffington C (1991) A Systemic Approach to Consultation. London: Karnac Books.

Campbell J (1985) Myths To Live By. London: Paladin, Granada.

Campbell PA, McMahon EM (1985) Bio-Spirituality: Focusing as a Way to Grow. Chicago: Loyola University Press.

Capra F (1992) The Tao of Physics. London: Flamingo.

Casey D (1993) Managing Learning in Organizations. Buckingham: Open University Press.

Castañeda C (1970) The Teachings of Don Juan. London: Penguin.

Castañeda C (1973) Journey to Ixtlan.

London: The Bodley Head.

Castañeda C (1974) Tales of Power. London: Hodder and Stoughton.

Chopra D (1990) Quantum Healing: Exploring the Frontiers of Mind Body Medicine. New York: Bantam Books.

Clance PR (1985) The Impostor Phenomenon: Overcoming the Fear that Haunts Your Success. Atlanta: Peachtree Publishers.

Clance PR, Imes SA (1978) The impostor phenomenon in high achieving women: dynamics and therapeutic intervention. Psychotherapy: Theory, Research and Practice 15(3): 241–47.

Clance PR, O'Toole MA (1988) The impostor phenomenon: an internal barrier to empowerment and achievement. Women and Therapy 6: 51–64.

Claremont de Castilleja I (1973) Knowing Woman: A Feminine Psychology. New York: Perennial Library, Harper and Row.

Clark N (1994) Team-Building: A Practical Guide for Trainers. London: McGraw-Hill.

Clarkson P (1989) Gestalt Counselling in Action. London: Sage.

Clarkson P, Lapworth P (1992) Systemic integrative psychotherapy. In Dryden W (Ed.) Integrative and Eclectic Therapy: A Handbook. Milton Keynes: Open University Press.

Clarkson P, Mackewn J (1993) Fritz Perls. London: Sage.

Claxton G (1997) Hare Brain Tortoise Mind. London: Fourth Estate.

Cockman P, Evans B, Reynolds P (1998) Consulting for Real People. London: McGraw-Hill.

Coffield D (Ed.) (1999) Why's the Beer Always Stronger up North?: Studies of Lifelong Learning in Europe. Bristol: The Policy Press.

Collins D (1998) Organizational Change: Sociological Perspectives. London: Routledge.

Coopersmith S (1967) The Antecedents of Self-Esteem. San Francisco: WH Freeman.

Covey SR (1992) The Seven Habits of Highly Effective People. New York: Simon and Schuster.

Csikszentmihalyi M (1990) Flow: The Psychology of Optimal Experience. New York: Harper and Row.

Culley S (1992) Counselling skills: an integrative framework. In Dryden W (Ed.) Integrative and Eclectic Therapy: A Handbook. Milton Keynes: Open University Press.

Danforth LM (1990) Firewalking and Religious Healing: The Anastenaria of Greece and the American Firewalking Movement. Princeton University Press.

Davidson D (1997) Memories of Josephes. London: The Leaders Partnership.

Davis M, McKay M, Eshelman ER (2000) The Relaxation and Stress Reduction Workbook. (5th edn) Oakland, CA: New Harbinger Publications.

de Board R (1978) The Psychoanalysis of Organizations. London: Tavistock Publications.

de Bono E (1990) Lateral Thinking. London: Penguin.

de Shazer S (1988) Clues: Investigating Solutions in Brief Therapy. New York: WW Norton and Company.

Dickson A (1982) A Woman in Your Own Right: Assertiveness and You. London: Quartet Books.

Dilts R (1991) Changing Belief Systems with NLP. California: Meta Publications.

Dilts R (1996) Positive intention – bringing light into the darkness: the principle of positive intention. Available online at www.scruz.net/~rdilts/Articles/article2; accessed 5 Feb. 2001.

Dilts R (1997) The NLP spelling strategy. Available online at www.nlpu.com/Articles/artic10.htm; accessed 5 Feb. 2001.

Dilts R (1998a) Fourth position. Available online at www.scruz.net/~rdilts/Articles/artic21.htm; accessed 18 Dec. 2000.

Dilts R (1998b) Harnessing the imagination. Available online at www.scruz.net/~rdilts/Articles/artic16.htm; accessed 18 Dec. 2000.

Dilts R (1998c) Presuppositions. Available online at www.scruz.net/~rdilts/Articles/artic20.htm; accessed 18 Dec. 2000.

Dilts R (1999) Anchoring. Available online at www.scruz.net/~rdilts/Articles/artic28.htm; accessed 9 Jan. 2001.

Dilts R, Epstein T (1995) Dynamic Learning. California: Meta Publications.

Dowling C (2000) Rebirthing and Breathwork. London: Piatkus Books.

Dryden W (1998) Developing Self-Acceptance: A Brief, Educational, Small Group Approach. Chichester: Wiley.

Dryden W (1999) Rational Emotive Behavioural Counselling in Action. (2nd edn) London: Sage.

Edinger EF (1992) Ego and Archetype: Individuation and the Religious Function of the Psyche. Boston: Shambhala.

Egan G (1994) Working the Shadow Side. San Francisco: Jossey Bass.

English F (1971) The substitute factor: rackets and real feelings. Transactional Analysis Journal 2(1): 23–25.

Epstein P (1978) Kabbalah: The Way of the Jewish Mystic. Boston: Shambhala.

Erikson EH (1977) Childhood and Society. (Revised edn) London: Paladin.

Erikson EH (1994) Identity: Youth and Crisis. New York: WW Norton.

Ernst S, Goodison L (1981) In Our Own Hands: A Handbook of Self-help Therapy. London: The Women's Press.

Erskine R (1993) Inquiry, attunement and involvement in the psychotherapy of dissociation. Journal of Transactional Analysis 23(4): 184–90.

Erskine R, Zalcman M (1979) The racket system: a model for racket analysis. Transactional Analysis Journal 9(1): 51–59.

Evans N (1992) Experiential Learning: Assessment and Accreditation. London: Routledge.

Evans-Wentz WY (1960) The Tibetan Book of the Dead. London: Oxford Press.

Farthing GA (1974) Life, Death And Dreams. The Blavatsky Lecture, 25 May 1974. London: The Theosophical Society in England.

Feltman C, Horton I (2000) The Handbook of Counselling and Psychotherapy. London: Sage.

Ferner JD (1995) Successful Time Management: A Self Teaching Guide. (2nd edn) Chichester: Wiley.

Fisher D, Rooke D, Torbert WR (2001) Personal and Organisational Transformations. Boston: Edge\Work Press.

Fisher D, Torbert WR (1995) Personal and Organizational Transformations. London: McGraw-Hill.

Flemons D (1991) Completing Distinctions. Boston: Shambhala.

Fordham F (1966) An Introduction to Jung's Psychology. London: Penguin.

Foster S, Little M (1989) The Book of the Vision Quest. New York: Prentice Hall.

Frankl VE (1994) Man's Search for Meaning. New York: Pocket Books.

Freire P (1972) Pedagogy of the Oppressed. Harmondsworth, Middlesex: Penguin Books.

French WL, Bell CH, Zawacki RA (Eds) (1994) Organization Development and Transformation. (4th edn) Burr Ridge, IL: Irwin.

Freud S (1923) The Ego and the Id. In Strachey J (Ed.) (1964) The Standard Edition of the Complete Psychological Works of Sigmund Freud, Vol. 19. London: Hogarth Press.

Frick WB (1987) The symbolic growth experience: paradigm for a humanistic-existential learning theory. Journal of Humanistic Psychology 27: 406–23.

Fritz R (1994) Creating. London: Butterworth-Heinemann.

Fromm E (1975) The Art of Loving. London: Unwin Paperbacks.

Fromm E (1978) To Have or to Be. London: Unwin Paperbacks.

Fromm E (1982) Greatness and Limitations of Freud's Thought. London: Abacus, Sphere Books.

Frost WP (1992) What is the New Age?: Defining Third Millennium Consciousness. New York: The Edwin Mellen Press.

Gallwey T (1986) The Inner Game of Tennis. London: Pan.

Gallwey T (1999) The Inner Game of Work. New York: Random House.

Gardner H (1993) Frames of Mind: The

Theory of Multiple Intelligences. (2nd edn) London: Fontana.

Gardner H, Kornhaber ML, Wake WK (1996) Intelligence: Multiple Perspectives. New York: Holt, Rinehart and Winston.

Gawain S (1995) Creative Visualisation. California: New World Library.

Gemmill G, Costello M (1990) Group mirroring as a means for exploring the group shadow: a perspective for organizational consulting. Consultation 9(4).

Gendlin ET (1978) Focusing. New York: Bantam New Age Books.

Gendlin ET (1996) Focusing-Oriented Psychotherapy. New York: The Guilford Press.

Gersie A, King N (1990) Storymaking in Education and Therapy. London: Jessica Kingsley.

Geshe Kelsang Gyatso (1995) The Meditation Handbook. (3rd edn) New York: Tharpa Publications.

Giroux HA (1981) Ideology, Culture, and the Process of Schooling. Philadelphia, PA: Temple University Press.

Glassman WE (1995) Approaches to Psychology. Buckinghamshire: Open University Press.

Glouberman D (1989) Life Choices and Life Changes Through Imagework: The Art of Developing Personal Vision. London: Unwin Hyman.

Glover J (1989) I: The Philosophy and Psychology of Personal Identity. London: Penguin.

Goffman E (1959) The Presentation of Self in Everyday Life. Garden City, NY: Doubleday.

Goldfried MR, Newman CF (1992) A history of psychotherapy integration. In Norcross JC, Goldfried MR (Eds) Handbook of Psychotherapy Integration. New York: Basic Books. pp 46–93.

Goleman D (1996) Emotional Intelligence. London: Bloomsbury.

Gordon D (1978) Therapeutic Metaphors. California: Meta Publications.

Gordon WJJ (1961) Synectics: The Development of Creative Capacity. New York: Harper and Row.

Grasse R (1996) The Waking Dream: Unlocking the Symbolic Language of our Lives. Wheaton, IL: Theosophical Publishing House.

Gray J (1993) Men Are From Mars, Women Are From Venus. London: Thorsons.

Greene L (1977) Relating: An Astrological Guide to Living with Others on a Small Planet. London: Coventure Ltd.

Greene L (1990) Saturn: A New Look at an Old Devil. London: Arkana.

Greene L, Sharman-Burke J (2000) The Mythic Journey: The Meaning of Myth as a Guide to Life. Glastonbury: Gothic Image Publications.

Greenleaf RK (1970) The Servant as Leader. Indianapolis: The Robert Greenleaf Center.

Gregory J (1994) A grounded theory study of the education of hospital nurses: how education for interpersonal relating influences the way nurses relate to each other in the college and on the wards. Unpublished Doctoral Thesis, School of Educational Studies, University of Surrey, Guildford.

Gregory J (1996) The Psycho-Social Education of Nurses. Aldershot: Avery.

Gregory J, Tosey P (2000) Self and Peer Assessment of Experiential Learning in Higher Education. Human Potential Research Group, School of Educational Studies, University of Surrey.

Grinder J, Bandler R (1976) The Structure of Magic II: A Book about Communication and Change. Palo Alto, CA: Science and Behaviour Books.

Grinder J, DeLozier J (1996) Turtles All the Way Down. Pontland, OR: Metamorphous Press.

Grof S (1988) The Adventure of Self-Discovery. Albany, NY: State University of New York Press.

Grof S, Grof C (Eds) (1989) Spiritual Emergency: When Personal Transformation Becomes a Crisis. Los Angeles: JP Tarcher.

Grosskurth P (1991) The Secret Ring: Freud's Inner Circle and the Politics of Psychoanalysis. London: Cape. Cited in Young R (1996) The culture of British psychoanalysis. Available online at www.shef.ac.uk/~psysc/culture/paper5h.html; accessed 18 Dec. 2000.

Gulbenkian S (Ed.) (2000) The Future Is Now: Anthroposophy at the New Millennium. London: Temple Lodge Publishers.

H.H. The Dalai Lama (1998) The Tibetan Book of the Dead (Trans. RAF Thurman) London: Thorsons.

Hamelink CJ (1994) Trends in World Communication: On Disempowerment and Self-empowerment. Penang, Malaysia: Southbound Third World Network.

Hampden-Turner C (1981) Maps of the Mind. London: Mitchell Beazley.

Hanson P (1973) The Johari window: a model for soliciting and giving feedback. In Pfeiffer JW, Jones JE (Eds) Annual Handbook for Group Facilitators. La Jolla, CA:University Associates.

Hardy J (1989) A Psychology with a Soul: Psychosynthesis in Evolutionary Context. London: Arkana.

Hare B (1996) Be Assertive: The Positive Way to Communicate Effectively. London: Vermilion.

Harman W (1988) Global Mind Change. Indianapolis: Knowledge Systems Inc.

Harré R, Gillett G (1994) The Discursive Mind. London: Sage.

Harrison R (1995) Consultant's Journey. London: McGraw-Hill.

Hartley P (1999) Interpersonal Communication. (2nd edn) London: Routledge.

Harvey C, Harvey S (1999) Principles of Astrology. London: Thorsons.

Hassan S (1990) Combatting Cult Mind Control. (2nd edn) Rochester, VT: Inner Traditions International.

Hassan S (2000) Releasing the Bonds: Empowering People to Think for Themselves. Aitan Publishing Company.

Hastings A (1991) With the Tongues of Men and Angels: A Study of Channeling. UK: The Dryden Press.

Heider J (1986) The Tao of Leadership. Aldershot: Wildwood House, Gower.

Hendricks G (1995) Conscious Breathing: Breathwork for Health, Stress Release,

and Personal Mastery. New York: Bantam Books.

Heron J (1974a) The Concept of a Peer Learning Community. Human Potential Research Project, University of Surrey.

Heron J (1974b) Reciprocal Counselling. Human Potential Research Project, University of Surrey, Guildford.

Heron J (1981) Paradigm Papers. Human Potential Research Project, University of Surrey.

Heron J (1982) Education of the Affect. Human Potential Research Project, University of Surrey.

Heron J (1987) Confessions of a Janus-Brain. London: Endymion Press.

Heron J (1989) The Facilitator's Handbook. London: Kogan Page.

Heron J (1990) Helping the Client. London: Sage.

Heron J (1991) The politics of facilitation: balancing facilitator authority and learner autonomy. In Mulligan J, Griffin C (Eds) Empowerment Through Experiential Learning: Exploration of Good Practice. London: Kogan Page. pp 66–75.

Heron J (1992) Feeling and Personhood: Psychology in Another Key. London: Sage.

Heron J (1996) Co-operative Inquiry: Research into the Human Condition. London: Sage.

Heron J (1998a) Co-counselling. (3rd edn) Available online at: www.dpets.demon.co.uk/cciuk/resources/manuals.html; accessed 30 Nov. 2000.

Heron J (1998b) Intensive Counselling. (Revised version) Available online at www.dpets.demon.co.uk/cciuk/practice/intensive.html; accessed 30 Nov. 2000.

Heron J (1998c) Sacred Science: Person-centred Inquiry into the Spiritual and the Subtle. Ross-on-Wye: PCCS Books.

Heron J (1999) The Complete Facilitator's Handbook. London: Kogan Page.

Herrigel E (1972) Zen in the Art of Archery. London: Routledge and Kegan Paul.

Hersey P, Blanchard KH (1969) Management of Organizational Behaviour. Englewood Cliffs, NJ: Prentice Hall.

Hillman J (1983) Archetypal Psychology. Woodstock, CT: Spring Publications Inc.

Hillman J (1985) Anima: An Anatomy of a Personified Notion. Dallas: Spring Publications.

Hillman J (1996) The Soul's Code. Toronto: Bantam Books.

Hillman J (1997) Suicide and the Soul. (2nd edn) Woodstock, CT: Spring Publications Inc.

Hillman J, Ventura M (1992) We've Had a Hundred Years of Psychotherapy and the World's Getting Worse. New York: Harper.

Hogan C (2000) Facilitating Empowerment. London: Kogan Page.

Holm J, Bowker J (Eds) (1994) Rites of Passage. London: Pinter Publishers.

Holmes P, Karp M (Eds) (1991) Psychodrama: Inspiration and Technique. London: Routledge.

Holmes P, Karp M, Watson M (Eds) (1994) Psychodrama Since Moreno. London: Routledge.

Honey P, Mumford A (1992) The Manual of Learning Styles. (3rd edn) Maidenhead: P Honey.

Hooper D, Dryden W (Eds) (1991) Couple Therapy. Buckingham: Open University Press.

Hooper-Hensen G (1992) Suggestopedia: a way of learning for the 21st century. In Mulligan J, Griffin C (Eds) Empowerment Through Experiential Learning: Exploration of Good Practice. London: Kogan Page. pp 197–207.

Hopcke RH (1995) Persona: Where Sacred Meets Profane. Boston: Shambhala.

Houston J (1982) The Possible Human. Los Angeles: JP Tarcher Inc.

Huber B (1991) Astrological Psychosynthesis. London: Aquarian Press.

Huczynski AA (1983) Encyclopedia of Management Development Methods. Aldershot: Gower.

Huczynski AA (1993) Management Gurus: What Makes Them and How to Become One. London: Routledge.

Hudson L (1967) Contrary Imaginations. Middlesex: Penguin.

Hudson L, Jacot B (1991) The Way Men Think: Intellect, Intimacy and the Erotic Imagination. London: Yale UP.

Hunt C, Sampson F (Eds) (1998) The Self on the Page: Theory and Practice of Creative Writing in Personal Development. London: Jessica Kingsley Publishers.

Huss C (Ed.) (1990) The Banyan Tree: A Textbook for Holistic Health Practitioners. Available online at www.healthlibrary.com/reading/banyanIII/index.htm; accessed 31 Jan. 2001.

Huxley A (1946) The Perennial Philosophy. London: Chatto and Windus.

Hycner R (1993) Between Person and Person: Towards a Dialogical Psychotherapy. New York: Gestalt Journal Press.

Jackins H (1970) Fundamentals of Co-Counselling Manual. Seattle: Rational Island Publications.

Jackson H (Ed.) (1999) Creating Harmony: Conflict Resolution in Community. Denmark/East Meon: Gaia Trust/Permanent Publications.

Jacobs M (1998) The Presenting Past. Milton Keynes: Open University Press.

James K, Arroba T (1999) Energizing the Workplace: A Strategic Response to Stress. Aldershot: Gower Publishing Ltd.

James T (2000) Hypnosis Bancyfelin. Carmarthen: Crown House Publishing.

James T, Woodsmall W (1988) Time Line Therapy Cupertino. CA: Meta Publications.

James W (1982) The Varieties of Religious Experience. London: Penguin Books Ltd.

Janis IL (1972) Victims of Group Think. Boston: Houghton Mifflin.

Janov A (1973) The Primal Scream. London: Abacus.

Jarvis P (1995) Adult and Continuing Education. (2nd edn) London: Routledge.

Jarvis P, Holford J, Griffin C (1998) The Theory and Practice of Learning. London: Kogan Page.

Jeffers S (1996) Feel The Fear and Do It Anyway. London: Arrow.

Johnson SM (1987) Humanizing the Narcissistic Style. New York: WW Norton and Company.

Jourard S (1971) The Transparent Self. New York: van Nostrand Reinhold Company Inc.

Joy WB (1979) Joy's Way: A Map for the Transformational Journey. New York: Putnam Books.

Judith A (1996) Eastern Body, Western Mind. Berkeley, CA: Celestial Arts.

Jung CG (1953) Collected Works, Vol. 6. London: Routledge.

Jung CG (1963) Memories, Dreams, Reflections. Glasgow: Fontana Press, Harper Collins.

Jung CG (1964) Man and his Symbols. London: Aldus. (Republished 1990 by Penguin Books.)

Jung CG (1966) Two essays on analytical psychology. Collected Works, Vol.7. London: Routledge and Kegan Paul.

Jung CG (1968a) The structure and dynamics of the Psyche. Collected Works, Vol. 8. London: Routledge.

Jung CG (1968b) The Archetypes and the Collective Unconscious. Collected Works, Vol.9, Part 1. London: Routledge and Kegan Paul.

Jung CG (1968c) Aion. Collected Works, Vol. 9, Part 2. London: Routledge.

Jung CG. (1968d) Psychology and Alchemy. Collected Works, Vol. 12. (2nd edn) London: Routledge.

Jung CG (1969) The Structure and Dynamics of the Psyche. Collected Works, Vol.8. (2nd edn) London: Routledge and Kegan Paul. (Also included in this volume is 'On Synchronicity' – a translation of Jung's 1951 Eranos lecture.) References are to paragraph numbers.

Jung CG (1971) Psychological Types. Collected Works, Vol. 6. (2nd edn) London: Routledge and Kegan Paul.

Jung CG (1974) The Undiscovered Self. London: Routledge and Kegan Paul.

Jung CG (1982) Dreams. London: Ark Paperbacks, Routledge.

Jung CG (1983) Selected Writings. London: Fontana Press.

Jung CG (1995) The psychology of the child archetype. In Abrahams J (Ed.) Reclaiming the Inner Child. London: Thorsons.

Kahler T, Capers H (1974) The Miniscript. Transactional Analysis Journal 1(1): 79–87.

Kahn M (1991) Between Therapist and Client: The New Relationship. New York: Freeman And Company.

Karpman S (1968) Fairy tales and script drama analysis. Transactional Analysis Bulletin 7(26): 39–43.

Keeney B (1983) Aesthetics of Change. New York: Guilford Press.

Keleman S (1989) Living your Dying. (2nd edn) Berkeley, CA: Center Press.

Kelly G (1955) The Psychology of Personal Constructs, Vols 1 and 2. New York: Norton.

Kets de Vries M (1993) Leaders, Fools and Impostors. San Francisco: Jossey-Bass.

Kilty J (1979) Self and Peer Assessment and Peer Audit. Human Potential Research Project, University of Surrey.

Kirkpatrick DL (1971) A Practical Guide for Supervisory Training and Development. Reading, MA: Addison-Wesley Publishing Co.

Kleber RJ (1992) Coping with Trauma. Amsterdam/Lisse: Swets and Zeitlinger.

Knight J, Scott W (1998) Co-facilitation Partnerships. London: Kogan Page.

Knight S (1999) Introducing NLP. London: Chartered Institute of Personnel and Development.

Knowles MS (1980) The Modern Practice of Adult Education: From Pedagogy to Andragogy. (2nd edn) New York: Cambridge Books.

Knowles MS (1986) Using Learning Contracts. San Francisco: Jossey Bass.

Kohlberg, L (1981) Essays on Moral Development (Vol. 1). San Francisco: Harper and Row.

Kohut H (1984) How Does Analysis Cure? Chicago: University of Chicago Press.

Kolb D (1984) Experiential Learning: Experience as the Source of Learning and Development. New Jersey: Prentice-Hall.

Kovel J (1978) A Complete Guide to Therapy. London: Penguin Books.

Kübler-Ross E (1970) On Death and Dying. London: Tavistock.

Kubr M (Ed.) (1996) Management Consulting: A Guide to the Profession. Geneva: International Labour Office.

Kuhn T (1996) The Structure of Scientific Revolutions. (3rd edn) Chicago: University of Chicago Press.

Laing RD (1965) The Divided Self. London: Penguin Books.

Laing RD (1983) The Voice of Experience. Harmondsworth: Penguin.

Laing RD (1990a) The Divided Self. London: Penguin Books.

Laing RD (1990b) The Politics of Experience and The Bird of Paradise. London: Penguin Books.

Lakoff G, Johnson M (1980) Metaphors We Live By. Chicago: University of Chicago Press.

Lao Tzu (1969) Tao Te Ching. (Trans. DC Lau) Harmondsworth: Penguin Books.

La Tourelle M, Courtenay A (1997) Principles of Kinesiology. London: Thorsons.

Learning from Experience Trust (2000) Mapping APEL: Accreditation of Prior Experiential Learning in English Higher Education Institutions. Available online, Department for Education and Employment website: www.dfee.gov.uk/heqe/let_final.htm; accessed 29 Nov. 2000.

Lefcourt HM (1982) Locus of Control: Current Trends in Theory and Research. (2nd edn) Hillsdale, NJ: Erlbaum Associates.

Leonard J, Laut P (1983) Rebirthing: The Science of Enjoying All of Your Life. California: Trinity Publications.

Lerner I, Lerner M, Guilfol C (1992) Inner Child Cards: A Journey into Fairy Tale, Myth and Nature. Santa Fe, NM: Bear and Co.

Lessing D (1997) The Sufis and Idries Shah. Available online at www.clearlight.com/octagon/lessing.htm; accessed 3 Jan. 2001.

Levin M (2000) Spiritual Intelligence. London: Hodder and Stoughton.

Levine S (1993) A Gradual Awakening. Bath: Gateway Books.

Lewin K (1947) Frontiers in group dynamics, II: channels of group life; social planning and action research. Human Relations 1(2): 145–53.

Lewis CS (1977) Surprised by Joy. London: Fontana Books.

Loevinger J, Wessler E (1978) Measuring Ego Development, vols 1 and 2. San Francisco: Jossey-Bass.

Lowen A (1976) Bioenergetics. Harmondsworth, Middlesex: Penguin Books.

Lowen A, Lowen L (1977) The Vibrant Way to Health: A Manual of Exercises. New York: Harper and Row. Available online, website of the Dallas Society for Bioenergetic Analysis: bioenergetics-dallas.com/moronbio.htm; accessed 7 Dec. 2000.

Luft J, Ingram H (1967) Of Human Interaction: The Johari Model. Palo Alto, CA: Mayfield.

MacDonald G, MacDonald G (1998) The Complete Illustrated Guide to the Alexander Technique: A Practical Program for Health, Poise, and Fitness. Shaftsbury, Dorset: Element Books.

Maister DH (2000) Trusted Advisor. New York: Simon and Schuster.

Marcuse H (1987) Eros and Civilisation: A Philosophical Inquiry into Freud. London: Ark Paperbacks.

Margetson D (1997) Why is problem-based learning a challenge? In Boud D, Feletti G (Eds) The Challenge of Problem-Based Learning. (2nd edn) London: Kogan Page. pp 36–44.

Marshall J, Reason P (1997) Collaborative and self-reflective forms of inquiry in management research. In Burgoyne J, Reynolds M (Eds) (1997) Management Learning: Integrating Perspectives in Theory and Practice. London: Sage.

Marsick VJ, Watkins KE (1989) Informal and Incidental Learning in the Workplace. London: Routledge.

Marton D, Hounsell D, Entwistle N (1997) The Experience of Learning: Implications for Teaching and Studying in Higher Education. (2nd edn) Edinburgh: Scottish Academic Press.

Maslow A (1943) A theory of human motivation. Psychological Review 50(4): 370–96.

Maslow AH (1964) Religions, values and peak experiences. In Vardey L (Ed.) God in All Worlds: An Anthology of Contemporary Spiritual Writing. London: Chatto and Windus.

Maslow AH (1968) Towards a Psychology of Being. (2nd edn) Princeton, NJ: Van Nostrand Company.

Maslow A (1970) Motivation and Personality. (2nd edn) New York: Harper and Row.

Masson J (1992) Against Therapy. London: Fontana.

Matthews C, Matthews J (1985) The Western Way: A Practical Guide to the Western Mystery Tradition. London: Arkana.

Matthews C, Matthews J (1986) The Western Way: A Practical Guide to the Western Mystery Tradition, Vol 2: The Hermetic Tradition. London: Arkana.

May R (1953) Man's Search for Himself. New York: WW Norton and Company, Inc.

May R (1976) The Courage To Create. New York: Bantam Books.

May R (1996) The Meaning of Anxiety. New York: Norton.

McCrone J (1998) Going Inside: A Tour Around a Single Moment of Consciousness. London: Faber.

McCrone J (1999) Left brain, right brain. New Scientist 163. Available online at www.newscientist.com/ns/19990703/leftbrainr.html; accessed 2 Jan. 2001.

McGregor Burns J (1978) Leadership. New York: Harper and Row.

McKay M, Fanning P (2000) Self-Esteem. Oakland, CA: New Harbinger Publications.

McKenzie E (1998) Healing Reiki. London: Hamlyn.

McMahon EM (1993) Beyond the Myth of Dominance: An Alternative to a Violent Society. Kansas City: Sheed and Ward.

McNeely DA (1991) Animus Aeternus: Exploring the Inner Masculine. (Studies in Jungian Psychology by Jungian Analysts, 49). Toronto: Inner City Books.

McNiff J, Lomax P, Whitehead J (1996) You and Your Action Research Project. London: Routledge.

Meade M (1993) Men and The Water of Life: The Initiation and Tempering of Men. San Francisco: Harper.

Meier D (2000) The Accelerated Learning Handbook. San Francisco: Berrett-Koehler.

Mellor K, Sigmund E (1975) Discounting. Transactional Analysis Journal 5(3): 295–302.

Mezirow J (1991) Transformative Dimensions of Adult Learning. San Francisco: Jossey-Bass.

Miller A (1990) Banished Knowledge: Facing Childhood Injuries. London: Virago.

Miller G, Galanter E, Pribram K (1960) Plans and the Structure of Behaviour. New York: Henry Holt and Co.

Millman D (2000) The Way of the Peaceful Warrior: A Book That Changes Lives. (20th anniversary edn) Novato, CA: HJ Kramer.

Moore T (1992) Care of the Soul: How to Add Depth and Meaning to Everyday Life. London: Piatkus.

Morgan G (1997) Images of Organization. (2nd edn) London: Sage.

Moustakas C (1990) Heuristic Research: Design, Methodology, and Applications. London: Sage.

Moustakas C (1994) Phenomenological Research Methods. London: Sage.

Mulligan J (1988) The Personal Management Handbook. London: Sphere.

Mulligan J, Griffin C (Eds) (1992) Empowerment Through Experiential Learning: Exploration of Good Practice. London: Kogan Page.

Mumford A (1995) Effective Learning. London: Institute of Personnel and Development.

Murray Parkes C (1996) Bereavement. London: Routledge.

Myss C (1997) Anatomy of the Spirit. London: Bantam Books.

Naess A (1989) Ecology, Community and Lifestyle. New York: Cambridge University Press.

Nolan V (1989) The Innovator's Handbook: The Skills of Innovative Management – Problem Solving, Communication, and Teamwork. USA: Penguin.

Nonaka I, Takeuchi H (1995) The Knowledge-Creating Company. Oxford: Oxford University Press.

Noyes L (1998) The Enlightenment Intensive: Dyad Communication as a Tool for Self-realization. Berkely, CA: Frog Ltd, North Atlantic Books.

O'Connor J, Seymour J (1993) Neuro-Linguistic Programming: An Introduction. (2nd edn) London: Thorsons.

Ogden TH (1991) Projective Identification and Psychotherapeutic Technique. London: Jason Aronson.

O'Hanlon B, Wilk J (1987) Shifting Contexts: The Generation of Effective Psychotherapy. New York: The Guilford Press.

Ornstein R (1972) The Psychology of Consciousness. London: Penguin Books.

Owen H (Ed.) (1995) Tales from Open Space. Maryland: Abbott Publishing. Available online at www.mindspring.com/~owenhh/Tales.htm; accessed 5 Feb. 2001.

Ozaniec N (1990) The Chakras. Dorset: Element Books.

Palazzoli MS, Cecchin G, Prata G, Boscolo L (1978) Paradox and Counter-Paradox: A New Model in the Therapy of the Family in Schizophrenic Transition. (Trans. EV Burt) New York: Jason Aronson.

Palmer H (1995) The Enneagram in Love and Work. San Francisco: Harper and Row.

Palmer S, Woolfe R (Eds) (2000) Integrative and Eclectic Counselling and Psychotherapy. London: Sage.

Parks P (1994) The Counsellor's Guide to Parks Inner Child Therapy. London: Souvenir Press.

Parlett M, Hemming J (1996) Gestalt therapy. In Dryden W (Ed.) Handbook of Individual Therapy. London: Sage. Chap. 9.

Paul M (1992) Inner Bonding: Becoming a Loving Adult to Your Inner Child. San Francisco: Harper.

Peale N (1953) The Power of Positive Thinking. London: Cedar Books, Heinemann.

Pearson CS (1991) Awakening the Heroes Within. San Francisco: Harper Collins.

Pearson J (1999) A phenomenological inquiry into the experience of bringing a loving perspective into professional relationships. Unpublished MSc Thesis, University of Surrey, Guildford.

Pease A (1997) Body Language. London: Sheldon Press.

Pedler M (1997) Interpreting action learning. In Burgoyne J, Reynolds M (Eds) Management Learning: Integrating Perspectives in Theory and Practice. London: Sage.

Peiffer V (1996) Principles of Hypnotherapy. London: Thorsons.

Penrose R (1994) Shadows of the Mind. Oxford: Oxford University Press.

Perls FS (1969) Gestalt Therapy Verbatim. Moab, UT: Real People Press.

Pettifor E (1995) Process of individuation: a quick pencil sketch by Eric Pettifor. Available online at www.wynja.com/personality/jungarchf.html; accessed 5 Feb. 2001.

Phillips K, Shaw P (1998) A Consultancy Approach for Trainers and Developers. (2nd edn) Aldershot: Gower.

Pinkola Estes C (1992) Women Who Run with the Wolves: Contacting the Power of the Wild Woman. London: Random House.

Pirsig R (1974) Zen and the Art of Motorcycle Maintenance. London: Corgi Books, Transworld Publishers.

Plato (1973) Phaedrus and the Seventh and Eighth Letters. (Trans. W Hamilton) London: Penguin Books.

Polanyi M (1966) The Tacit Dimension. London: Routledge and Kegan Paul.

Pollack R (1997) Seventy-Eight Degrees of Wisdom. London: Thorsons.

Poppeliers W (1998) Inner and Outer Sexuality: New Oedipal Approaches to Healthy Intimacy. Nijmegen, NL.

Postle D (1988) The Mind Gymnasium. London: Macmillan/Papermac. (Digital edition available in 2001 at: www.mind-gymnasium.com.)

Postle D (1993) Putting the heart back into learning. In Boud D, Cohen R, Walker D (Eds) Using Experience for Learning. Buckingham: Society for Research into Higher Education and Open University Press. pp 33–45.

Pressman S (1993) Outrageous Betrayal. New York: St Martins Press. Extracts available online at perso.wanadoo.fr/eldon.braun/awareness/pressmn1.

Quenk NL (1993) Beside Ourselves: Our Hidden Personality in Everyday Life. Palo Alto, CA: Davies-Black.

Quest P (1999) Reiki. London: Piatkus.

Raelin JA (2000) Work-Based Learning: The New Frontier of Management Development. New Jersey: Prentice Hall.

Ramsden P (1992) The Action Profile® system of movement assessment for self-development. In Payne H (Ed.) Dance Movement Therapy: Theory and Practice. London: Tavistock/Routledge. pp 218–41.

Randall R, Southgate J (1980) Co-operative and Community Group Dynamics. London: Barefoot Books.

Raphael DD (1994) Moral Philosophy. Oxford: Oxford University Press.

Rawlinson A (1997) The Book of Enlightened Masters. Chicago: Open Court.

Reagan H (1980) Shamanic Wheels and Keys. Scotsdale, AZ: DTMMS.

Reason P (Ed.) (1988) Human Inquiry in Action: Developments in New Paradigm Research. London: Sage.

Reason P (Ed.) (1994) Participation in Human Inquiry. London: Sage.

Reason P, Heron J (1995) Co-operative inquiry. In Smith JA, Harre R, Van Langenhove L (Eds) Rethinking Methods in Psychology. London: Sage. Available online at zeus.sirt.pisa.it/icci/welcome.html#ICCI; accessed 18 Dec. 2000.

Reddin WJ (1970) Managerial Effectiveness. London: McGraw-Hill.

Redfield J (1994) The Celestine Prophecy. London: Bantam Books.

Reich W (1972) Character Analysis. (3rd edn) New York: Farrar, Straus and Giroux.

Revans R (1983) Action learning: its origins and nature. In Pedler M (Ed.) Action Learning in Practice. Aldershot: Gower.

Reynolds M (1997a) Learning styles: a critique. Management Learning 28(2): 115–33.

Reynolds M (1997b) Towards a critical management pedagogy. In Burgoyne J, Reynolds M (Eds) Management Learning: Integrating Perspectives in Theory and Practice. London: Sage.

Rinpoche S (1992) The Tibetan Book of Living and Dying. London: Rider.

Riso DR, Hudson R (1999) The Wisdom of the Enneagram. New York: Bantam Books.

Rogers CR (1951) Client-centered Therapy, its Current Practice, Implications, and Theory. Boston: Houghton Mifflin.

Rogers CR (1961) On Becoming a Person: A Therapist's View of Psychotherapy. Boston: Houghton Mifflin.

Rogers CR (1967) On Becoming a Person. London: Constable.

Rogers CR (1983) Freedom to Learn for the 1980s. Columbus, OH: Merrill.

Rosenthal R (1968) Pygmalion in the Classroom: Teacher Expectation and Pupils' Intellectual Development. New York: Holt, Rinehart and Winston.

Roszak T (1992) The Voice of the Earth. New York: Touchstone Books.

Roszak T, Gomer ME, Kanner AD (1995) Ecopsychology. San Francisco: Sierra Club Books.

Rotter JB (1966) Generalized expectancies for internal versus external control of reinforcement. Psychological Monographs: General and Applied 80(1): 1–28.

Rousseau DM (1995) Psychological Contracts in Organizations. Thousand Oaks, CA: Sage.

Rowan J (1976) Ordinary Ecstasy: Humanistic Psychology in Action. London: Routledge.

Rowan J (1983) The Reality Game. London: Routledge.

Rowan J (1988) Ordinary Ecstasy: Humanistic Psychology in Action. (2nd edn) London: Routledge.

Rowan J (1990) Subpersonalities: The People Inside Us. London: Routledge.

Rowan J (1993) The Transpersonal. London: Routledge.

Rowan J (1996) Body work. In: A Guide to Humanistic Psychology. Available online at ahpweb.org/rowan_bibliography/chapter12.html; accessed 11 Dec. 2000.

Rowan J (1998) The Reality Game. (2nd edn) London: Routledge.

Rycroft C (1971) Reich. Glasgow: Fontana/Collins.

Rylatt A, Lohan K (1995) Creating Training Miracles. New Jersey: Prentice Hall.

Sagan C (1977) The Dragons of Eden: Speculations on the Evolution of Human Intelligence. New York: Random House.

Salaman G (1979) Work Organisations: Resistance and Control. London: Longman.

Sams J, Carson D (1988) Medicine Cards: The Discovery of Power Through the Ways of Animals. Santa Fe: Bear and Co.

Samuels MD, Samuels NS (1975) Seeing With the Mind's Eye: The History, Techniques and Uses of Visualization. New York: Random House.

Sarafino EP (1996) Principles of Behaviour Change. Chichester: John Wiley.

Sartre J-P (1985) Existentialism and Human Emotions. New Jersey: Citadel Press.

Schein E (1969) Process Consultation. Reading, MA: Addison-Wesley.

Schiff JL, Schiff AW (1975) The Cathexis Reader: Transactional Analysis Treatment for Psychosis. New York: Harper and Row.

Schön D (1983) The Reflective Practitioner: How Professionals Think in Action. New York: Basic Books.

Schön D (1987) Educating the Reflective Practitioner. San Francisco: Jossey-Bass.

Schröder M (1974) The shadow consultant. Journal of Applied Behavioural Science 10(4).

Schutz WC (1971) Joy: Expanding Human Awareness. London: Souvenir Press.

Scott Peck M (1990) The Different Drum. London: Arrow Books.

Seligman MEP (1975) Helplessness: On Depression, Development and Death. New York: WH Freeman.

Senge P (1990) The Fifth Discipline. London: Century Business, Random Century.

Senge PM, Roberts C, Ross RB, Smith BJ, Kleiner A (1994) The Fifth Discipline Fieldbook: Strategies and Tools for Building a Learning Organization. London: Nicholas Brealey.

Sheldrake R (1988) The Presence of the Past. London: Fontana.

Shohet R (1985) Dream Sharing. Wellingborough: Turnstone Press.

Sills C, Fish S, Lapworth P (1995) Gestalt Counselling. Oxon: Winslow.

Singer J (1994) Boundaries of the Soul. New York: Anchor Books, Random House Inc.

Singer J (1998) Modern Woman in Search of Soul. York Beach, Maine: Nicolas-Hays Inc.

Skinner BF (1938) The Behaviour of Organisms: An Experimental Analysis. New York: Appleton-Century-Crofts.

Skinner BF (1971) Beyond Freedom and Dignity. New York: Knopf.

Smiles S (1996) Self-Help. London Civitas: (Institute for the Study of Civil Society).

Snow H (1997) Indoor/Outdoor Team Building Games for Trainers: Powerful Activities from the World of Adventure-Based Team Building and Ropes Courses. London: McGraw-Hill.

Snyder BR (1971) The Hidden Curriculum. New York: Knopf.

Somé MP (1994) Of Water and the Spirit: Ritual, Magic, and Initiation in the Life of an African Shaman. New York: Tarcher.

Soskin J (1996) Insight and Intuition. London: Light Publications.

Spears LC (1998) The Power of Servant Leadership. San Francisco: Berrett-Koehler.

Sperry R (1964) The great cerebral commissure. Scientific American 210: 142–52. Offprint no. 174.

Spinelli E (1989) The Interpreted World: An Introduction to Phenomenological Psychology. London: Sage.

Stamp G (1993) Well-being at work: aligning purposes, people, strategies and structures. International Journal of Career Management 5(3).

Steiner R (1993) Understanding the Human Being: Selected Writings of Rudolf Steiner. Bristol: Rudolf Steiner Press.

Stephenson J (Ed.) (1998) Mentoring: The New Panacea? Dereham, Norfolk: Peter Francis Publishers.

Stevens JO (1971) Awareness: Exploring, Experimenting, Experiencing. Moab, UT: Real People Press.

Stewart I (1989) Transactional Analysis Counselling in Action. London: Sage. (New edition 2000)

Stewart I (1996) Developing Transactional Analysis Counselling. London: Sage.

Stewart I, Joines (1987) TA Today: An Introduction to Transactional Analysis. Nottingham: Lifespace.

Stewart RJ (1988) The Merlin Tarot: Images, Insight and Wisdom from the Age of Merlin. London: Aquarian Press.

Stone H, Winkleman S (1985) Embracing Our Selves. Marina Del Rey, CA: Devross.

Storr A (Ed.) (1983) Jung: Selected Writings, Introduced by Anthony Storr. Glasgow: Fontana Press.

Sun Bear, Wabun Wind, Crysalis Mulligan (1991) Dancing with the Wheel: The Medicine Wheel Workbook. Tucsan, AZ: Treasure Chest Books.

Tannenbaum R, Schmidt HW (1958) How to choose a leadership pattern. Harvard Business Review, March-April.

Tart CT (Ed.) (1997) Body, Mind and Spirit: Exploring the Parapsychology of Spirituality. Charlottesville, VA: Hampton Roads Publishing Co. Inc.

Teilhard de Chardin P (1959) The Phenomenon of Man. London: Collins.

Thomas AB (1993) Controversies in Management. London: Routledge.

Thompson JD (1967) Organizations in Action. New York: McGraw-Hill.

Tilney T (1998) Dictionary of Transactional Analysis. London: Whurr Publishers.

Torbert WR (1991) The Power of Balance. Newbury Park, CA: Sage.

Torbert WR, Fisher D (1992) Autobiographical awareness as a catalyst for managerial and organisational learning. Management Education and Development 23(3): 184–98.

Tosey P (1999) EnergyScapes: a human potential approach to experiences of organizations and change. Counselling at Work 27: 9–10.

Tosey P, Gregory J (1998) The peer learning community in higher education: reflections on practice. Innovations in Education and Training International 35(1): 74–81.

Tosey P, McNair S (2000) Work-related learning. In Jarvis P (Ed.) The Age of Learning. London: Kogan Page.

Tripp D (1993) Critical Incidents in Teaching: Developing Professional Judgement. London: Routledge.

Trungpa C (1988) Shambhala: The Sacred Path of the Warrior. Boston: Shambhala.

Tuckman BW (1965) Developmental sequence in small groups. Psychological Bulletin 63: 384–99.

Tuckman BW, Jensen MAC (1977) Stages of small group development revisited. Group and Organizational Studies 2: 419–27.

Underhill E (1999) Mysticism: The Nature and Development of Spiritual Consciousness. Oxford: One World Publications.

Usher R, Bryant I, Johnston R (1997) Adult Education and the Postmodern Challenge. London: Routledge.

van Deurzen E (1987) Existential Counselling in Practice. London: Sage.

Vardey L (1995) Mother Teresa: A Simple Path. London: Rider.

Vich MA (1988) Some historical sources of the term 'transpersonal'. Journal of Transpersonal Psychology 20(2): 107–10.

Von Franz M-L (1971) The inferior function. In Lectures on Jung's Typology. Dallas: Spring Publications.

Von Franz M-L (1997) Archetypal Dimensions of the Psyche. Boston: Shambhala Publications.

Vroom VH, Deci EL (Eds) (1992) Management and Motivation. (2nd edn) London: Penguin.

Watson TJ (1996) Motivation: that's Maslow, isn't it? Management Learning 27(4): 447–64.

Watts A (1961) Psychotherapy East and West. New York: Pantheon.

Watts A (2000) What is Tao? Novato, CA: New World Library.

Watzlawick P (1990) Muenchhausen's Pigtail or Psychotherapy and 'Reality': Essays and Lectures. New York: WW Norton and Company.

Watzlawick P, Beavin JH, Jackson DD (1967) Pragmatics of Human Communication. New York: WW Norton and Co.

Watzlawick P, Weakland JH (Eds) (1977) The Interactional View: Studies at the Mental

Research Institute 1965–74. New York: WW Norton and Company.

Watzlawick P, Weakland J, Fisch R (1974) Change: Principles of Problem Formation and Problem Resolution. New York: WW Norton.

Weaver JB (1985) The Polarity Response. Obtained through Southern Institute Press, www.intl-nlp.com/Books.

Weber M (1947) The Theory of Social and Economic Organization. Oxford University Press.

Wehr DS (1988) Jung and Feminism. London: Routledge.

Weisbord MR (1987) Productive Workplaces: Organising and Managing for Dignity, Meaning and Community. Oxford: Jossey-Bass.

Welwood J (Ed.) (1983) Awakening The Heart: East/West Approaches to Psychotherapy and the Healing Relationship. Boston: Shambhala.

Weschler IR, Reisler J (1959) Inside a Sensitivity Training Group. Los Angeles: Institute of Industrial Relations, University of California.

Wheatley MJ (1992) Leadership and the New Science: Learning about Organization from an Orderly Universe. San Francisco: Berrett-Koehler.

Whitmore J (1996) Coaching for Performance. London: Nicholas Brealey.

Wilber K (1980) The Atman Project. Wheaton, Illinois: Quest Books.

Wilber K (1983) Up From Eden. London: Routledge.

Wilber K (1996a) Eye to Eye. Boston: Shambhala.

Wilber K (1996b) How big is our umbrella? Noetic Sciences Review 40(Winter). Available online at www.noetic.org/Ions/archivelisting.asp; accessed 12 Dec. 2000.

Wilber K (1996c) A Brief History of Everything. Boston: Shambhala.

Wilber K (2000a) A Theory of Everything. Boston: Shambhala.

Wilber K (2000b) Integral Psychology: Consciousness, Spirit, Psychology, Therapy. Boston: Shambhala.

Wilhelm R (1968) I Ching. (3rd edn) London: Routledge and Kegan Paul. Introduction available online at www.iging.com/intro/introduc.htm; accessed 4 Jan. 2001.

Wilhelm R, Jung CG (1992) The Secret of the Golden Flower. New York: Arkana.

Wing RL (1979) The I Ching Workbook. Wellingborough: The Aquarian Press.

Winnicott DW (1986) Home Is Where We Start From. Harmondsworth: Penguin Books.

Winnicott D (1991) The Child, the Family and the Outside World. London: Penguin.

Witteveen HJ (1997) Universal Sufism. Dorset: Elements.

Wollams S, Brown M (1978) Transactional Analysis. Michigan: Huron Valley Institute Press.

Woodman M (1993) Leaving My Father's House: A Journey to Conscious Femininity. Boston: Shambhala.

Worden W (1991) Grief Counselling and Grief Therapy. London: Routledge.

Worell J, Remer P (1992) Feminist Perspectives in Therapy. New York: John Wiley.

Wright J (1987) B.F. Skinner: The pragmatic humanist. In Modgil S, Modgil C (Eds) B.F. Skinner: Consensus and Controversy. London: Falmer Press.

Yankura J, Dryden W (1994) Albert Ellis. London: Sage Publications.

Zeig J, Gilligan SG (1990) Brief Therapy: Myths, Methods and Metaphors. New York: Brunner Mazel Inc.

Zeig JK, Munion WM (1999) Milton H. Erickson. London: Sage.

Zinker J (1977) Creative Process in Gestalt Therapy. New York: Vintage Books.

Zohar D, Marshall I (2000) Spiritual Intelligence: The Ultimate Intelligence. London: Bloomsbury.

Zweig C, Wolff S (1997) Romancing the Shadow: How to Access the Power Hidden in Our Dark Side. London: Thorsons.